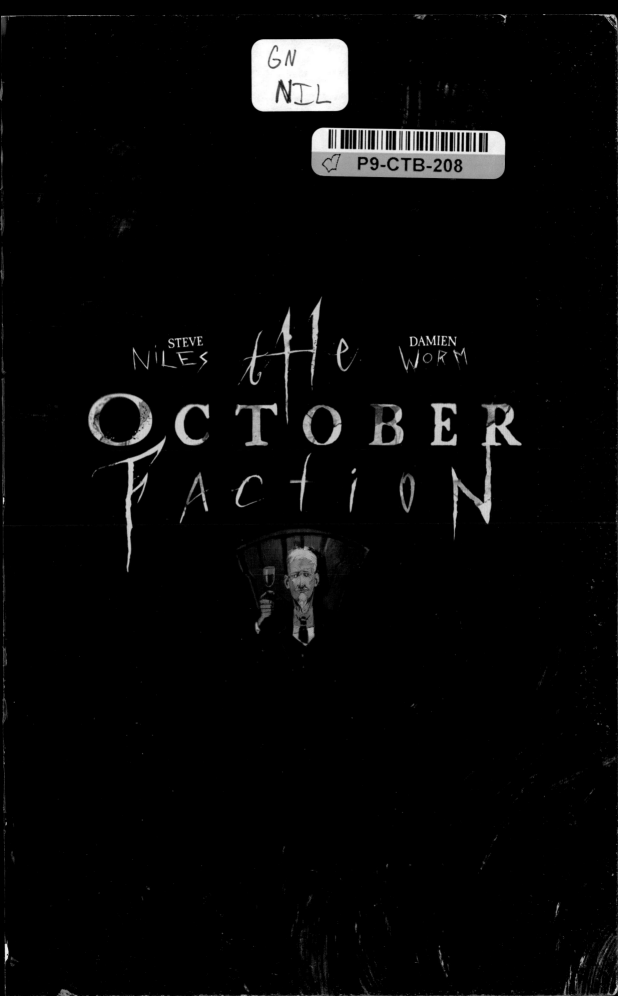

STEVE
NILES

DAMIEN
WORM

tHe
OCTOBER
FACtiON

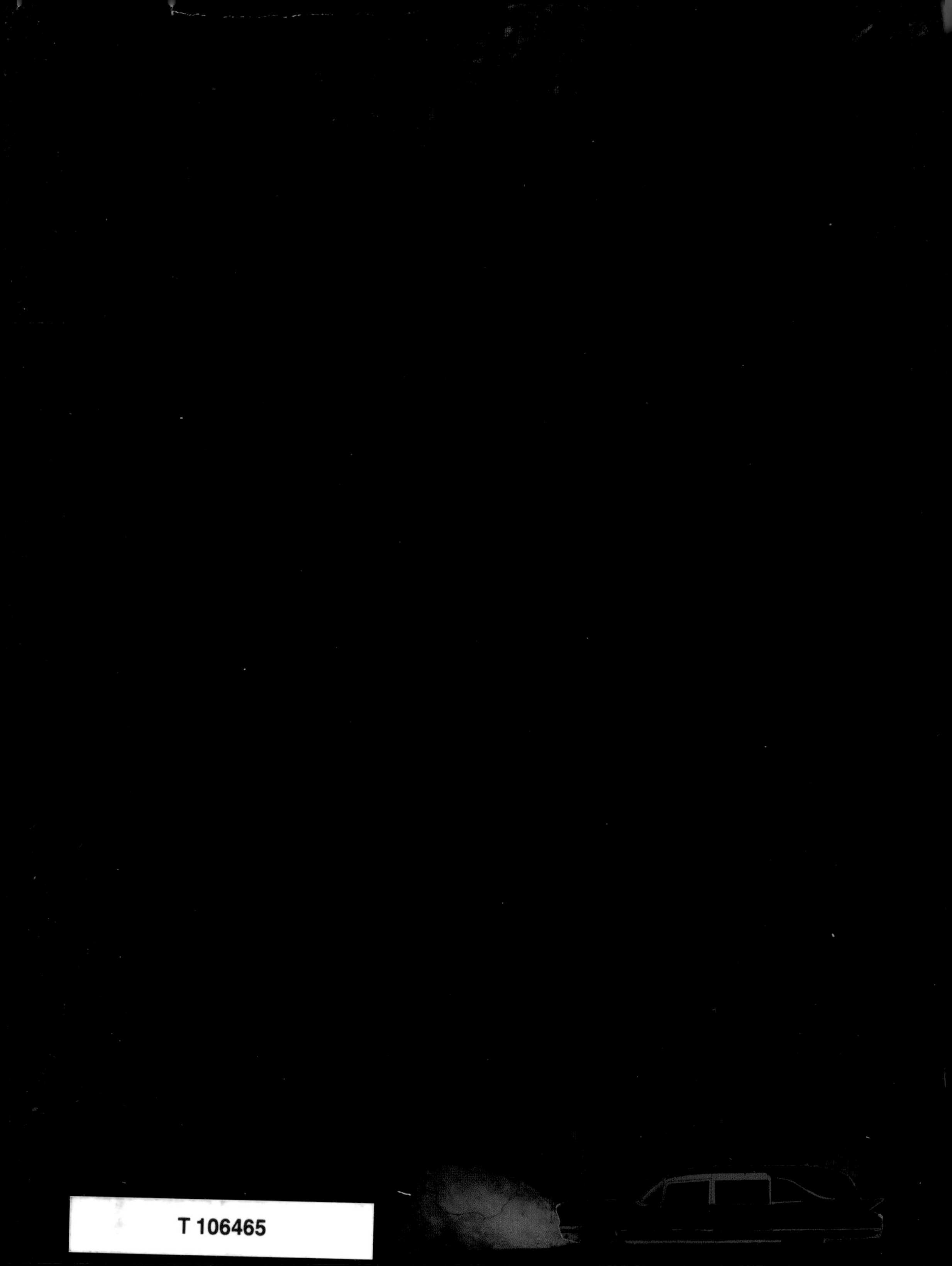

ISBN: 978-1-63140-251-7

18 17 16 15 1 2 3 4

www.IDWPUBLISHING.com
IDW founded by Ted Adams, Alex Garner, Kris Oprisko, and Robbie Robbins

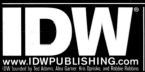

Ted Adams, CEO & Publisher
Greg Goldstein, President & COO
Robbie Robbins, EVP/Sr. Graphic Artist
Chris Ryall, Chief Creative Officer/Editor-in-Chief
Matthew Ruzicka, CPA, Chief Financial Officer
Alan Payne, VP of Sales
Dirk Wood, VP of Marketing
Lorelei Bunjes, VP of Digital Services
Jeff Webber, VP of Digital Publishing & Business Development

Facebook: **facebook.com/idwpublishing**
Twitter: **@idwpublishing**
YouTube: **youtube.com/idwpublishing**
Tumblr: **tumblr.idwpublishing.com**
Instagram: **instagram.com/idwpublishing**

Originally published as THE OCTOBER FACTION issues #1–6.

Created by
Steve Niles & **Damien Worm**

Written by **Steve Niles**
Illustrated by **Damien Worm**
Colors Assist by **Alyzia Zherno** (Ch. 6)
Letters by **Robbie Robbins** and **Shawn Lee**

Series Editors: **Chris Ryall** and **Michael Benedetto**

Cover by **Damien Worm**
Collection Edits by **Justin Eisinger** and **Alonzo Simon**
Collection Design by **Shawn Lee**

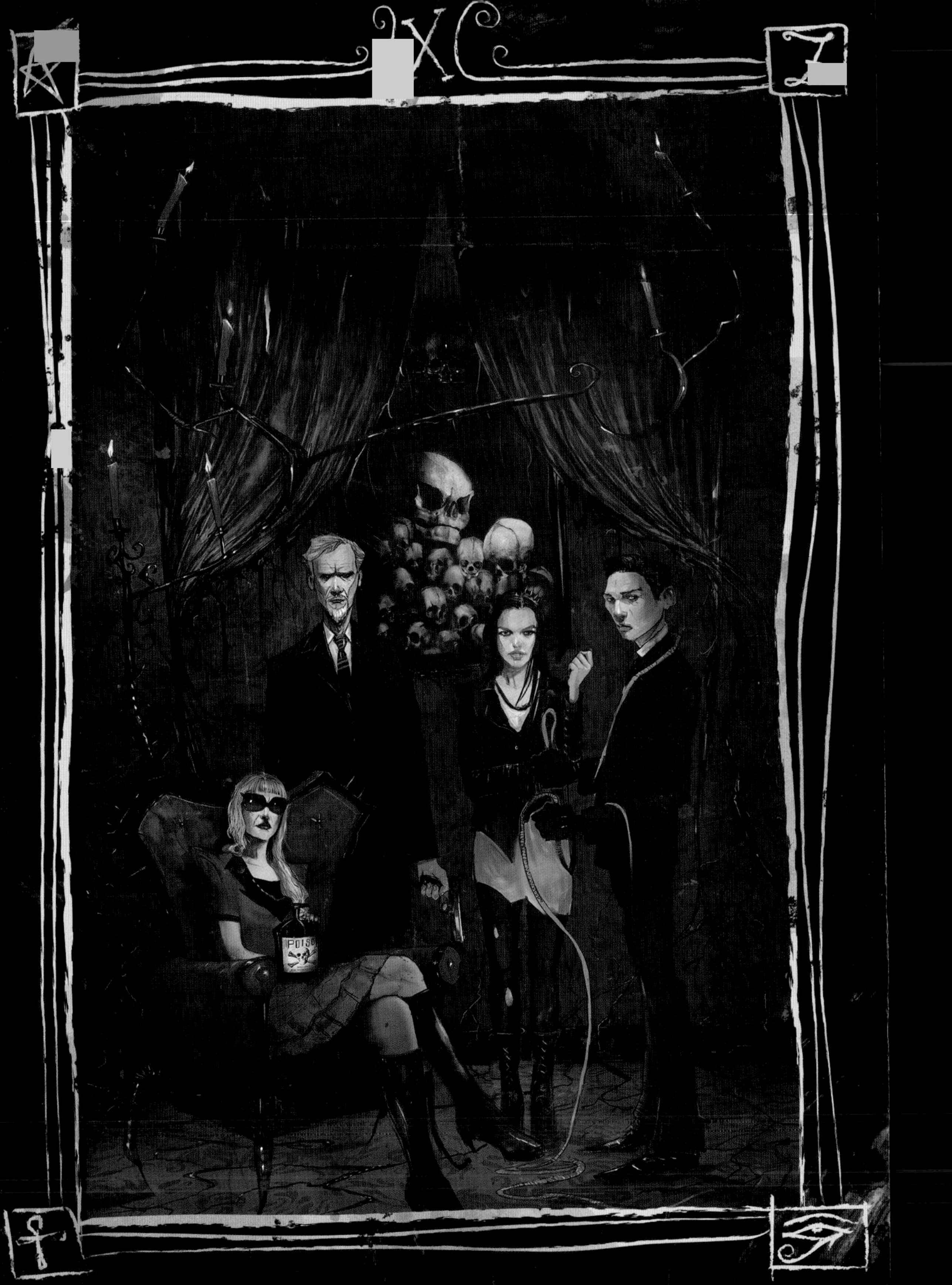

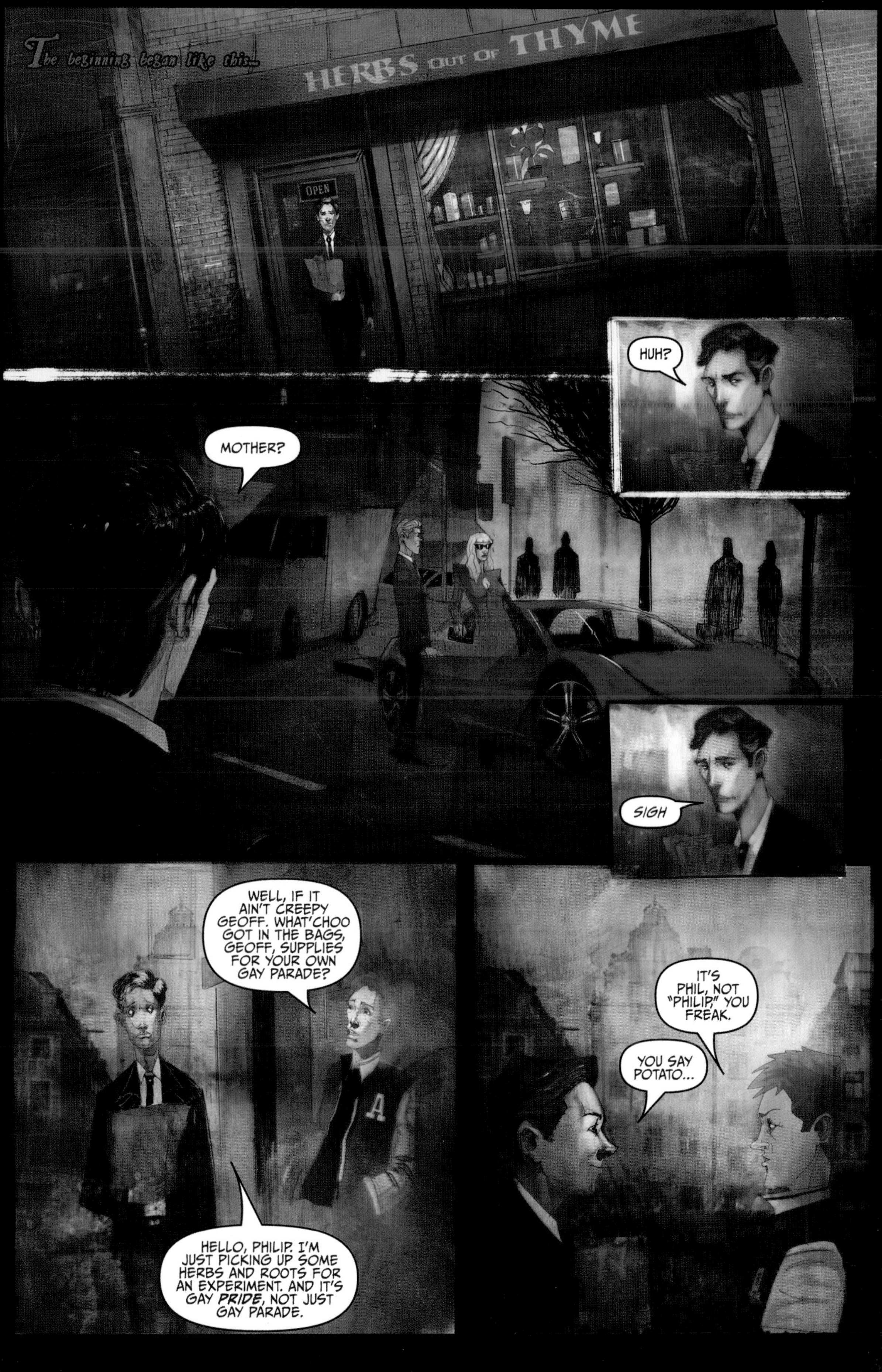

The beginning began like this...
HERBS OUT OF THYME
OPEN
HUH?
MOTHER?
SIGH
WELL, IF IT AIN'T CREEPY GEOFF. WHAT'CHOO GOT IN THE BAGS, GEOFF, SUPPLIES FOR YOUR OWN GAY PARADE?
HELLO, PHILIP. I'M JUST PICKING UP SOME HERBS AND ROOTS FOR AN EXPERIMENT. AND IT'S GAY *PRIDE*, NOT JUST GAY PARADE.
IT'S PHIL, NOT "PHILIP," YOU FREAK.
YOU SAY POTATO...

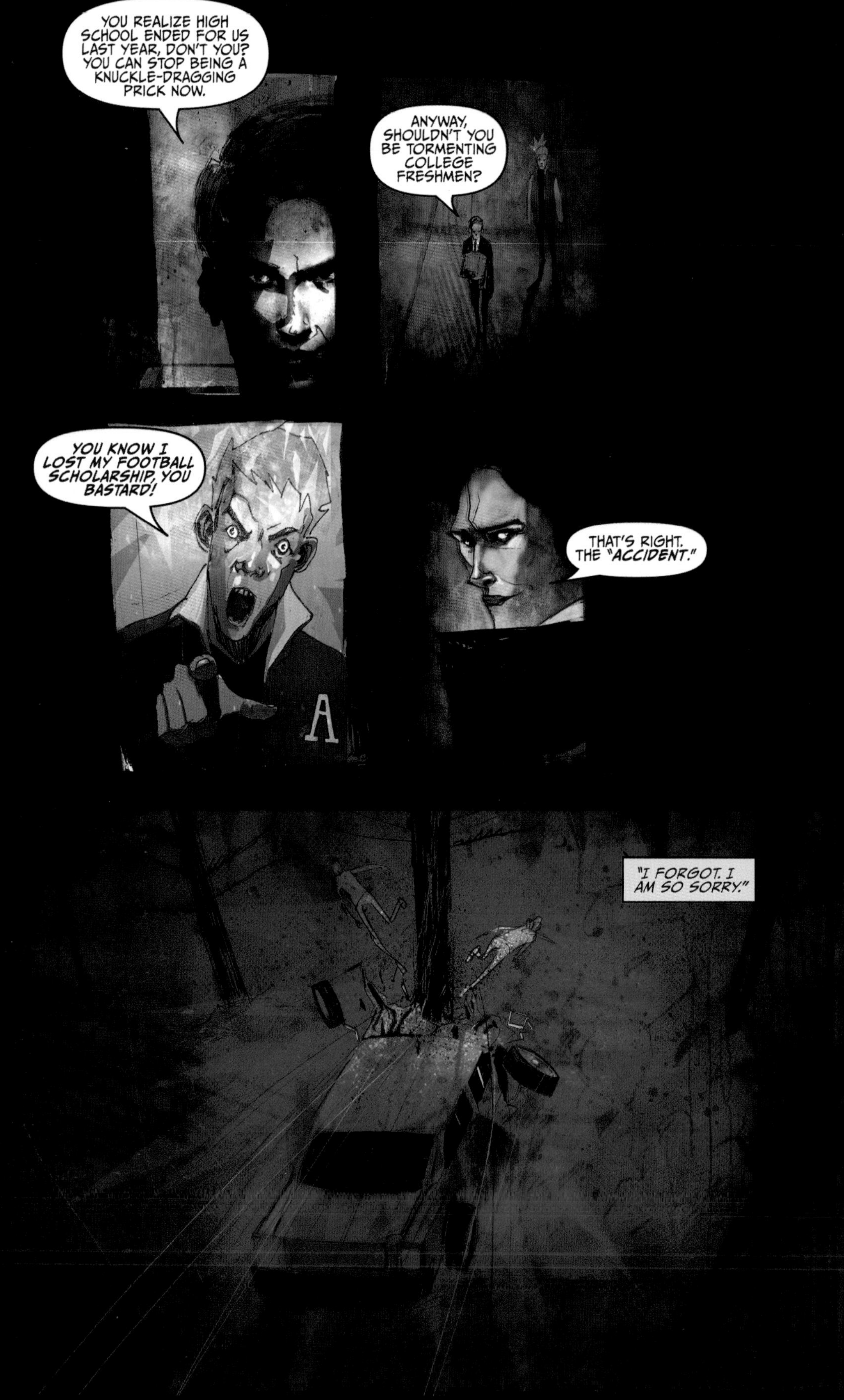
YOU REALIZE HIGH SCHOOL ENDED FOR US LAST YEAR, DON'T YOU? YOU CAN STOP BEING A KNUCKLE-DRAGGING PRICK NOW.
ANYWAY, SHOULDN'T YOU BE TORMENTING COLLEGE FRESHMEN?
YOU KNOW I LOST MY FOOTBALL SCHOLARSHIP, YOU BASTARD!
THAT'S RIGHT. THE "ACCIDENT."
"I FORGOT. I AM SO SORRY."

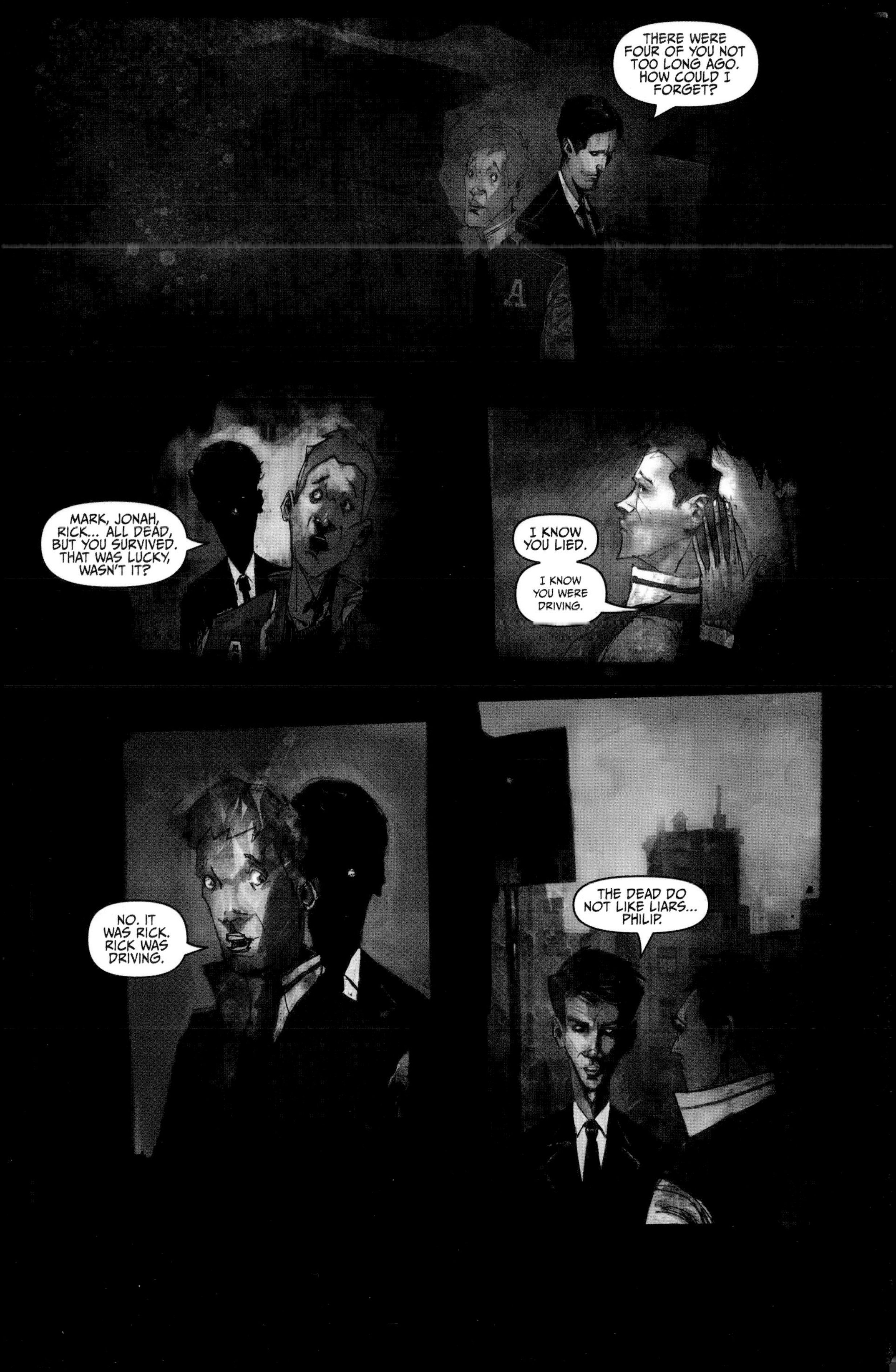
THERE WERE FOUR OF YOU NOT TOO LONG AGO. HOW COULD I FORGET?
MARK, JONAH, RICK... ALL DEAD, BUT YOU SURVIVED. THAT WAS LUCKY, WASN'T IT?
I KNOW YOU LIED.
I KNOW YOU WERE DRIVING.
NO. IT WAS RICK. RICK WAS DRIVING.
THE DEAD DO NOT LIKE LIARS... PHILIP.

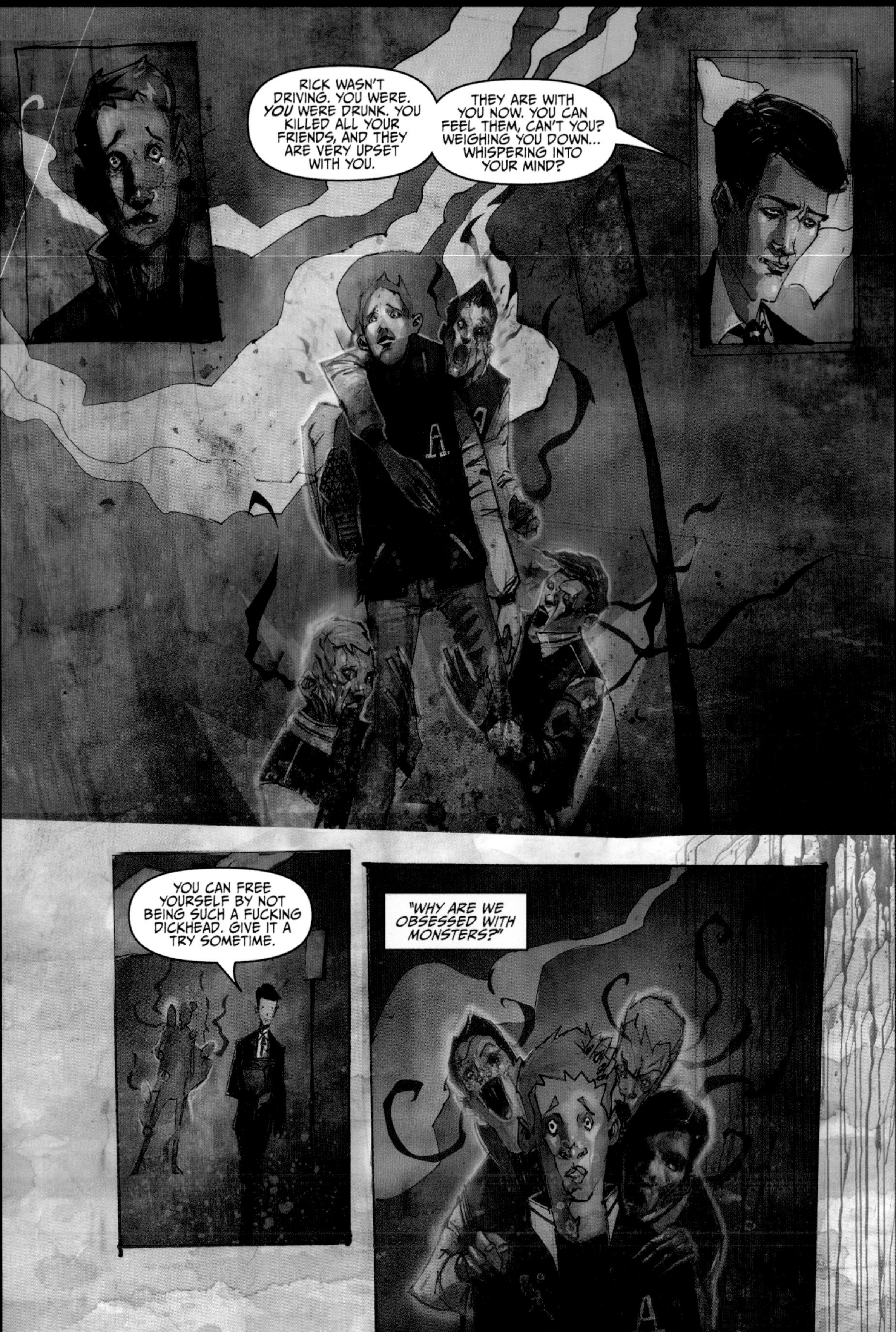
RICK WASN'T DRIVING. YOU WERE. YOU WERE DRUNK. YOU KILLED ALL YOUR FRIENDS, AND THEY ARE VERY UPSET WITH YOU.
THEY ARE WITH YOU NOW. YOU CAN FEEL THEM, CAN'T YOU? WEIGHING YOU DOWN... WHISPERING INTO YOUR MIND?
YOU CAN FREE YOURSELF BY NOT BEING SUCH A FUCKING DICKHEAD. GIVE IT A TRY SOMETIME.
"WHY ARE WE OBSESSED WITH MONSTERS?"

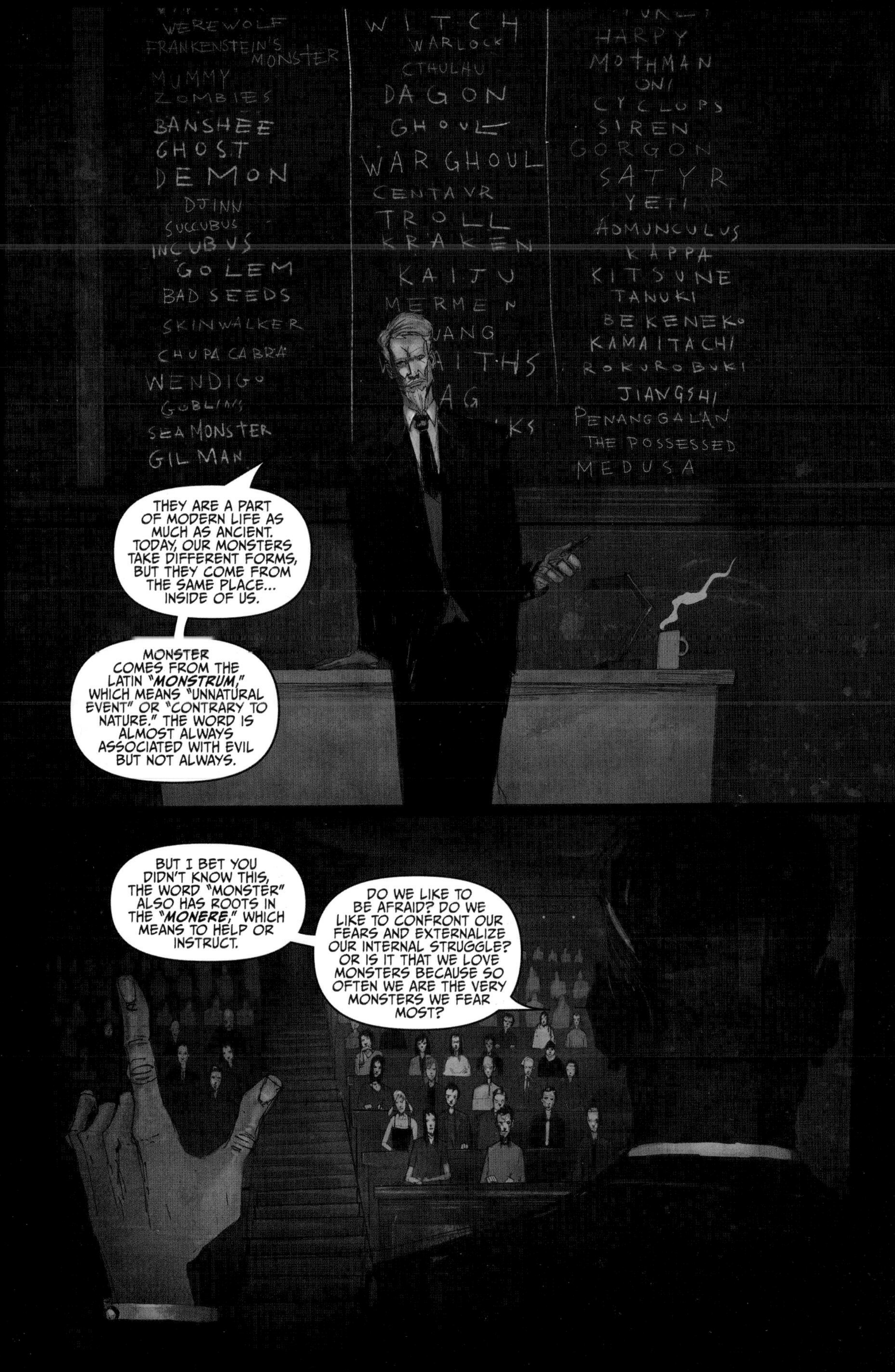
WEREWOLF
FRANKENSTEIN'S MONSTER
MUMMY
ZOMBIES
BANSHEE
GHOST
DEMON
DJINN
SUCCUBUS
INCUBUS
GOLEM
BAD SEEDS
SKINWALKER
CHUPA CABRA
WENDIGO
GOBLINS
SEA MONSTER
GILMAN
WITCH
WARLOCK
CTHULHU
DAGON
GHOUL
WAR GHOUL
CENTAVR
TROLL
KRAKEN
KAIJU
MERMEN
HARPY
MOTHMAN
ONI
CYCLOPS
SIREN
GORGON
SATYR
YETI
HOMUNCULUS
KAPPA
KITSUNE
TANUKI
BEKENEKO
KAMAITACHI
ROKUROBUKI
JIANGSHI
PENANGGALAN
THE POSSESSED
MEDUSA
THEY ARE A PART OF MODERN LIFE AS MUCH AS ANCIENT. TODAY, OUR MONSTERS TAKE DIFFERENT FORMS, BUT THEY COME FROM THE SAME PLACE... INSIDE OF US.
MONSTER COMES FROM THE LATIN "*MONSTRUM*," WHICH MEANS "UNNATURAL EVENT" OR "CONTRARY TO NATURE." THE WORD IS ALMOST ALWAYS ASSOCIATED WITH EVIL BUT NOT ALWAYS.
BUT I BET YOU DIDN'T KNOW THIS, THE WORD "MONSTER" ALSO HAS ROOTS IN THE "*MONERE*," WHICH MEANS TO HELP OR INSTRUCT.
DO WE LIKE TO BE AFRAID? DO WE LIKE TO CONFRONT OUR FEARS AND EXTERNALIZE OUR INTERNAL STRUGGLE? OR IS IT THAT WE LOVE MONSTERS BECAUSE SO OFTEN WE ARE THE VERY MONSTERS WE FEAR MOST?

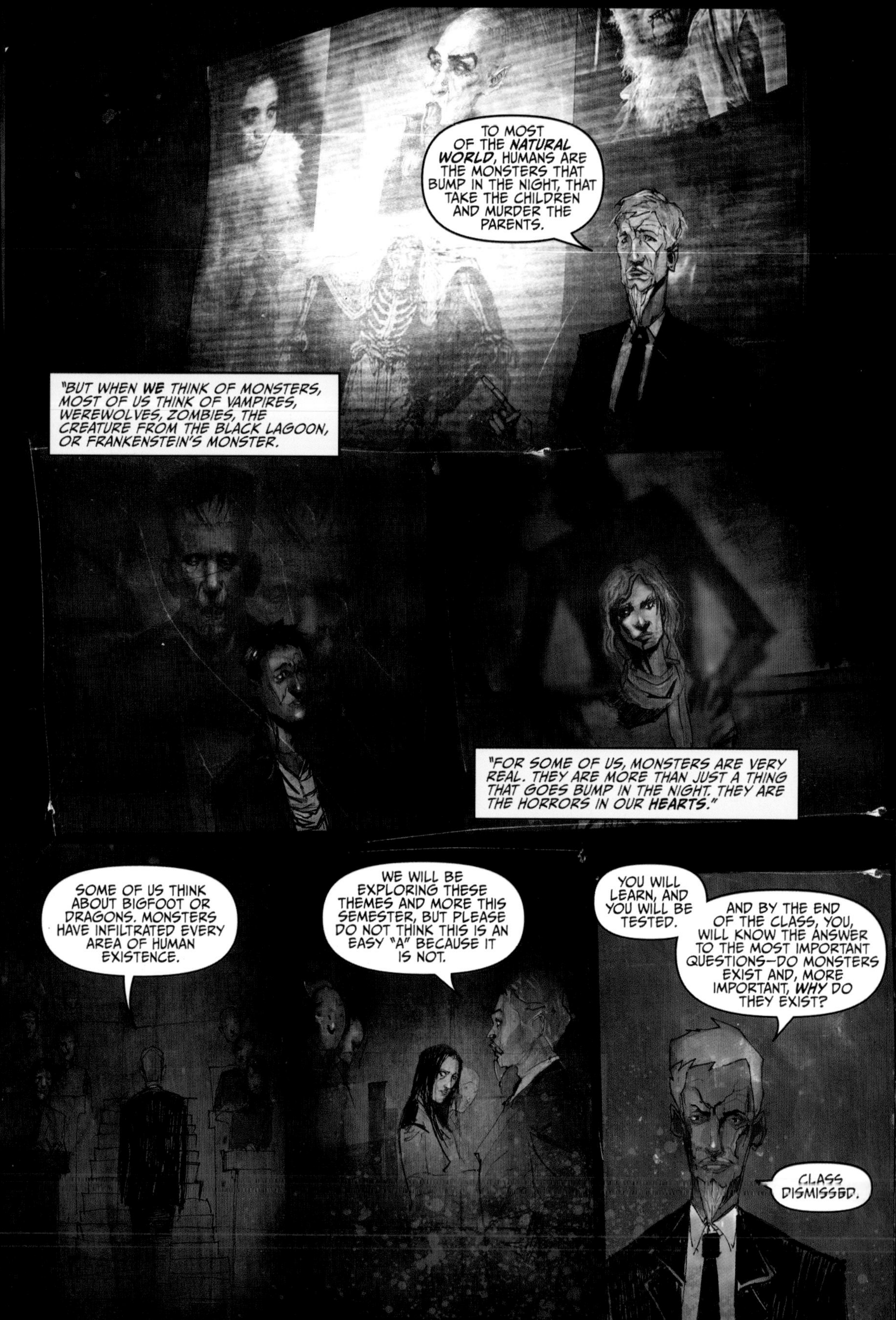
TO MOST OF THE **NATURAL WORLD**, HUMANS ARE THE MONSTERS THAT BUMP IN THE NIGHT, THAT TAKE THE CHILDREN AND MURDER THE PARENTS.
"BUT WHEN **WE** THINK OF MONSTERS, MOST OF US THINK OF VAMPIRES, WEREWOLVES, ZOMBIES, THE CREATURE FROM THE BLACK LAGOON, OR FRANKENSTEIN'S MONSTER.
"FOR SOME OF US, MONSTERS ARE VERY REAL. THEY ARE MORE THAN JUST A THING THAT GOES BUMP IN THE NIGHT. THEY ARE THE HORRORS IN OUR **HEARTS**."
SOME OF US THINK ABOUT BIGFOOT OR DRAGONS. MONSTERS HAVE INFILTRATED EVERY AREA OF HUMAN EXISTENCE.
WE WILL BE EXPLORING THESE THEMES AND MORE THIS SEMESTER, BUT PLEASE DO NOT THINK THIS IS AN EASY "A" BECAUSE IT IS NOT.
YOU WILL LEARN, AND YOU WILL BE TESTED.
AND BY THE END OF THE CLASS, YOU, WILL KNOW THE ANSWER TO THE MOST IMPORTANT QUESTIONS—DO MONSTERS EXIST AND, MORE IMPORTANT, **WHY** DO THEY EXIST?
CLASS DISMISSED.

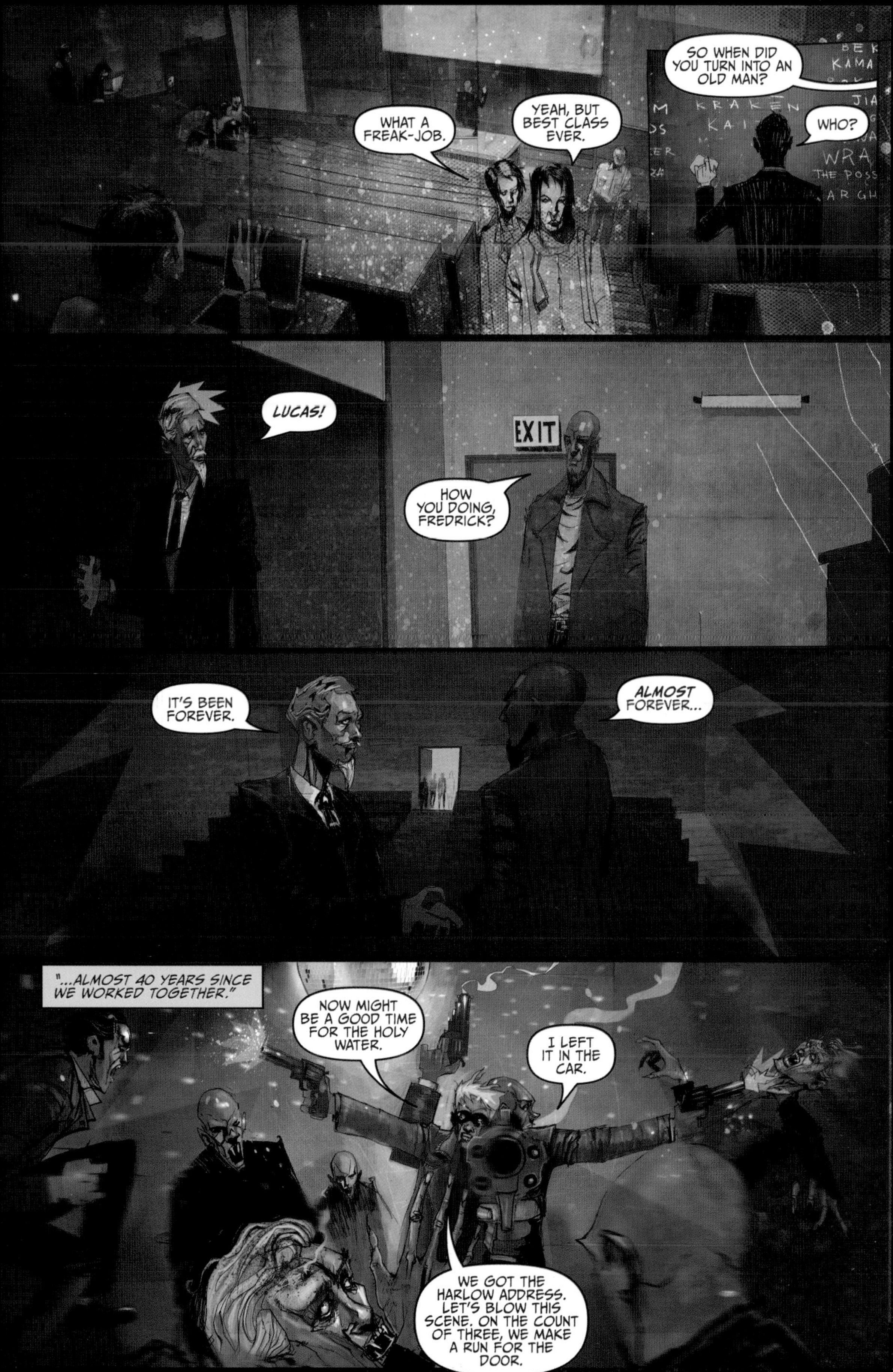
KRAKEN
WHAT A FREAK-JOB.
YEAH, BUT BEST CLASS EVER.
SO WHEN DID YOU TURN INTO AN OLD MAN?
WHO?
LUCAS!
EXIT
HOW YOU DOING, FREDRICK?
IT'S BEEN FOREVER.
ALMOST FOREVER...
"...ALMOST 40 YEARS SINCE WE WORKED TOGETHER."
NOW MIGHT BE A GOOD TIME FOR THE HOLY WATER.
I LEFT IT IN THE CAR.
WE GOT THE HARLOW ADDRESS. LET'S BLOW THIS SCENE. ON THE COUNT OF THREE, WE MAKE A RUN FOR THE DOOR.

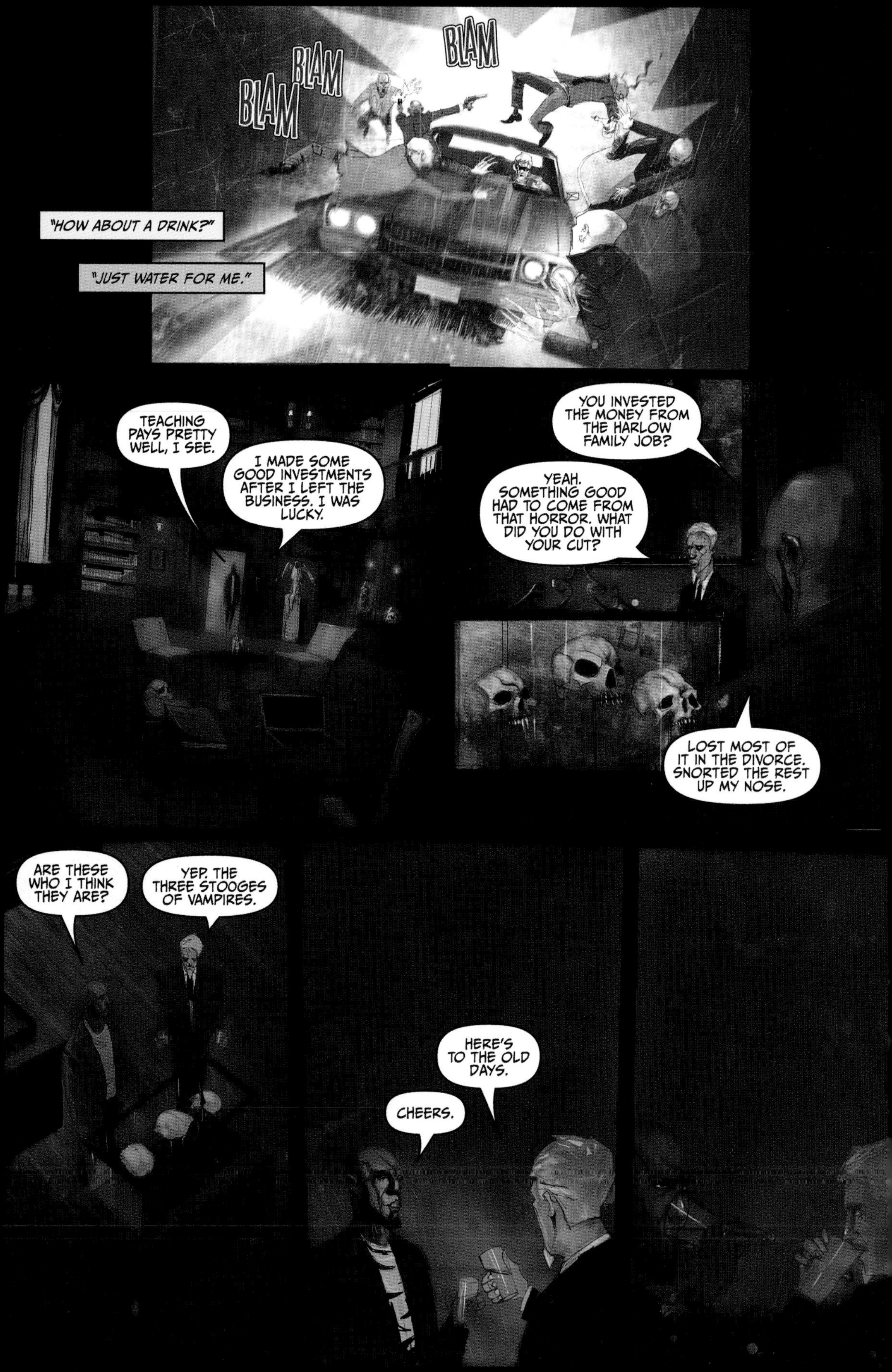
BLAM
BLAM
BLAM
"HOW ABOUT A DRINK?"
"JUST WATER FOR ME."
TEACHING PAYS PRETTY WELL, I SEE.
I MADE SOME GOOD INVESTMENTS AFTER I LEFT THE BUSINESS. I WAS LUCKY.
YOU INVESTED THE MONEY FROM THE HARLOW FAMILY JOB?
YEAH. SOMETHING GOOD HAD TO COME FROM THAT HORROR. WHAT DID YOU DO WITH YOUR CUT?
LOST MOST OF IT IN THE DIVORCE. SNORTED THE REST UP MY NOSE.
ARE THESE WHO I THINK THEY ARE?
YEP. THE THREE STOOGES OF VAMPIRES.
HERE'S TO THE OLD DAYS.
CHEERS.

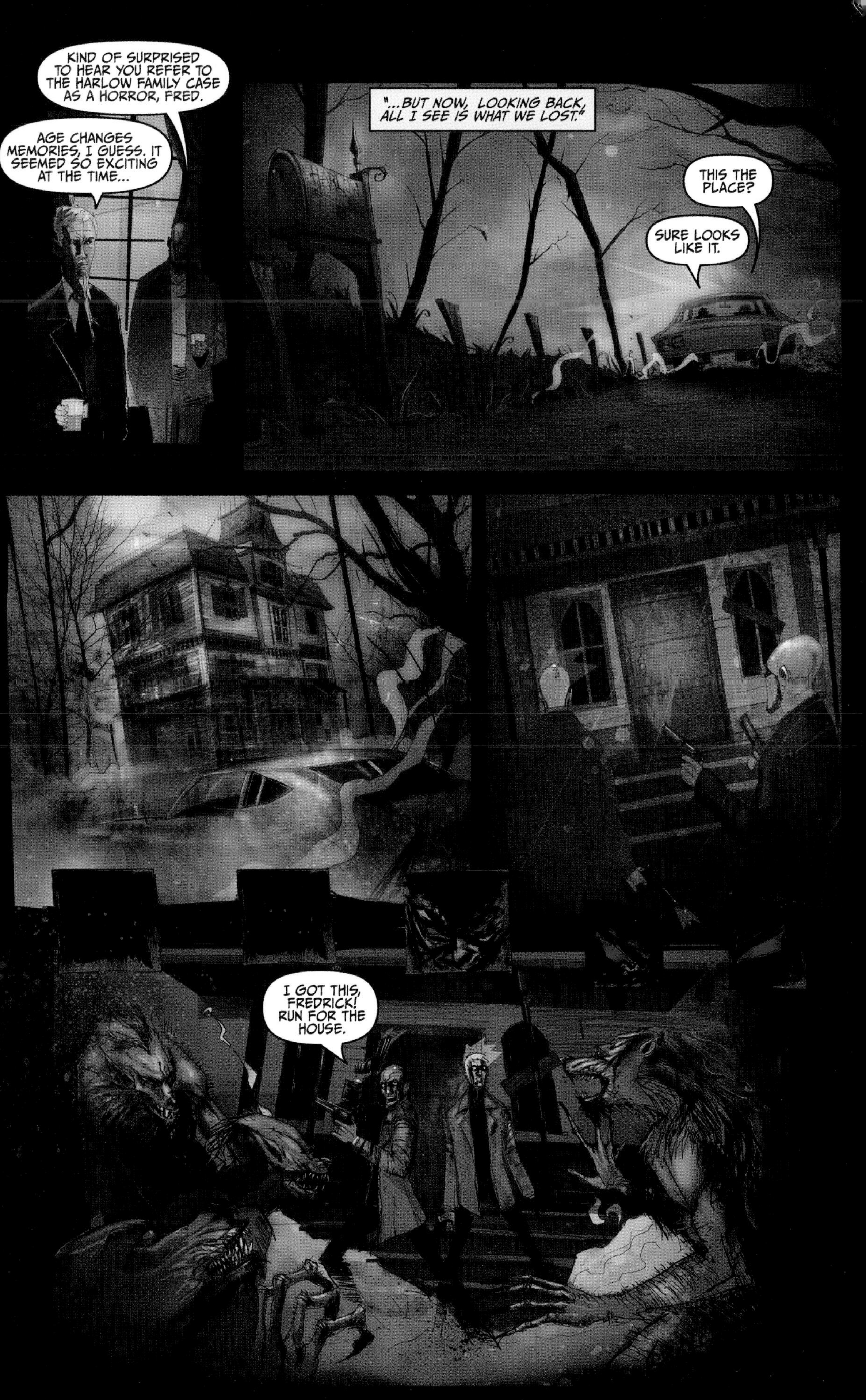
KIND OF SURPRISED TO HEAR YOU REFER TO THE HARLOW FAMILY CASE AS A HORROR, FRED.
AGE CHANGES MEMORIES, I GUESS. IT SEEMED SO EXCITING AT THE TIME...
"...BUT NOW, LOOKING BACK, ALL I SEE IS WHAT WE LOST."
THIS THE PLACE?
SURE LOOKS LIKE IT.
I GOT THIS, FREDRICK! RUN FOR THE HOUSE.

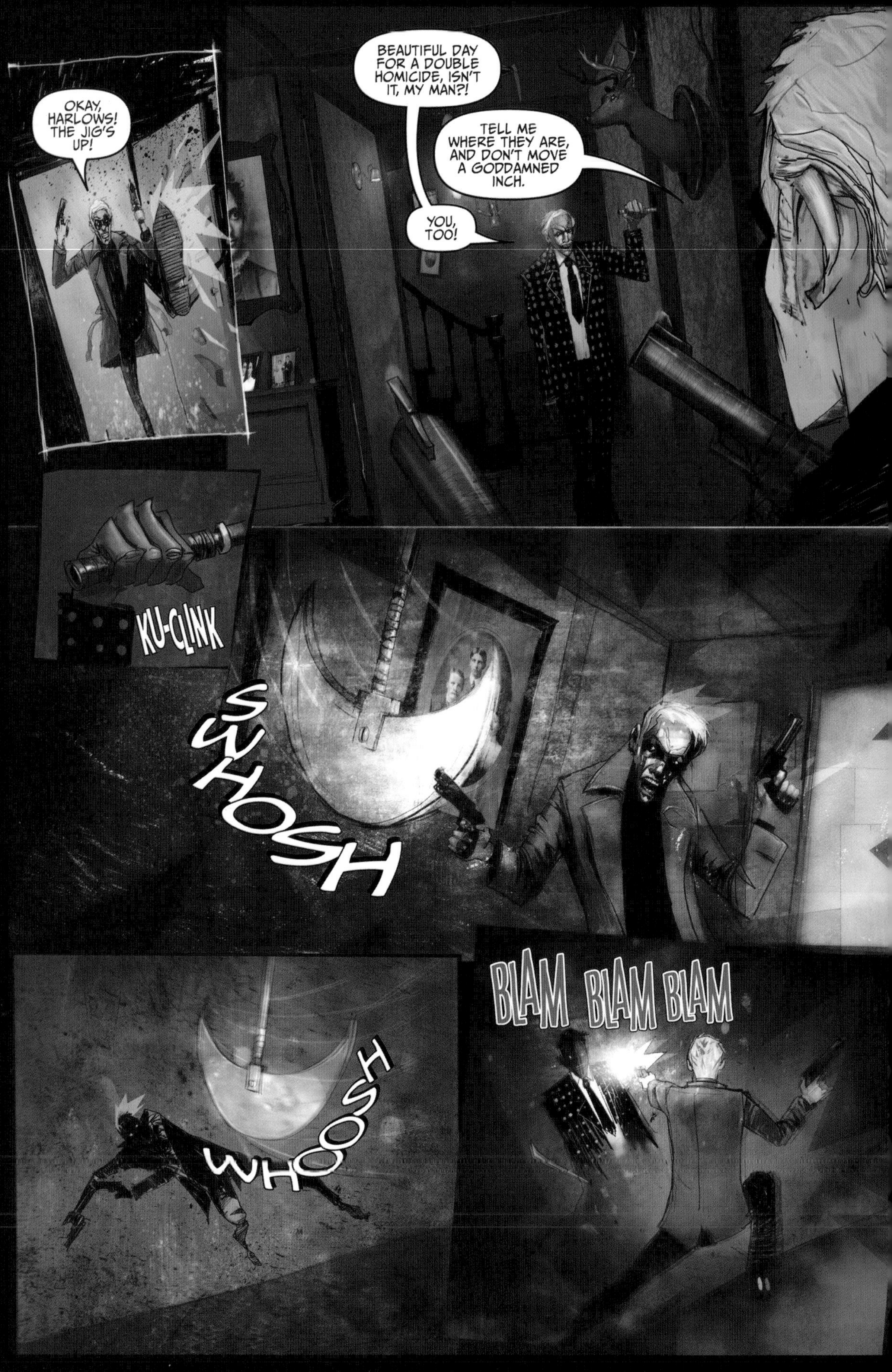
OKAY, HARLOWS! THE JIG'S UP!
BEAUTIFUL DAY FOR A DOUBLE HOMICIDE, ISN'T IT, MY MAN?!
TELL ME WHERE THEY ARE, AND DON'T MOVE A GODDAMNED INCH.
YOU, TOO!
KU-CLINK
SWHOSH
WHOOSH
BLAM BLAM BLAM

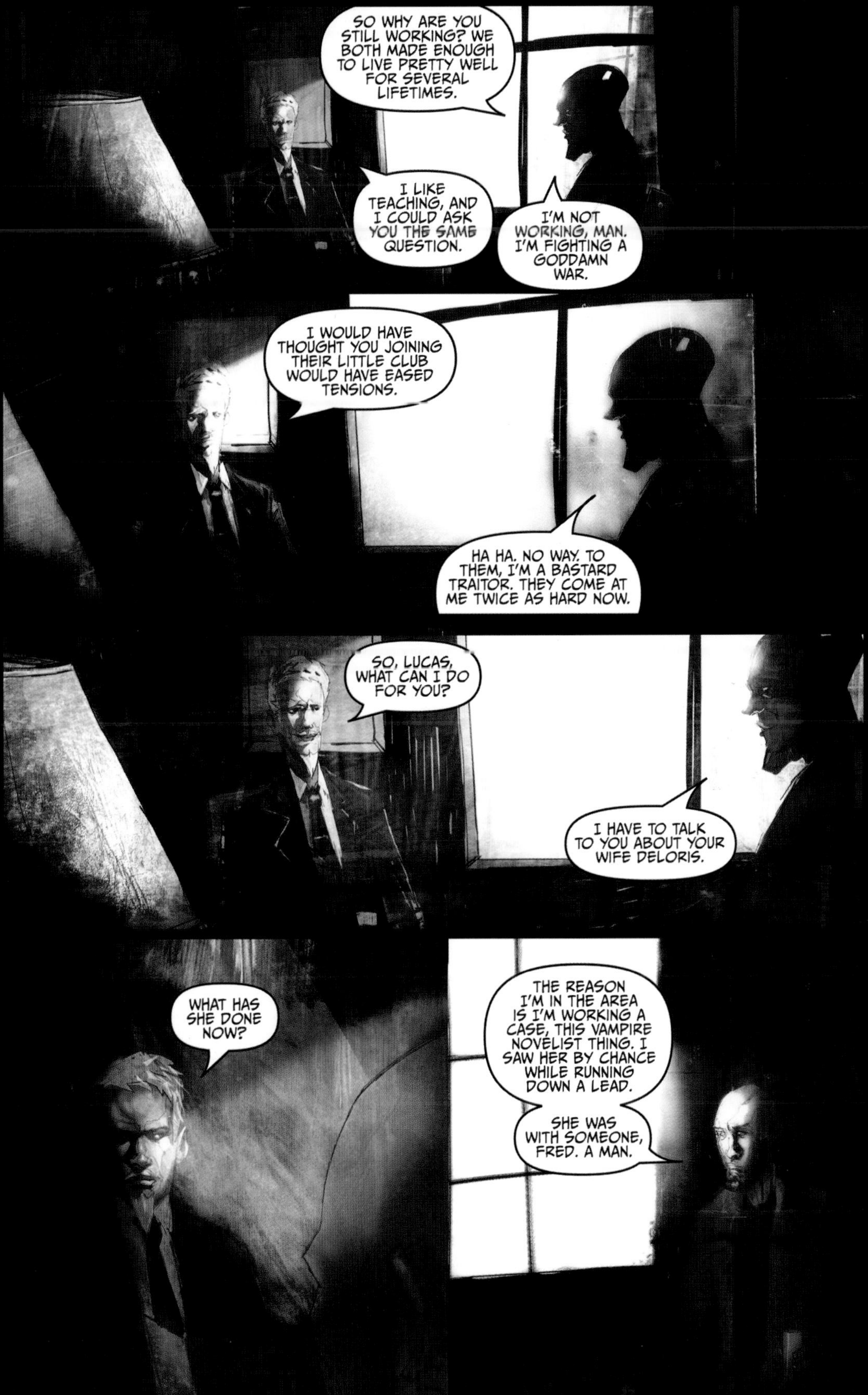
SO WHY ARE YOU STILL WORKING? WE BOTH MADE ENOUGH TO LIVE PRETTY WELL FOR SEVERAL LIFETIMES.
I LIKE TEACHING, AND I COULD ASK YOU THE SAME QUESTION.
I'M NOT WORKING, MAN. I'M FIGHTING A GODDAMN WAR.
I WOULD HAVE THOUGHT YOU JOINING THEIR LITTLE CLUB WOULD HAVE EASED TENSIONS.
HA HA. NO WAY. TO THEM, I'M A BASTARD TRAITOR. THEY COME AT ME TWICE AS HARD NOW.
SO, LUCAS, WHAT CAN I DO FOR YOU?
I HAVE TO TALK TO YOU ABOUT YOUR WIFE DELORIS.
WHAT HAS SHE DONE NOW?
THE REASON I'M IN THE AREA IS I'M WORKING A CASE, THIS VAMPIRE NOVELIST THING. I SAW HER BY CHANCE WHILE RUNNING DOWN A LEAD.
SHE WAS WITH SOMEONE, FRED. A MAN.

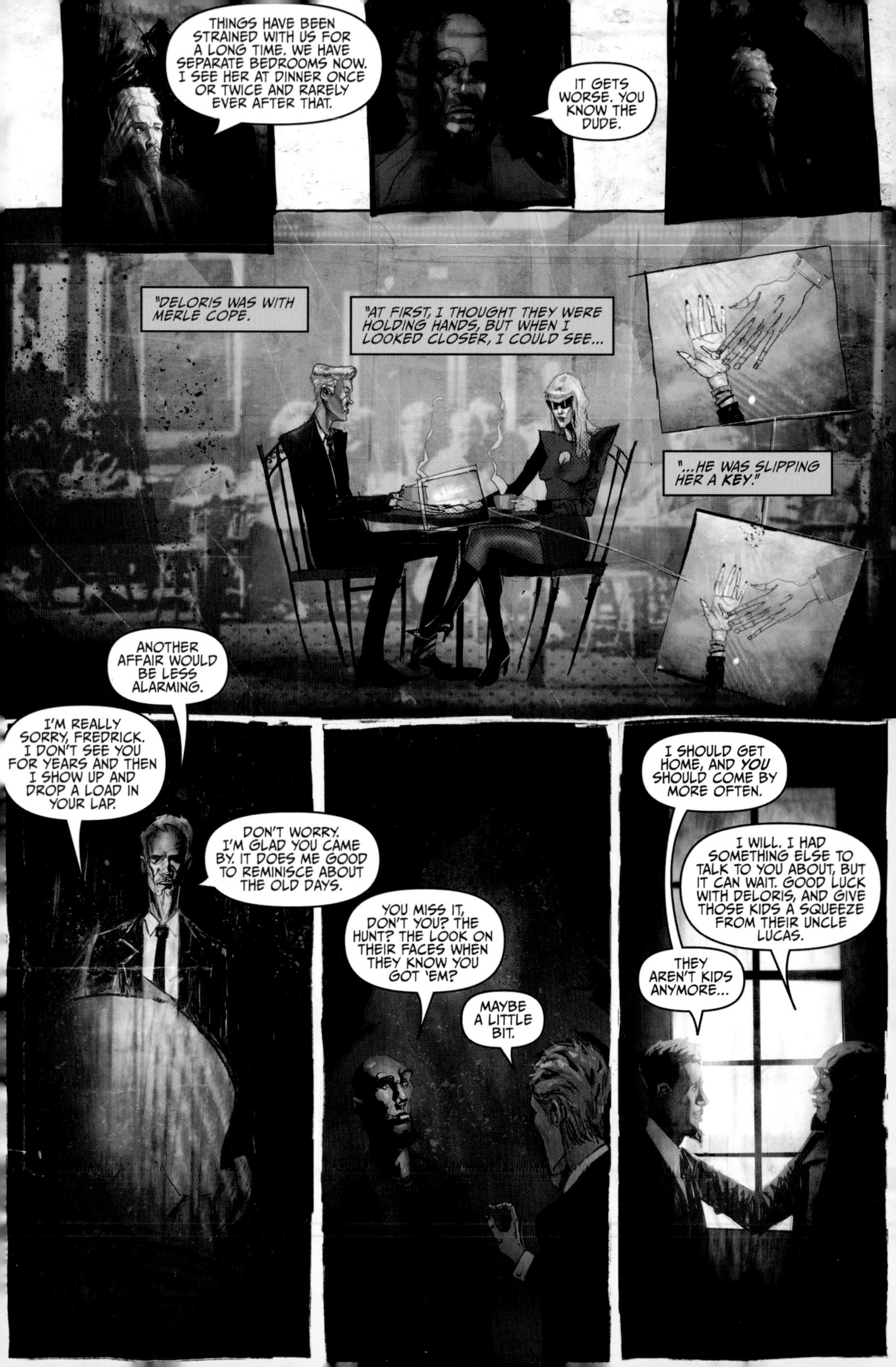
THINGS HAVE BEEN STRAINED WITH US FOR A LONG TIME. WE HAVE SEPARATE BEDROOMS NOW. I SEE HER AT DINNER ONCE OR TWICE AND RARELY EVER AFTER THAT.
IT GETS WORSE. YOU KNOW THE DUDE.
"DELORIS WAS WITH MERLE COPE.
"AT FIRST, I THOUGHT THEY WERE HOLDING HANDS, BUT WHEN I LOOKED CLOSER, I COULD SEE...
"...HE WAS SLIPPING HER A KEY."
ANOTHER AFFAIR WOULD BE LESS ALARMING.
I'M REALLY SORRY, FREDRICK. I DON'T SEE YOU FOR YEARS AND THEN I SHOW UP AND DROP A LOAD IN YOUR LAP.
DON'T WORRY. I'M GLAD YOU CAME BY. IT DOES ME GOOD TO REMINISCE ABOUT THE OLD DAYS.
YOU MISS IT, DON'T YOU? THE HUNT? THE LOOK ON THEIR FACES WHEN THEY KNOW YOU GOT 'EM?
MAYBE A LITTLE BIT.
I SHOULD GET HOME, AND YOU SHOULD COME BY MORE OFTEN.
I WILL. I HAD SOMETHING ELSE TO TALK TO YOU ABOUT, BUT IT CAN WAIT. GOOD LUCK WITH DELORIS, AND GIVE THOSE KIDS A SQUEEZE FROM THEIR UNCLE LUCAS.
THEY AREN'T KIDS ANYMORE...

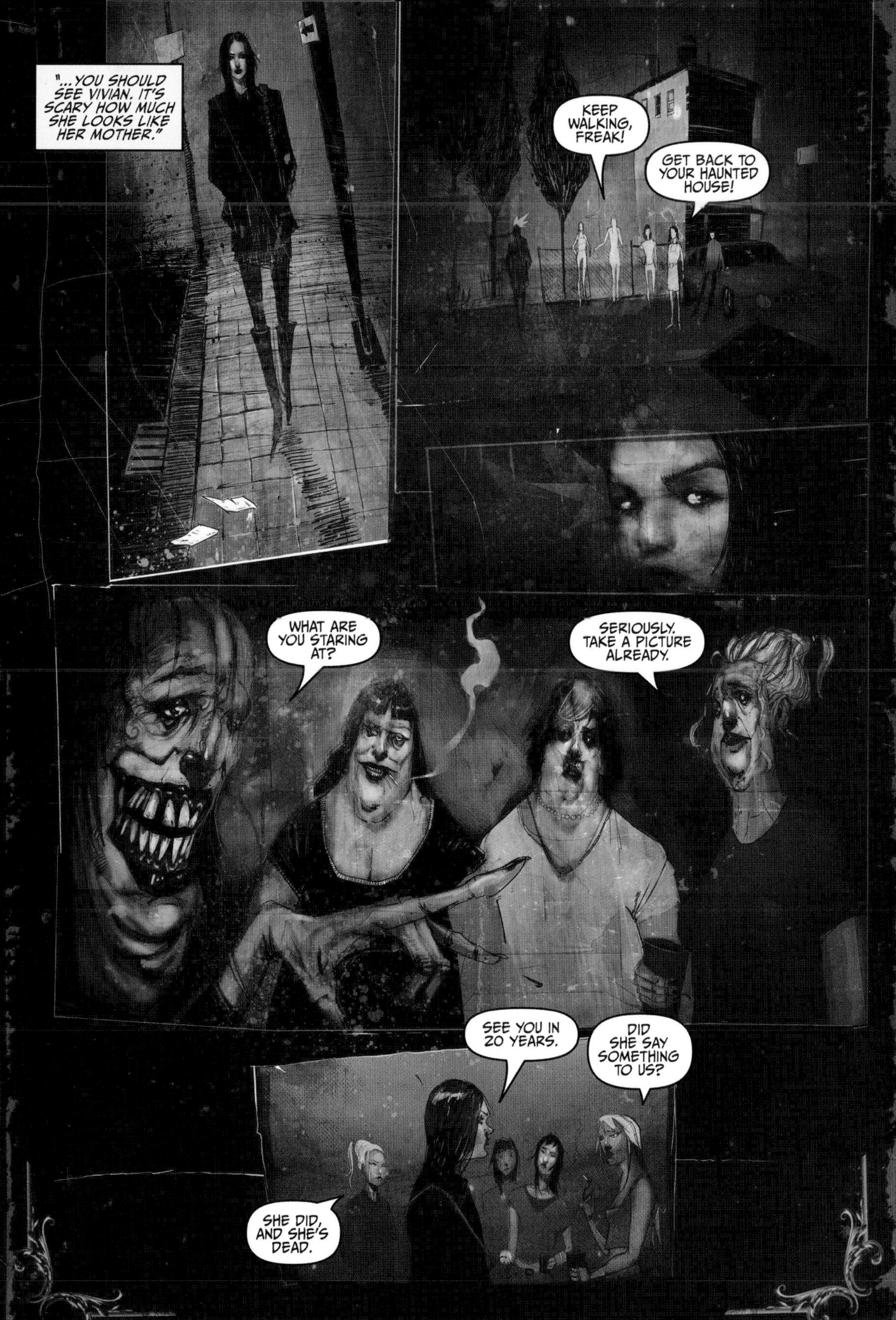

"...YOU SHOULD SEE VIVIAN. IT'S SCARY HOW MUCH SHE LOOKS LIKE HER MOTHER."
KEEP WALKING, FREAK!
GET BACK TO YOUR HAUNTED HOUSE!
WHAT ARE YOU STARING AT?
SERIOUSLY. TAKE A PICTURE ALREADY.
SEE YOU IN 20 YEARS.
DID SHE SAY SOMETHING TO US?
SHE DID, AND SHE'S DEAD.

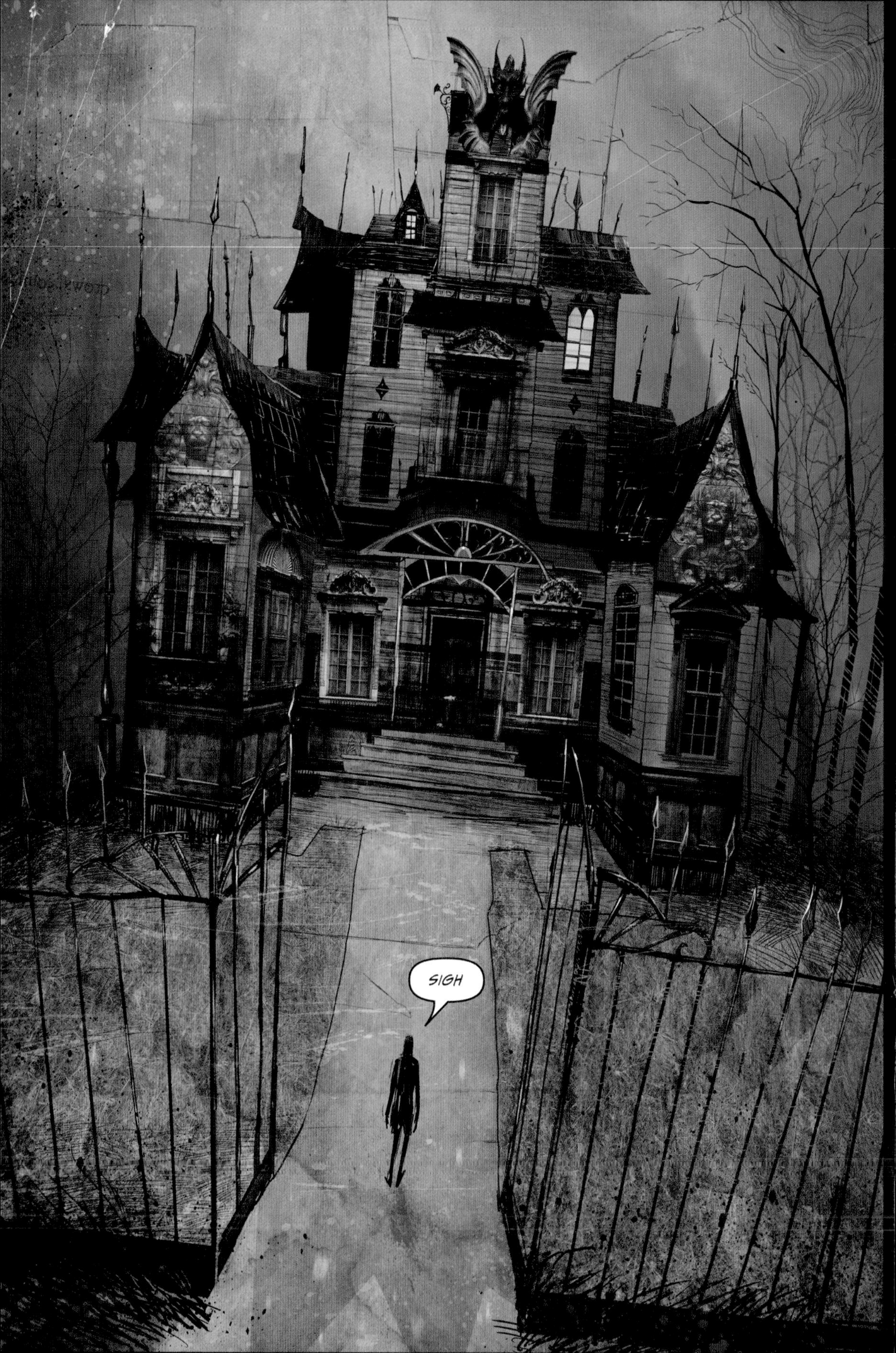
SIGH

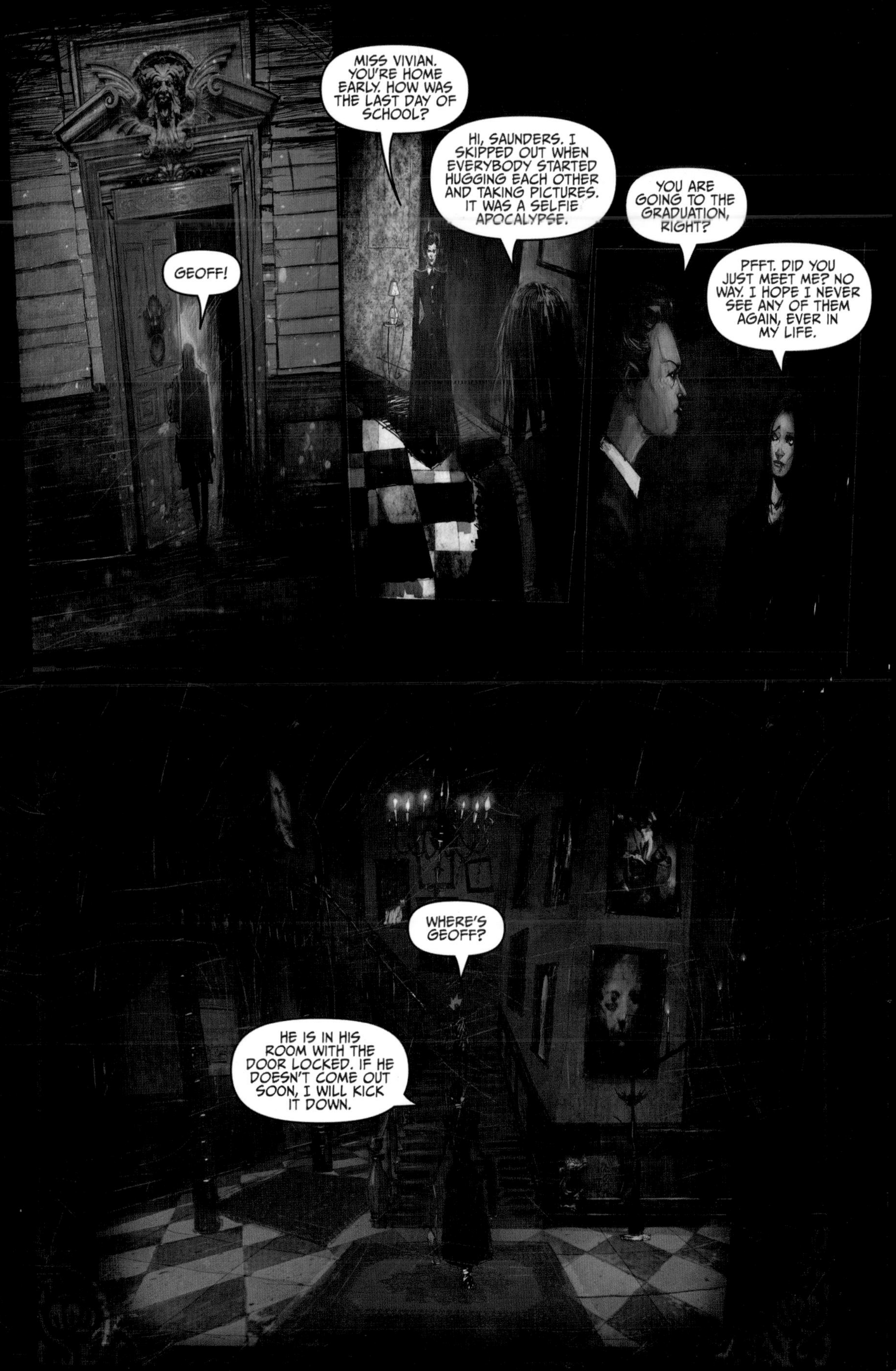
GEOFF!
MISS VIVIAN. YOU'RE HOME EARLY. HOW WAS THE LAST DAY OF SCHOOL?
HI, SAUNDERS. I SKIPPED OUT WHEN EVERYBODY STARTED HUGGING EACH OTHER AND TAKING PICTURES. IT WAS A SELFIE APOCALYPSE.
YOU ARE GOING TO THE GRADUATION, RIGHT?
PFFT. DID YOU JUST MEET ME? NO WAY. I HOPE I NEVER SEE ANY OF THEM AGAIN, EVER IN MY LIFE.
WHERE'S GEOFF?
HE IS IN HIS ROOM WITH THE DOOR LOCKED. IF HE DOESN'T COME OUT SOON, I WILL KICK IT DOWN.

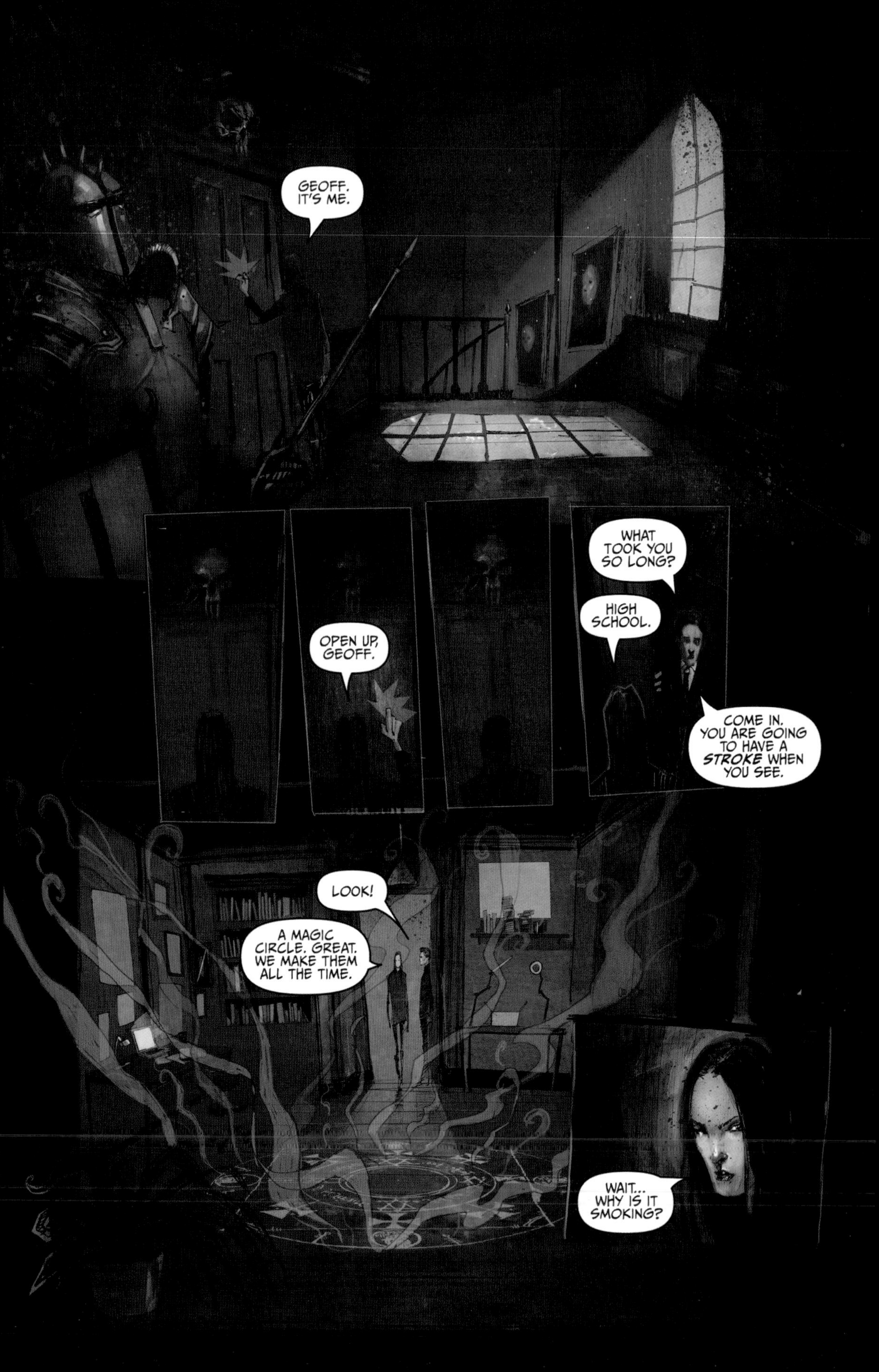
GEOFF. IT'S ME.
OPEN UP, GEOFF.
WHAT TOOK YOU SO LONG?
HIGH SCHOOL.
COME IN. YOU ARE GOING TO HAVE A STROKE WHEN YOU SEE.
LOOK!
A MAGIC CIRCLE. GREAT. WE MAKE THEM ALL THE TIME.
WAIT... WHY IS IT SMOKING?

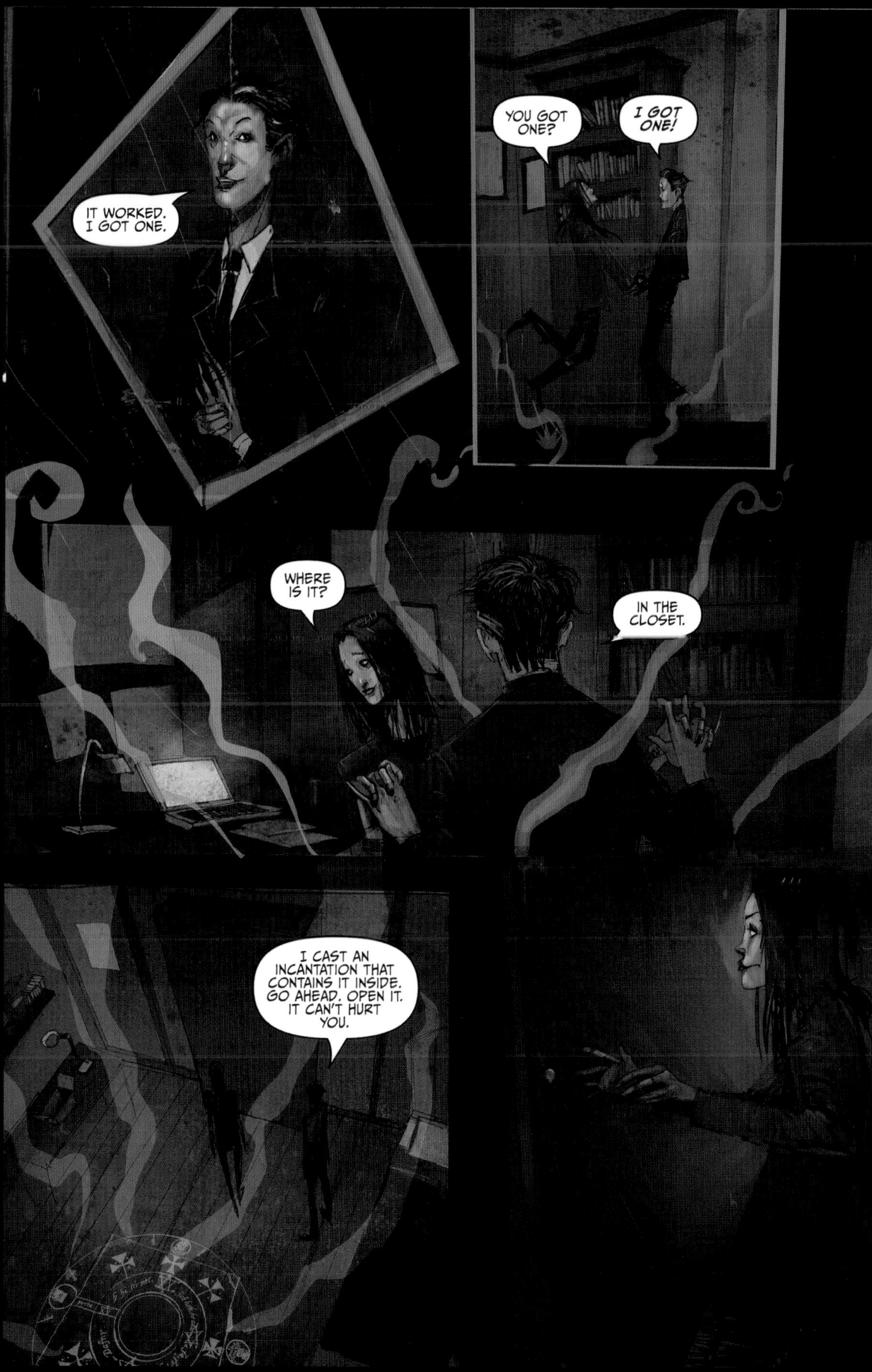
IT WORKED. I GOT ONE.
YOU GOT ONE?
I GOT ONE!
WHERE IS IT?
IN THE CLOSET.
I CAST AN INCANTATION THAT CONTAINS IT INSIDE. GO AHEAD. OPEN IT. IT CAN'T HURT YOU.

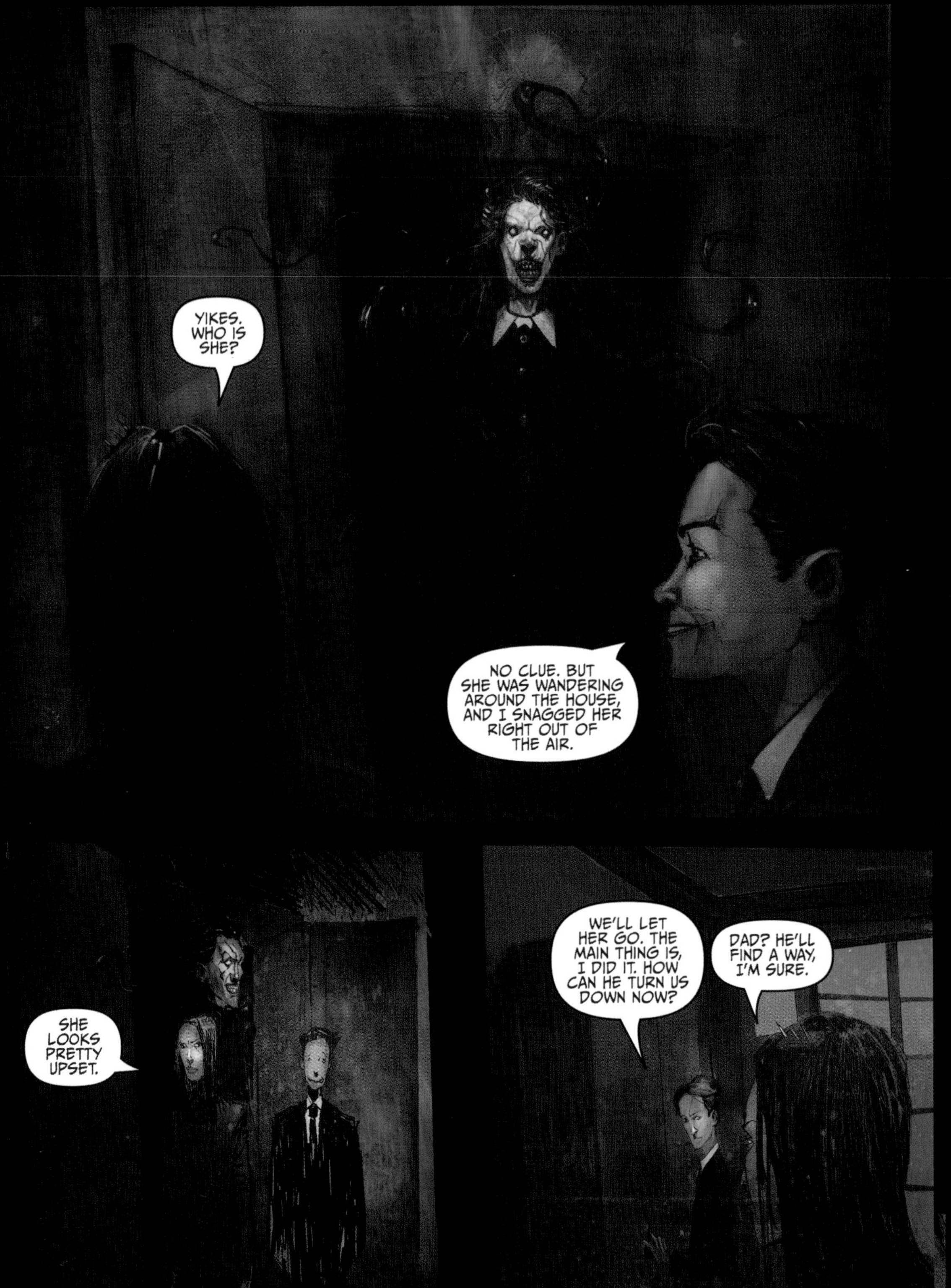
YIKES. WHO IS SHE?
NO CLUE. BUT SHE WAS WANDERING AROUND THE HOUSE, AND I SNAGGED HER RIGHT OUT OF THE AIR.
SHE LOOKS PRETTY UPSET.
WE'LL LET HER GO. THE MAIN THING IS, I DID IT. HOW CAN HE TURN US DOWN NOW?
DAD? HE'LL FIND A WAY, I'M SURE.

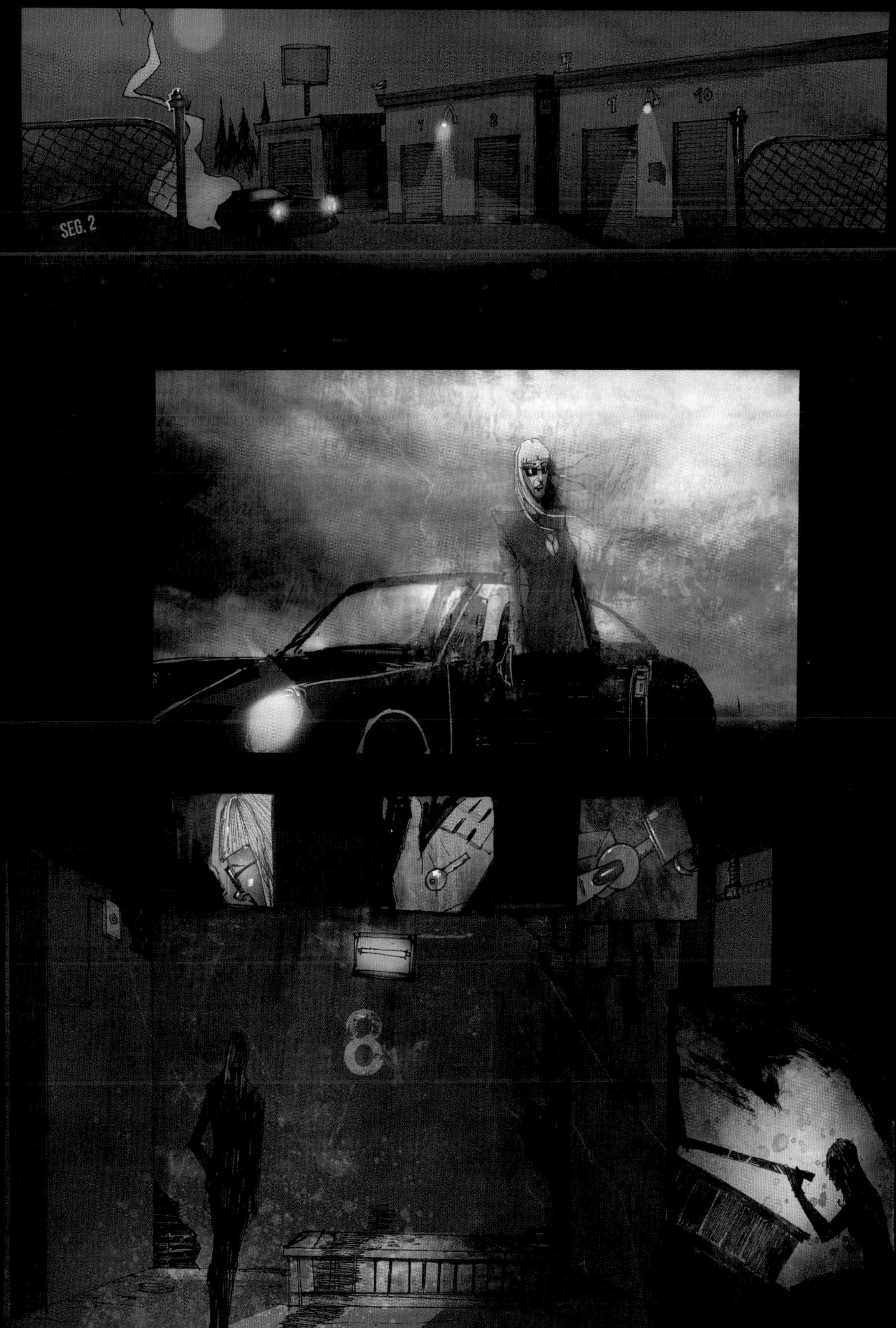
SEG. 2

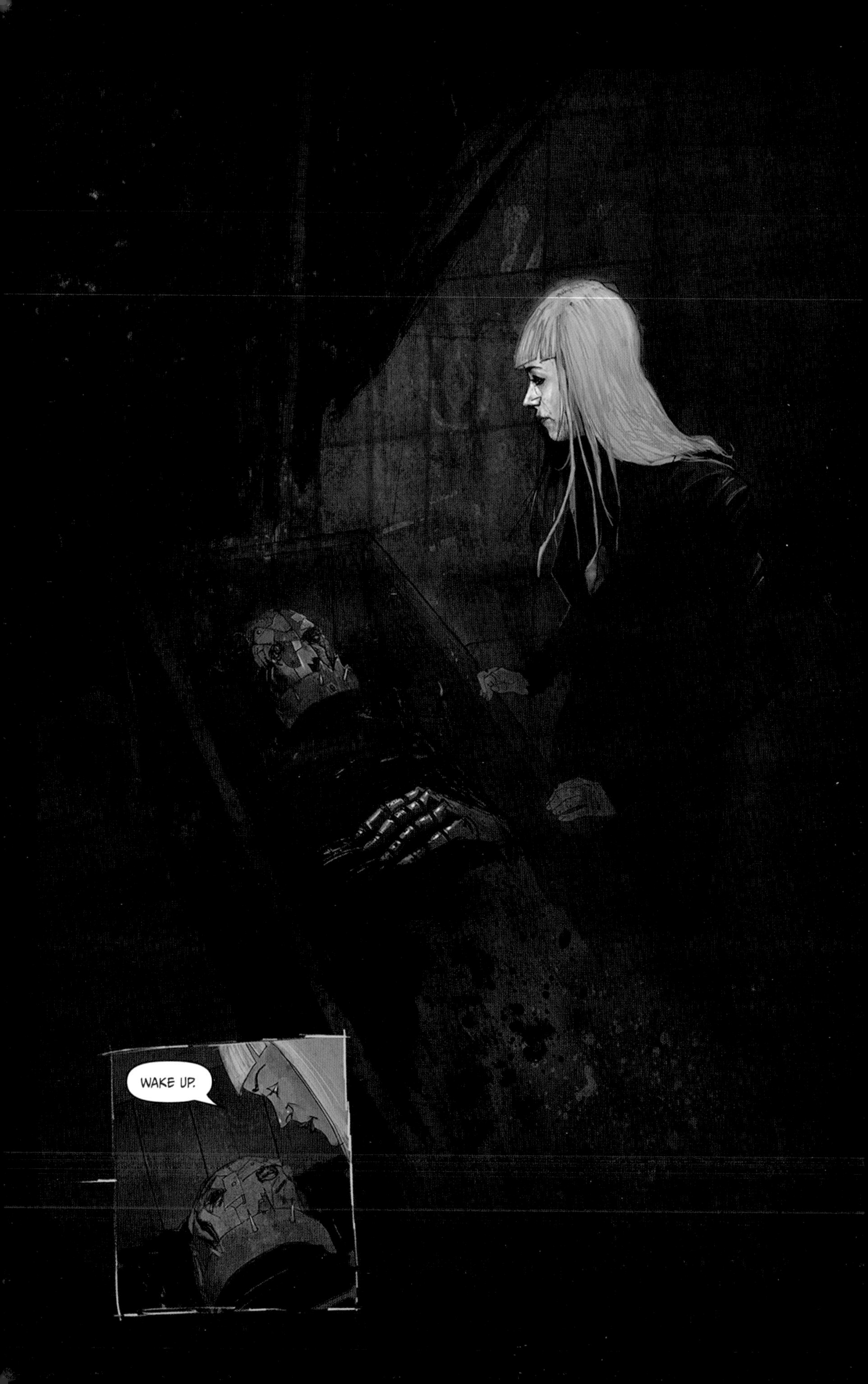
WAKE UP.

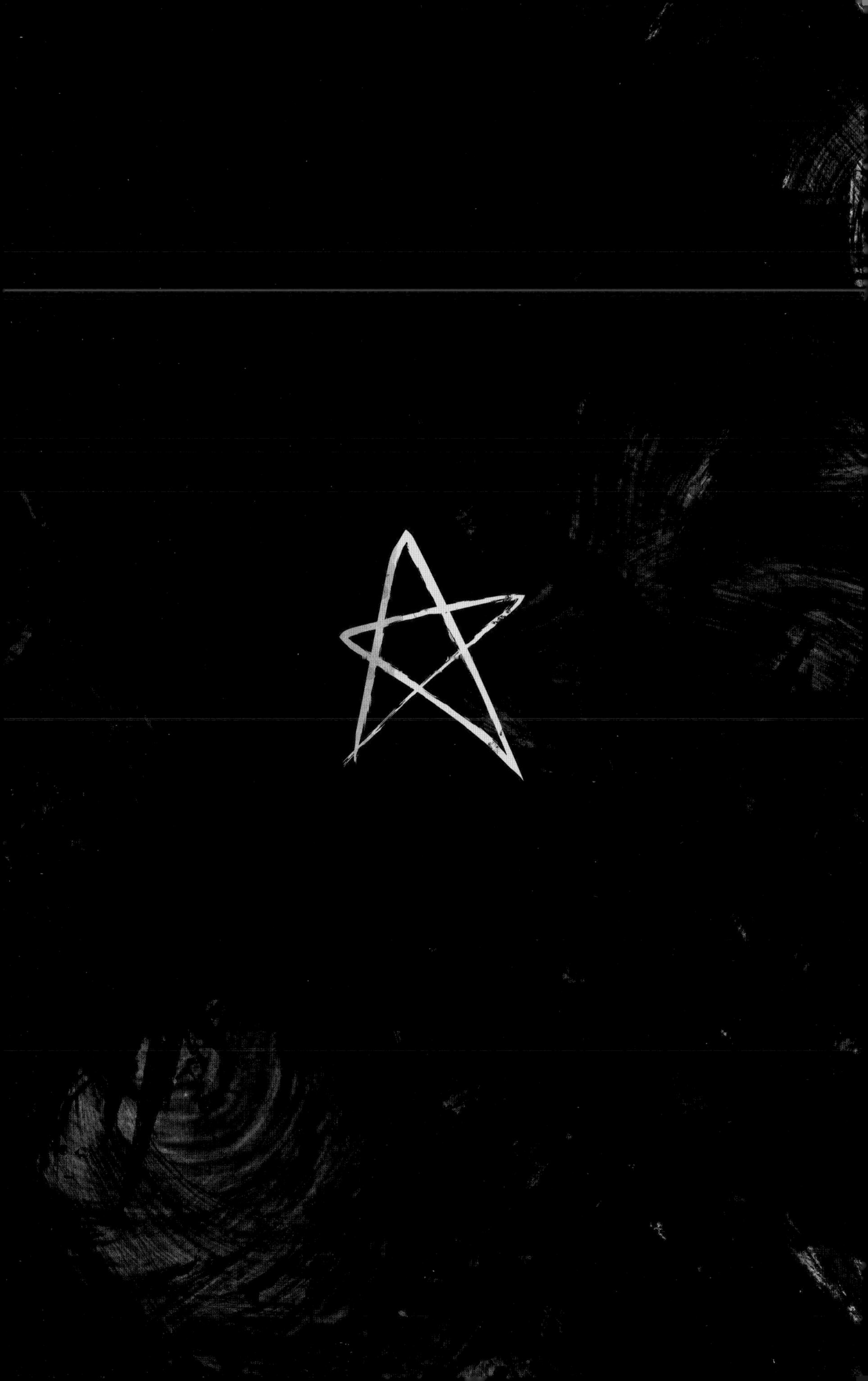

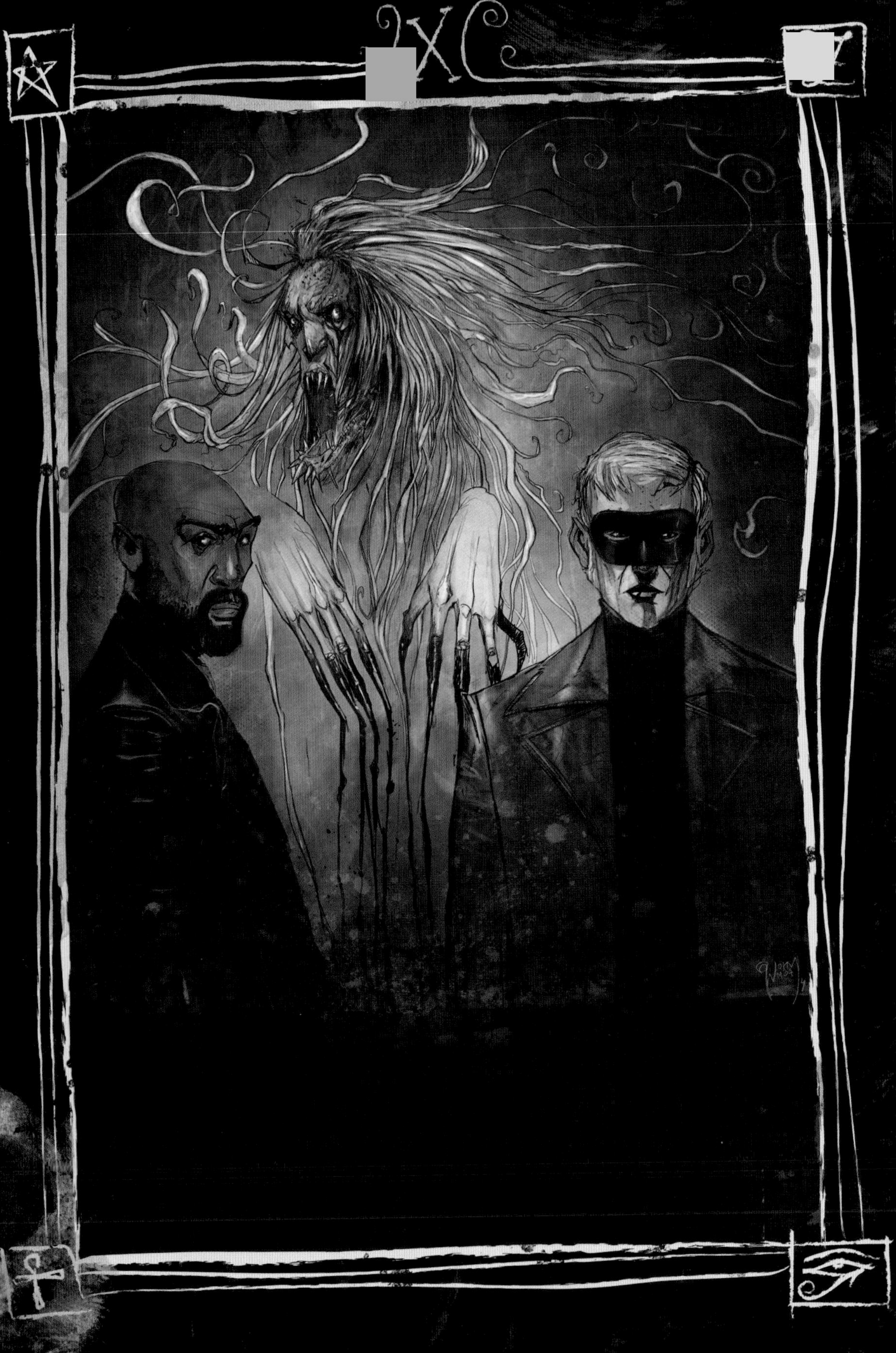
X

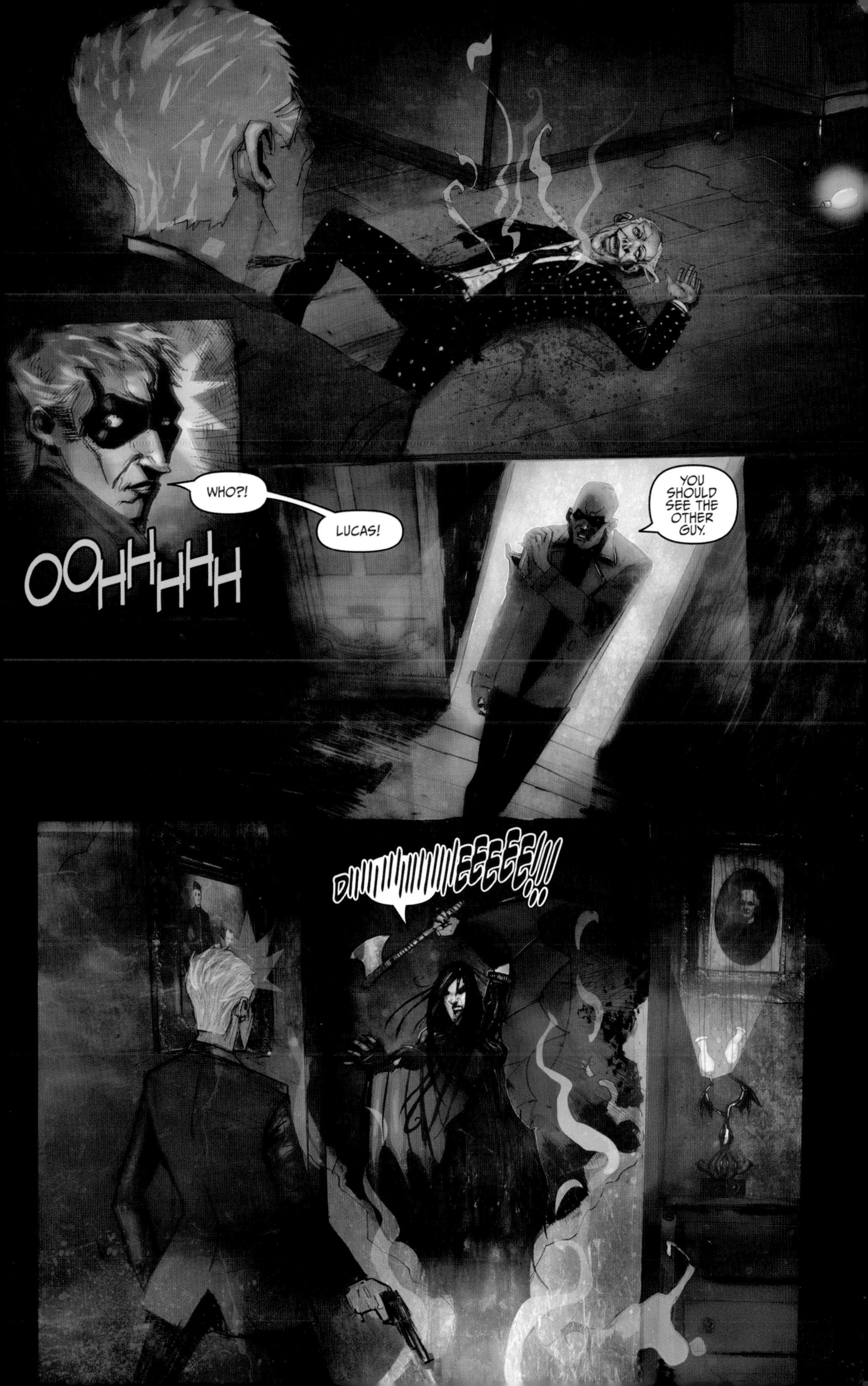
WHO?!
LUCAS!
YOU SHOULD SEE THE OTHER GUY.
OOHHHHHH
DIIIIIIIIIIIIIIEEEEE!!!

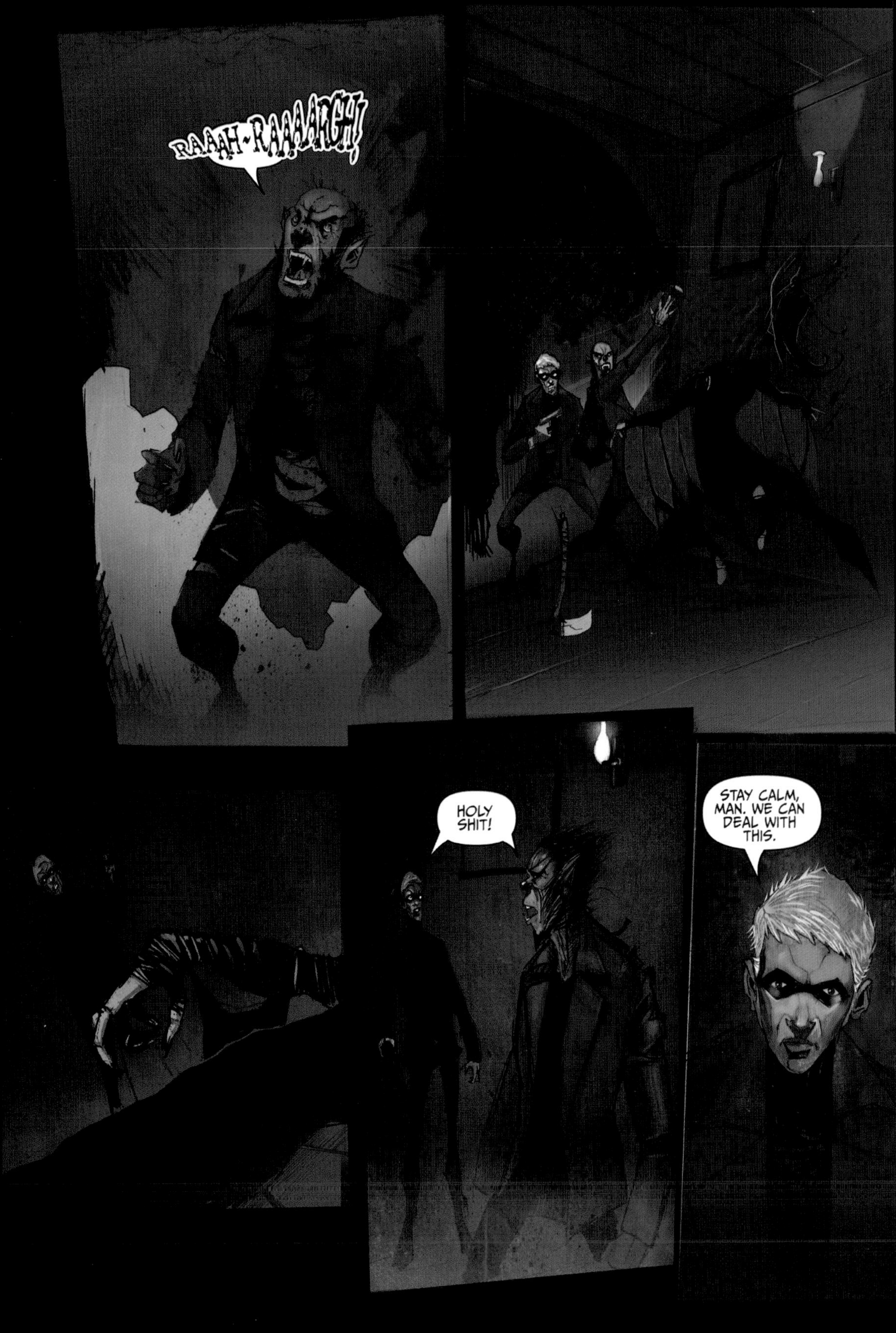
RAAAH-RAAAAARGH!
HOLY SHIT!
STAY CALM, MAN. WE CAN DEAL WITH THIS.

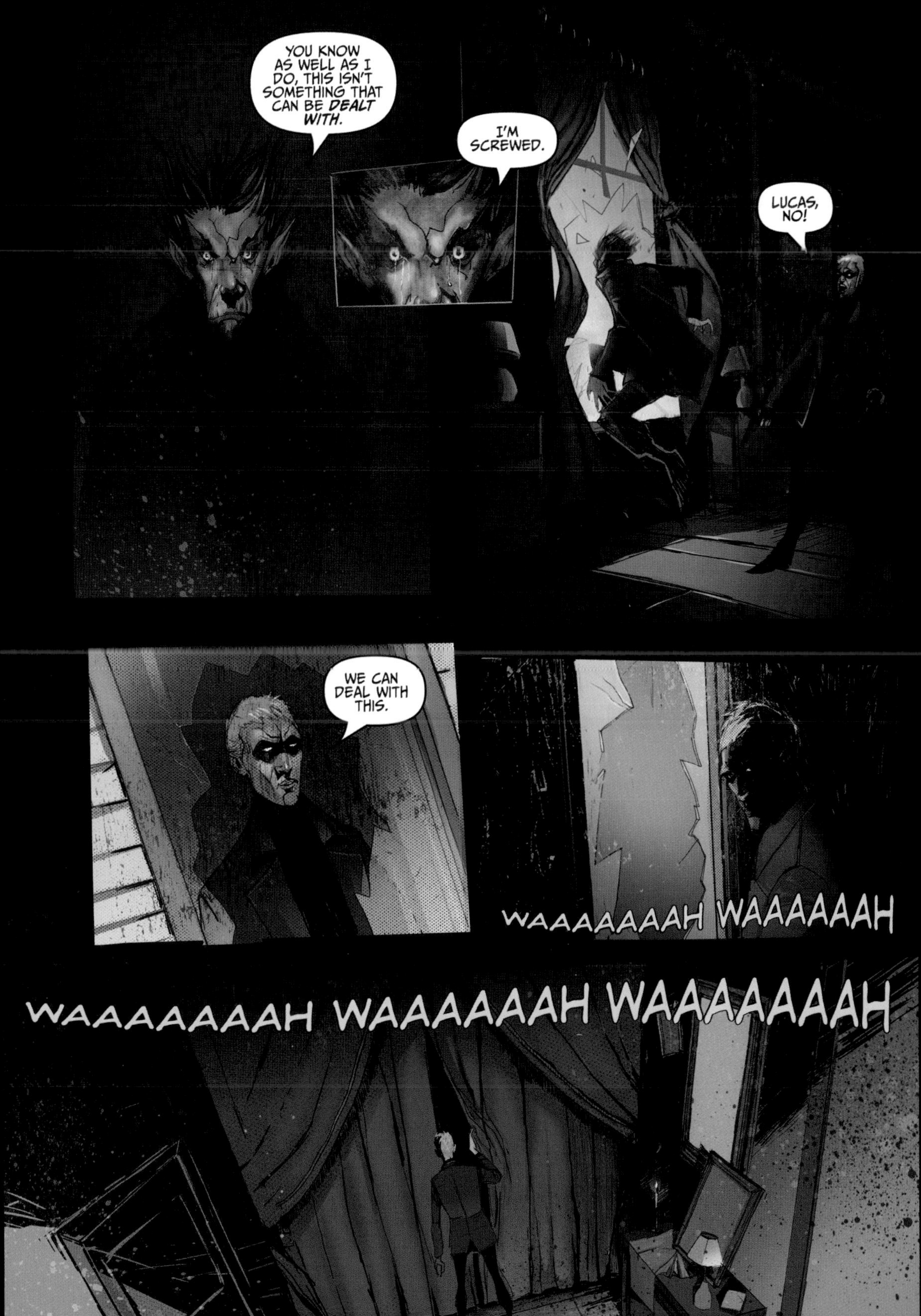
YOU KNOW AS WELL AS I DO, THIS ISN'T SOMETHING THAT CAN BE *DEALT WITH*.
I'M SCREWED.
LUCAS, NO!
WE CAN DEAL WITH THIS.
WAAAAAAAH WAAAAAAH
WAAAAAAAH WAAAAAAH WAAAAAAAH

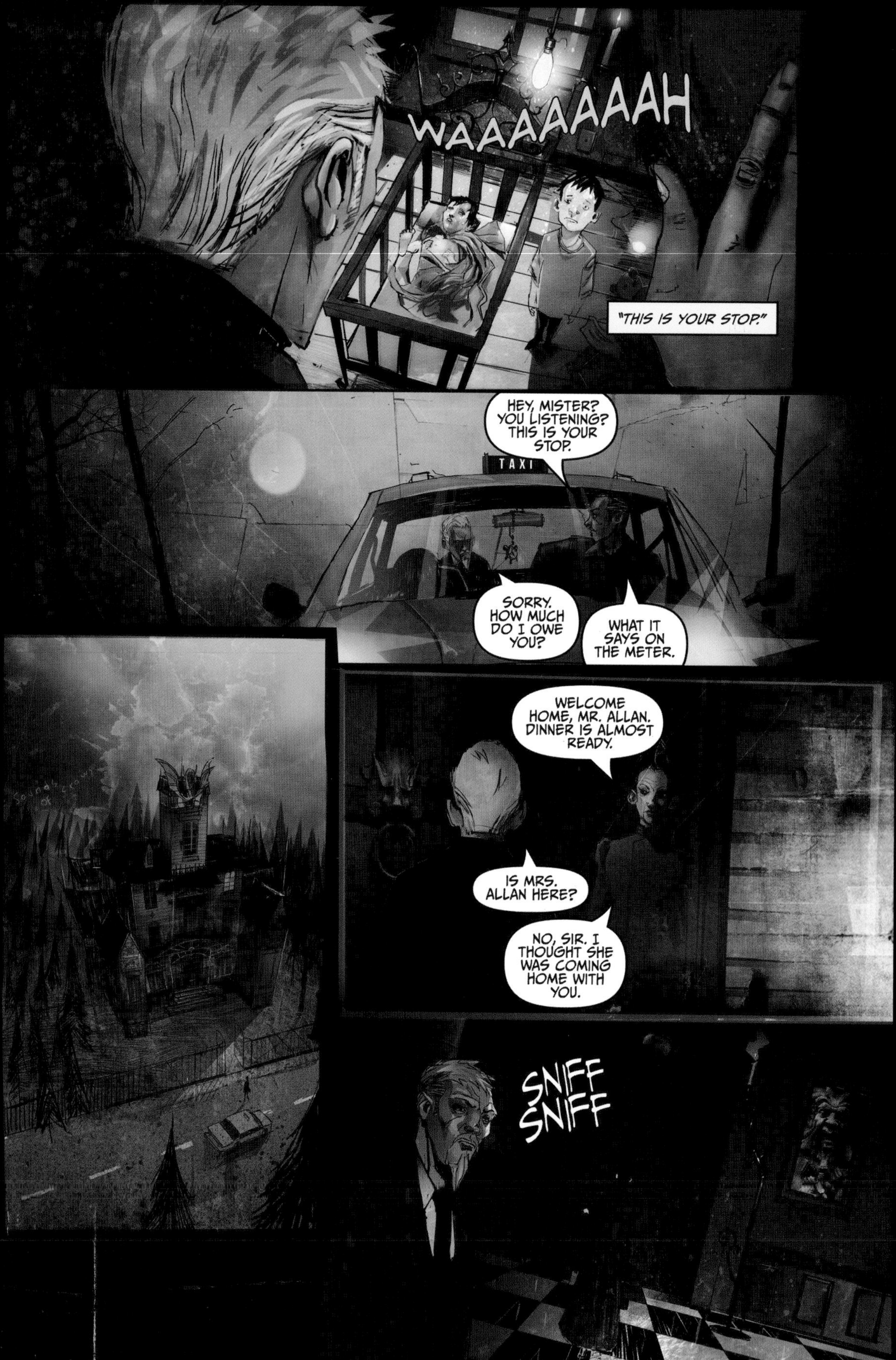
WAAAAAAAH
"THIS IS YOUR STOP."
HEY, MISTER? YOU LISTENING? THIS IS YOUR STOP.
TAXI
SORRY. HOW MUCH DO I OWE YOU?
WHAT IT SAYS ON THE METER.
WELCOME HOME, MR. ALLAN. DINNER IS ALMOST READY.
IS MRS. ALLAN HERE?
NO, SIR. I THOUGHT SHE WAS COMING HOME WITH YOU.
SNIFF SNIFF

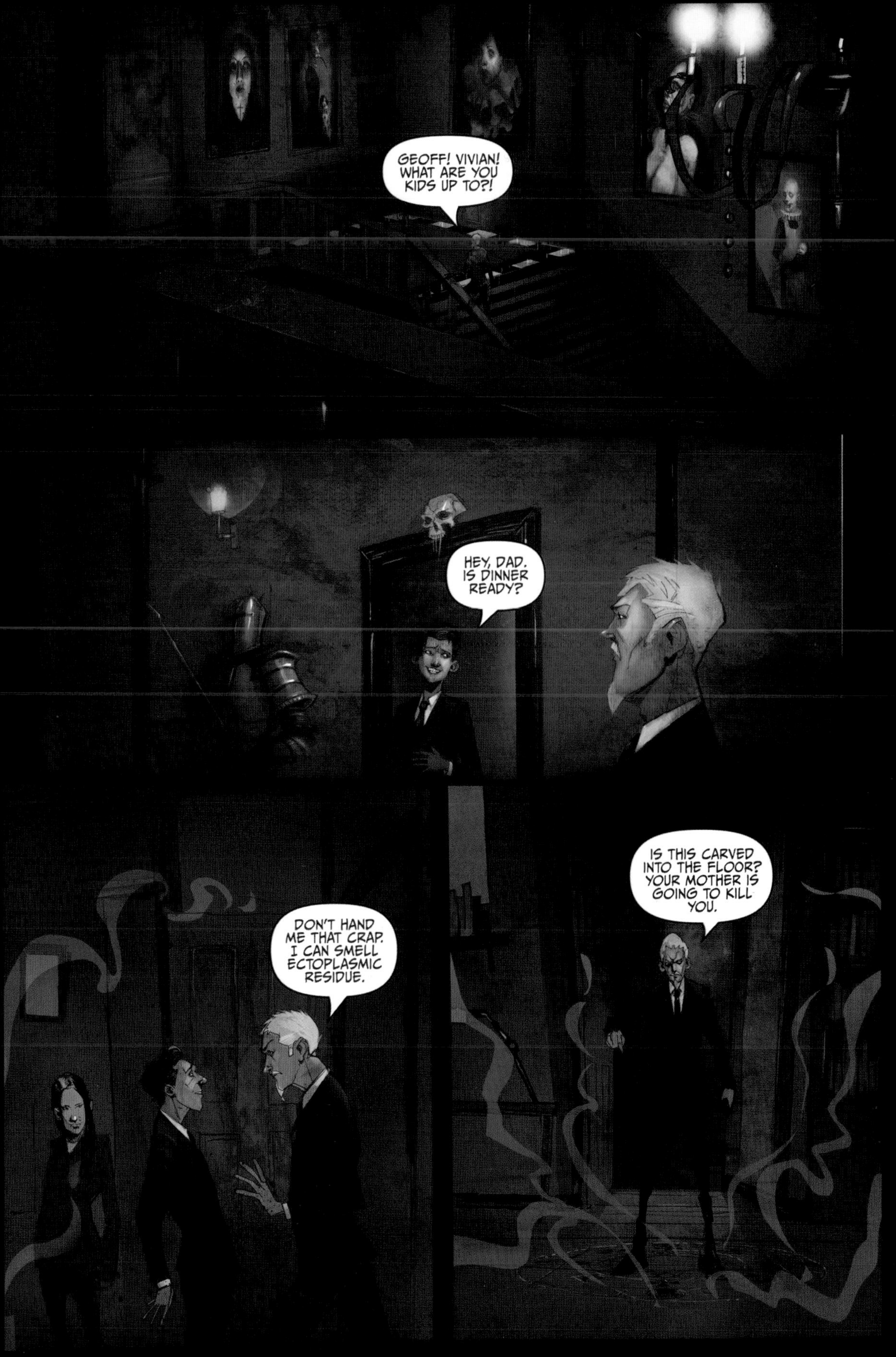
GEOFF! VIVIAN! WHAT ARE YOU KIDS UP TO?!
HEY, DAD. IS DINNER READY?
DON'T HAND ME THAT CRAP. I CAN SMELL ECTOPLASMIC RESIDUE.
IS THIS CARVED INTO THE FLOOR? YOUR MOTHER IS GOING TO KILL YOU.

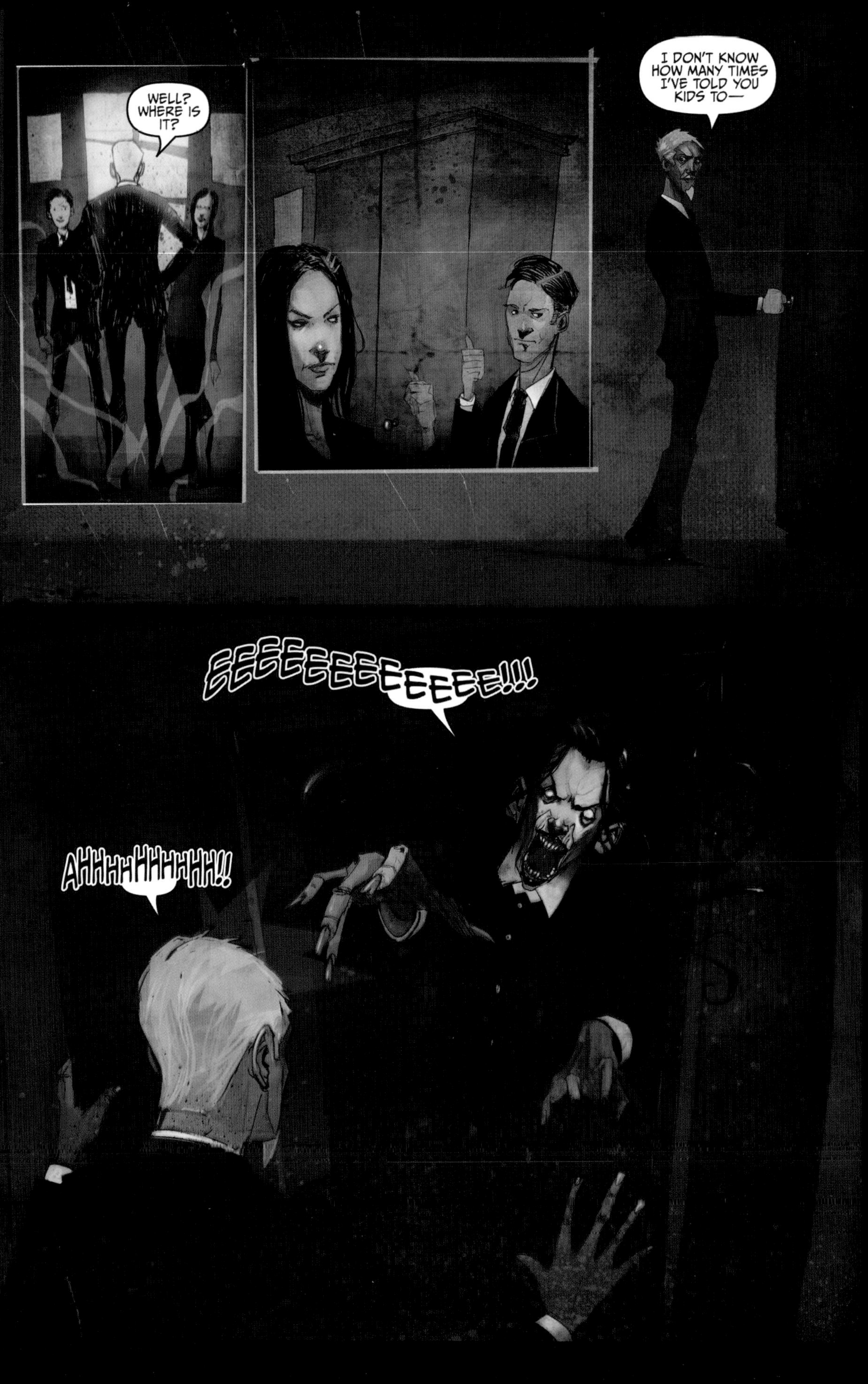
WELL? WHERE IS IT?
I DON'T KNOW HOW MANY TIMES I'VE TOLD YOU KIDS TO—
EEEEEEEEEEEEEEE!!!
AHHHHHHHHH!!

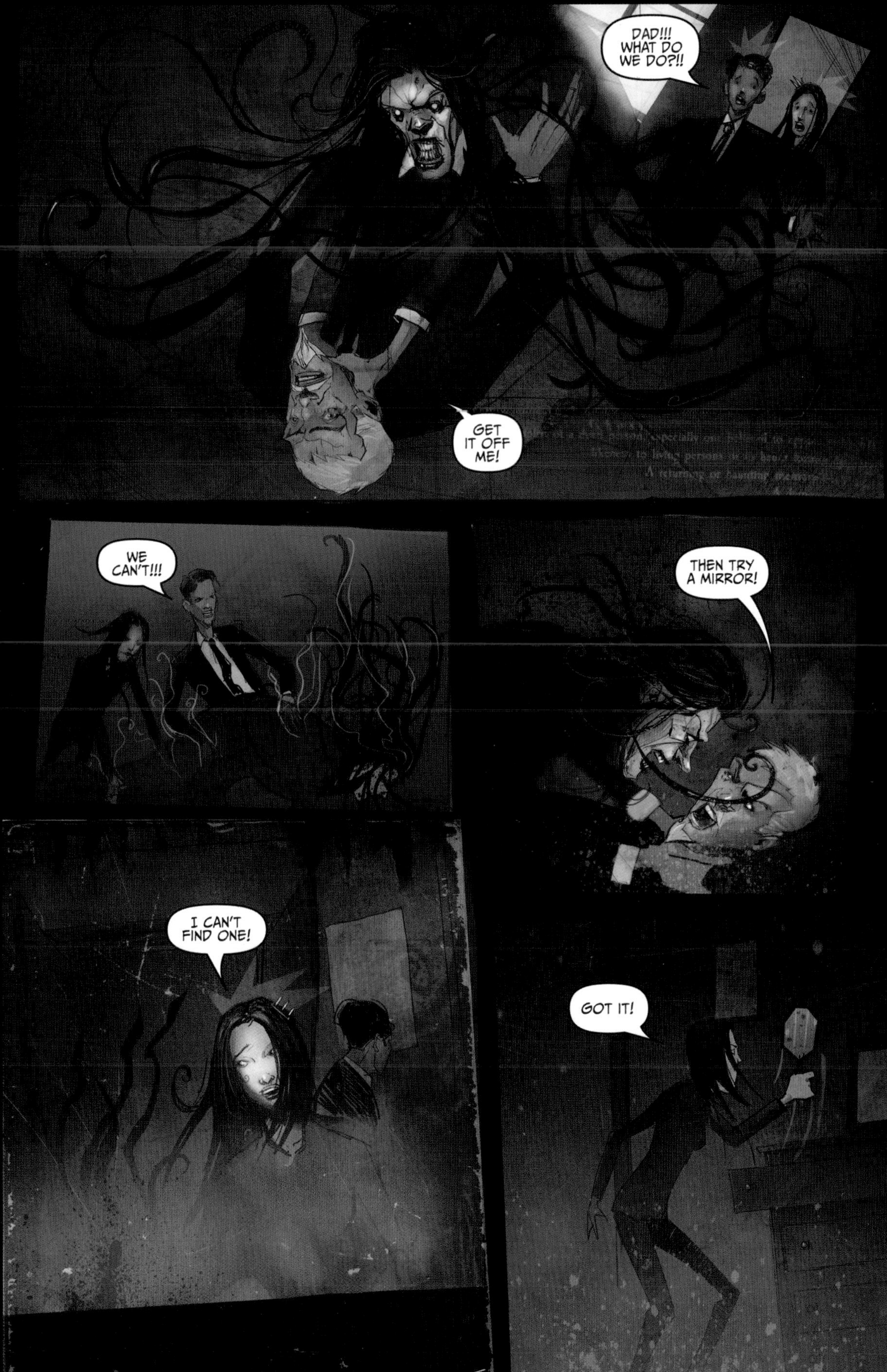
DAD!!! WHAT DO WE DO?!!
GET IT OFF ME!
WE CAN'T!!!
THEN TRY A MIRROR!
I CAN'T FIND ONE!
GOT IT!

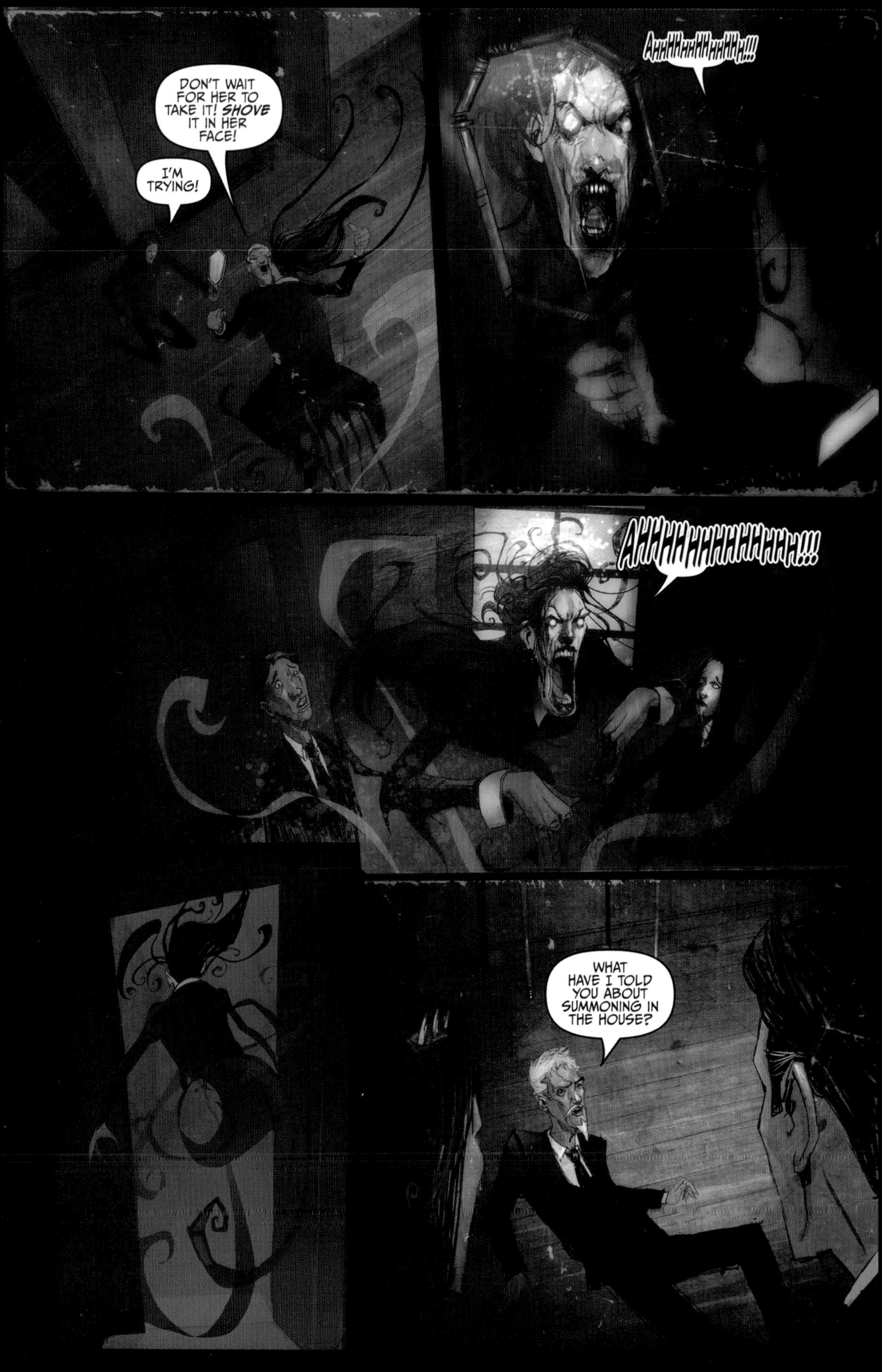
DON'T WAIT FOR HER TO TAKE IT! SHOVE IT IN HER FACE!
I'M TRYING!
AaaHHaaHHaaHHh!!!
AHHHHHHHHHHHHH!!!
WHAT HAVE I TOLD YOU ABOUT SUMMONING IN THE HOUSE?

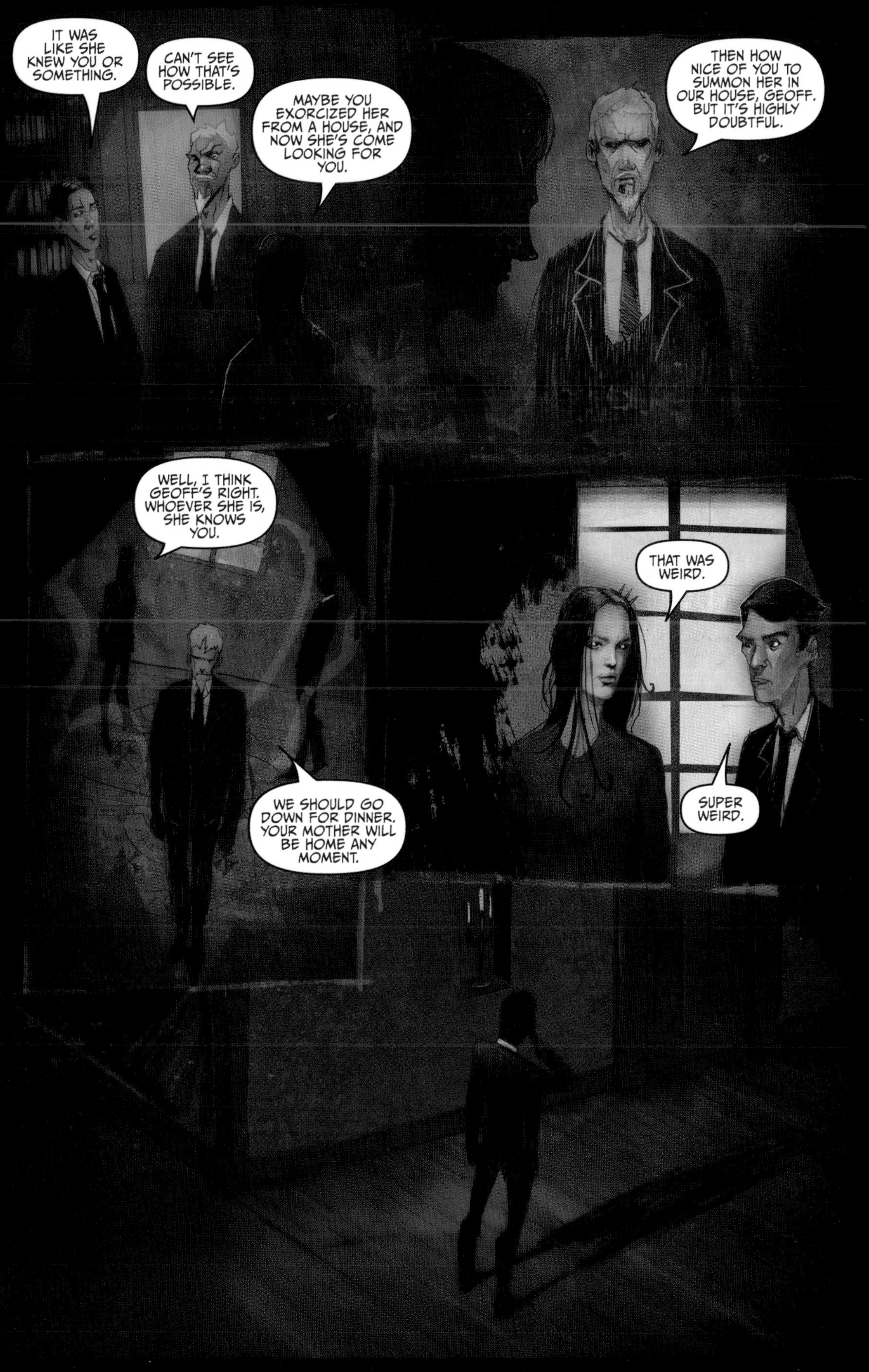
IT WAS LIKE SHE KNEW YOU OR SOMETHING.
CAN'T SEE HOW THAT'S POSSIBLE.
MAYBE YOU EXORCIZED HER FROM A HOUSE, AND NOW SHE'S COME LOOKING FOR YOU.
THEN HOW NICE OF YOU TO SUMMON HER IN OUR HOUSE, GEOFF. BUT IT'S HIGHLY DOUBTFUL.
WELL, I THINK GEOFF'S RIGHT. WHOEVER SHE IS, SHE KNOWS YOU.
WE SHOULD GO DOWN FOR DINNER. YOUR MOTHER WILL BE HOME ANY MOMENT.
THAT WAS WEIRD.
SUPER WEIRD.

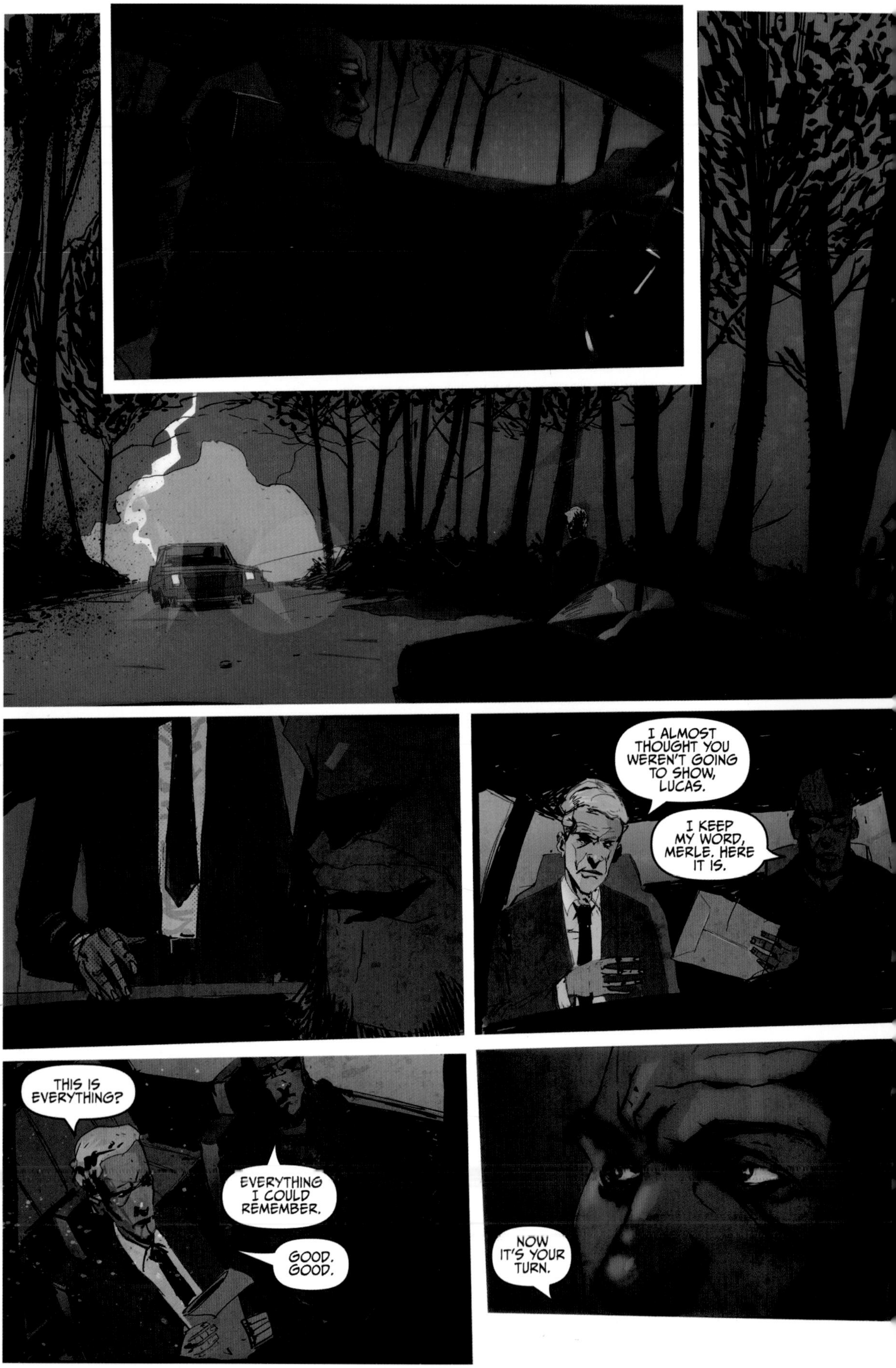
I ALMOST THOUGHT YOU WEREN'T GOING TO SHOW, LUCAS.
I KEEP MY WORD, MERLE. HERE IT IS.
THIS IS EVERYTHING?
EVERYTHING I COULD REMEMBER.
GOOD. GOOD.
NOW IT'S YOUR TURN.

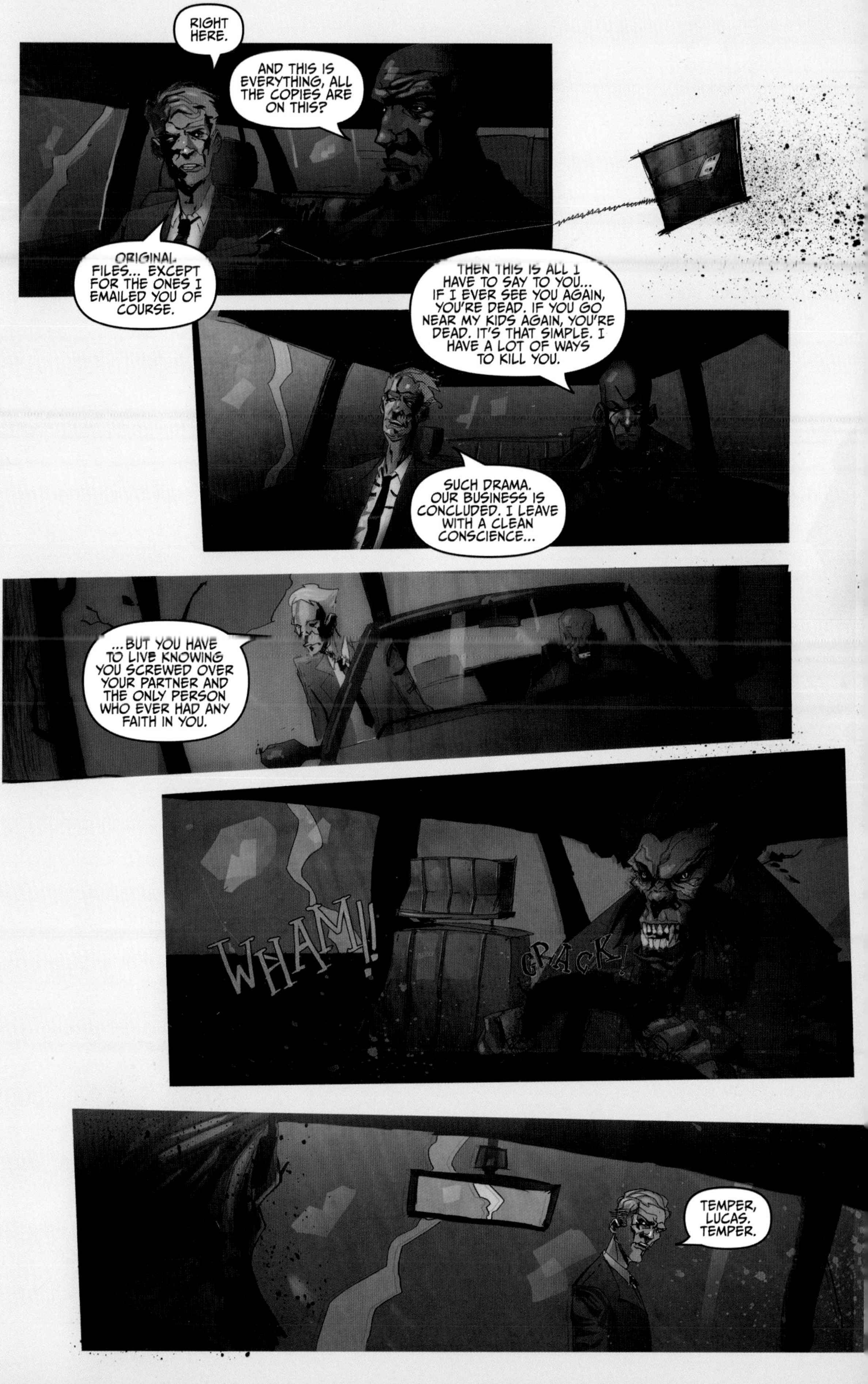

RIGHT HERE.
AND THIS IS EVERYTHING, ALL THE COPIES ARE ON THIS?
ORIGINAL FILES... EXCEPT FOR THE ONES I EMAILED YOU OF COURSE.
THEN THIS IS ALL I HAVE TO SAY TO YOU... IF I EVER SEE YOU AGAIN, YOU'RE DEAD. IF YOU GO NEAR MY KIDS AGAIN, YOU'RE DEAD. IT'S THAT SIMPLE. I HAVE A LOT OF WAYS TO KILL YOU.
SUCH DRAMA. OUR BUSINESS IS CONCLUDED. I LEAVE WITH A CLEAN CONSCIENCE...
...BUT YOU HAVE TO LIVE KNOWING YOU SCREWED OVER YOUR PARTNER AND THE ONLY PERSON WHO EVER HAD ANY FAITH IN YOU.
WHAM!!
CRACK!
TEMPER, LUCAS. TEMPER.

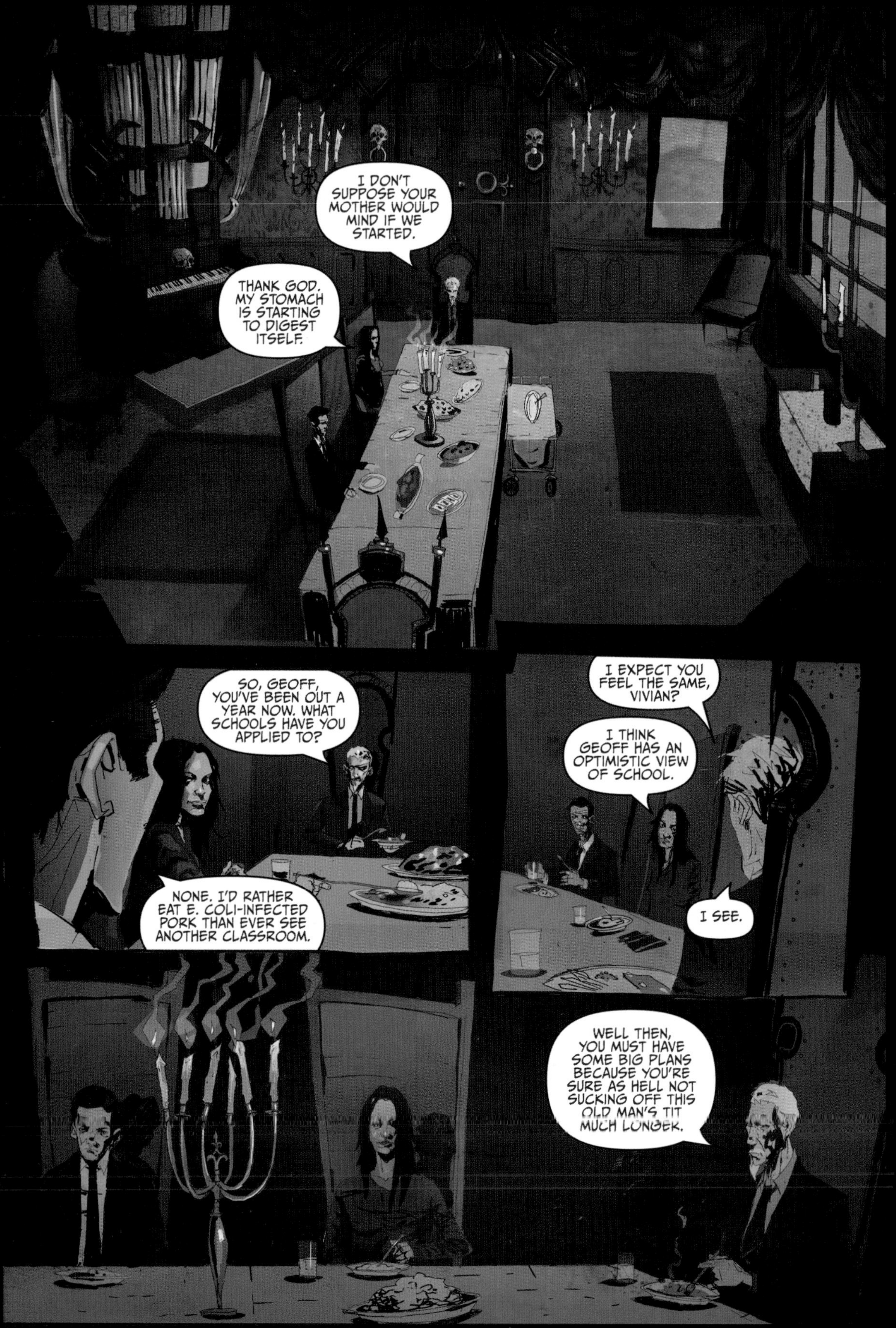
I DON'T SUPPOSE YOUR MOTHER WOULD MIND IF WE STARTED.
THANK GOD. MY STOMACH IS STARTING TO DIGEST ITSELF.
SO, GEOFF, YOU'VE BEEN OUT A YEAR NOW. WHAT SCHOOLS HAVE YOU APPLIED TO?
NONE. I'D RATHER EAT E. COLI-INFECTED PORK THAN EVER SEE ANOTHER CLASSROOM.
I EXPECT YOU FEEL THE SAME, VIVIAN?
I THINK GEOFF HAS AN OPTIMISTIC VIEW OF SCHOOL.
I SEE.
WELL THEN, YOU MUST HAVE SOME BIG PLANS BECAUSE YOU'RE SURE AS HELL NOT SUCKING OFF THIS OLD MAN'S TIT MUCH LONGER.

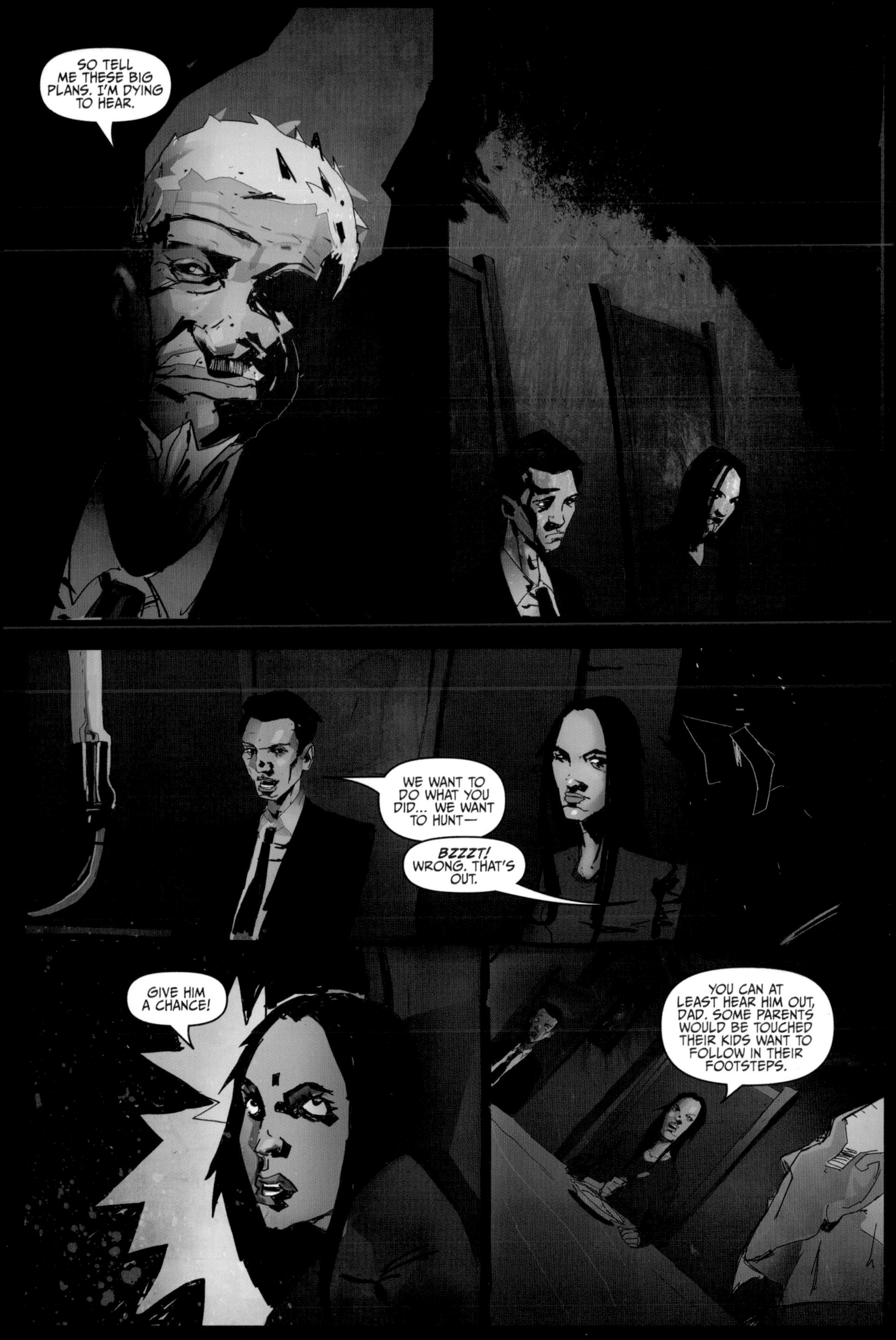
SO TELL ME THESE BIG PLANS. I'M DYING TO HEAR.
WE WANT TO DO WHAT YOU DID... WE WANT TO HUNT—
BZZZT! WRONG. THAT'S OUT.
GIVE HIM A CHANCE!
YOU CAN AT LEAST HEAR HIM OUT, DAD. SOME PARENTS WOULD BE TOUCHED THEIR KIDS WANT TO FOLLOW IN THEIR FOOTSTEPS.

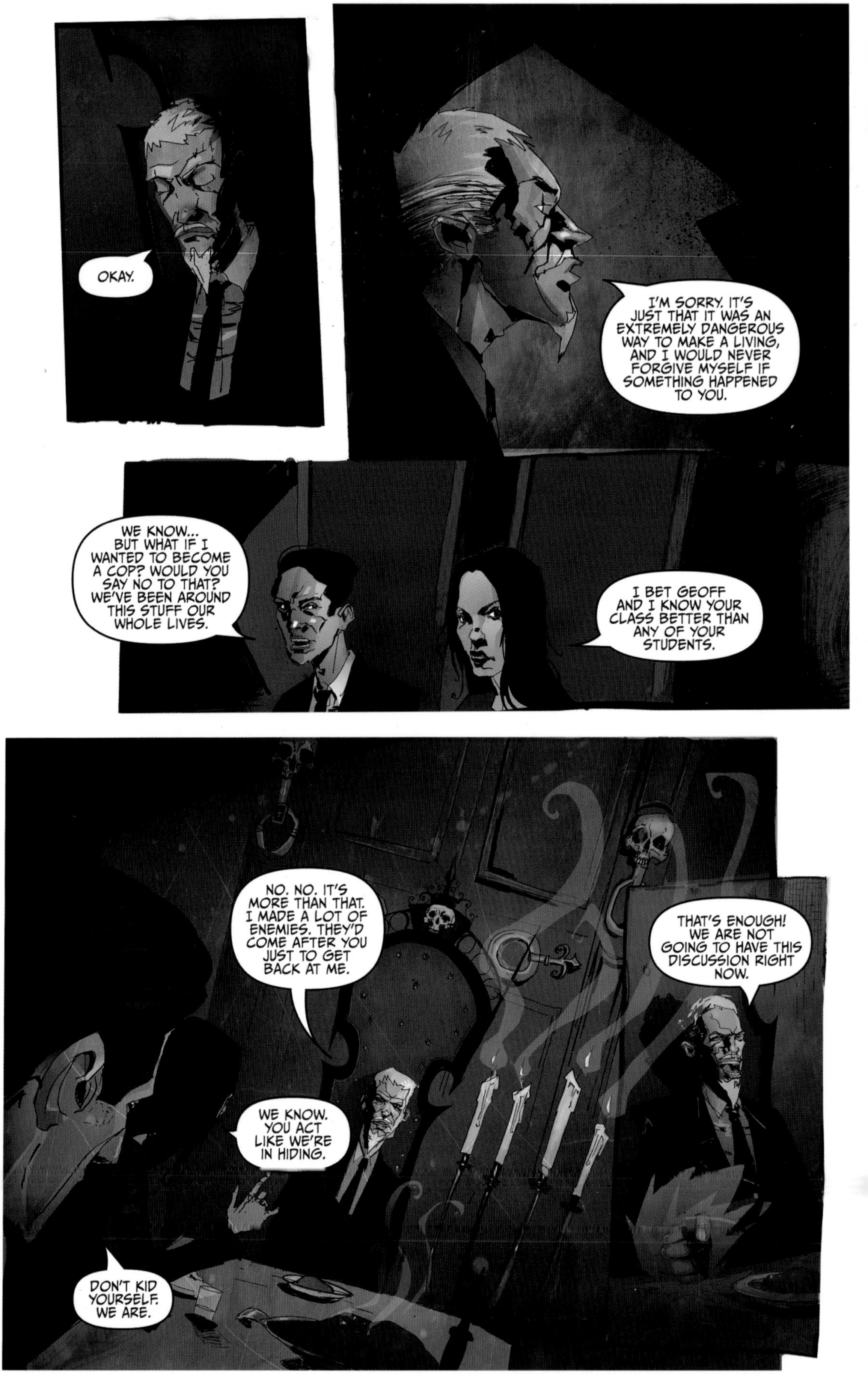
OKAY.
I'M SORRY. IT'S JUST THAT IT WAS AN EXTREMELY DANGEROUS WAY TO MAKE A LIVING, AND I WOULD NEVER FORGIVE MYSELF IF SOMETHING HAPPENED TO YOU.
WE KNOW... BUT WHAT IF I WANTED TO BECOME A COP? WOULD YOU SAY NO TO THAT? WE'VE BEEN AROUND THIS STUFF OUR WHOLE LIVES.
I BET GEOFF AND I KNOW YOUR CLASS BETTER THAN ANY OF YOUR STUDENTS.
NO. NO. IT'S MORE THAN THAT. I MADE A LOT OF ENEMIES. THEY'D COME AFTER YOU JUST TO GET BACK AT ME.
WE KNOW. YOU ACT LIKE WE'RE IN HIDING.
DON'T KID YOURSELF. WE ARE.
THAT'S ENOUGH! WE ARE NOT GOING TO HAVE THIS DISCUSSION RIGHT NOW.

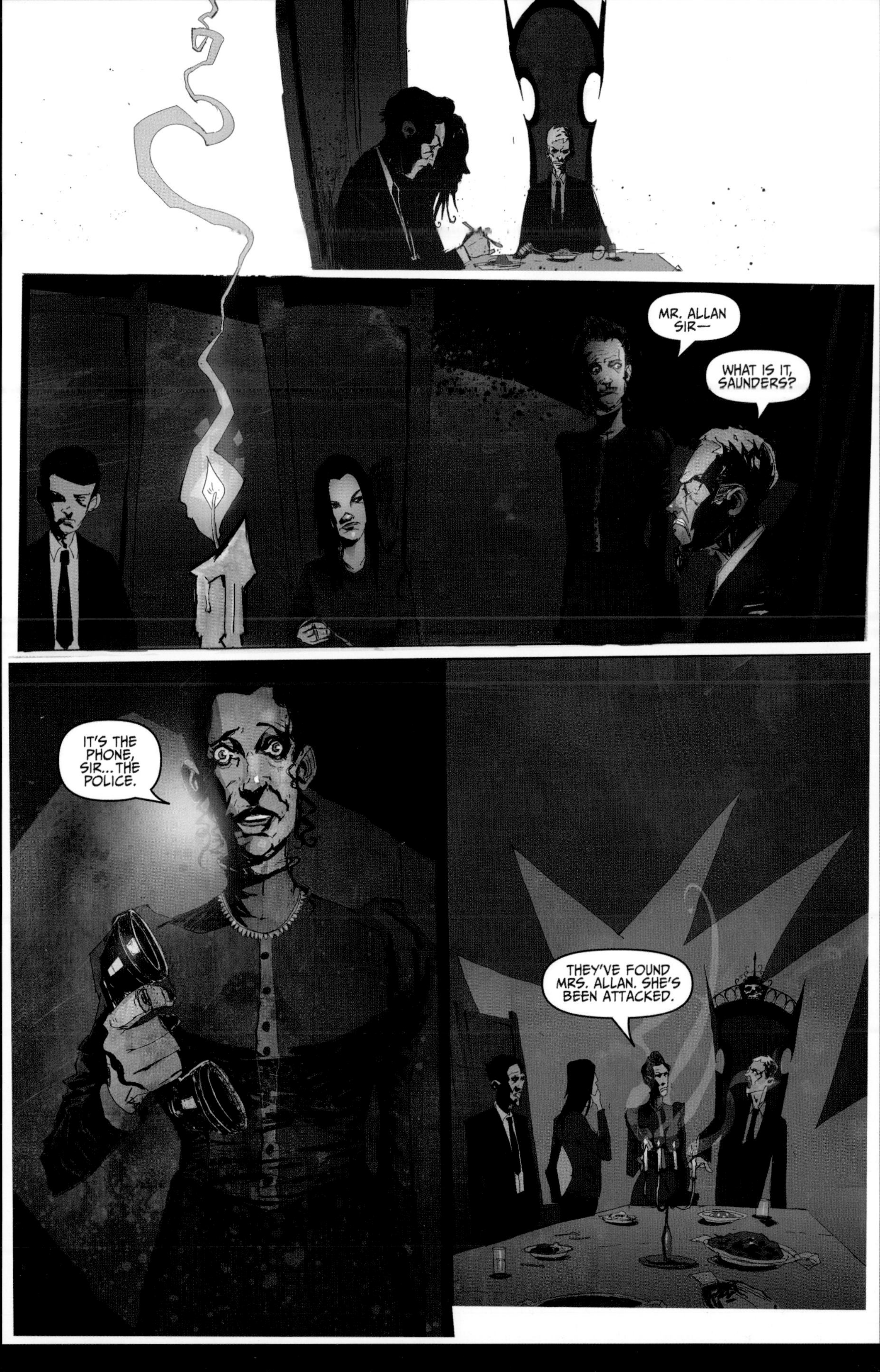
MR. ALLAN SIR—
WHAT IS IT, SAUNDERS?
IT'S THE PHONE, SIR... THE POLICE.
THEY'VE FOUND MRS. ALLAN. SHE'S BEEN ATTACKED.

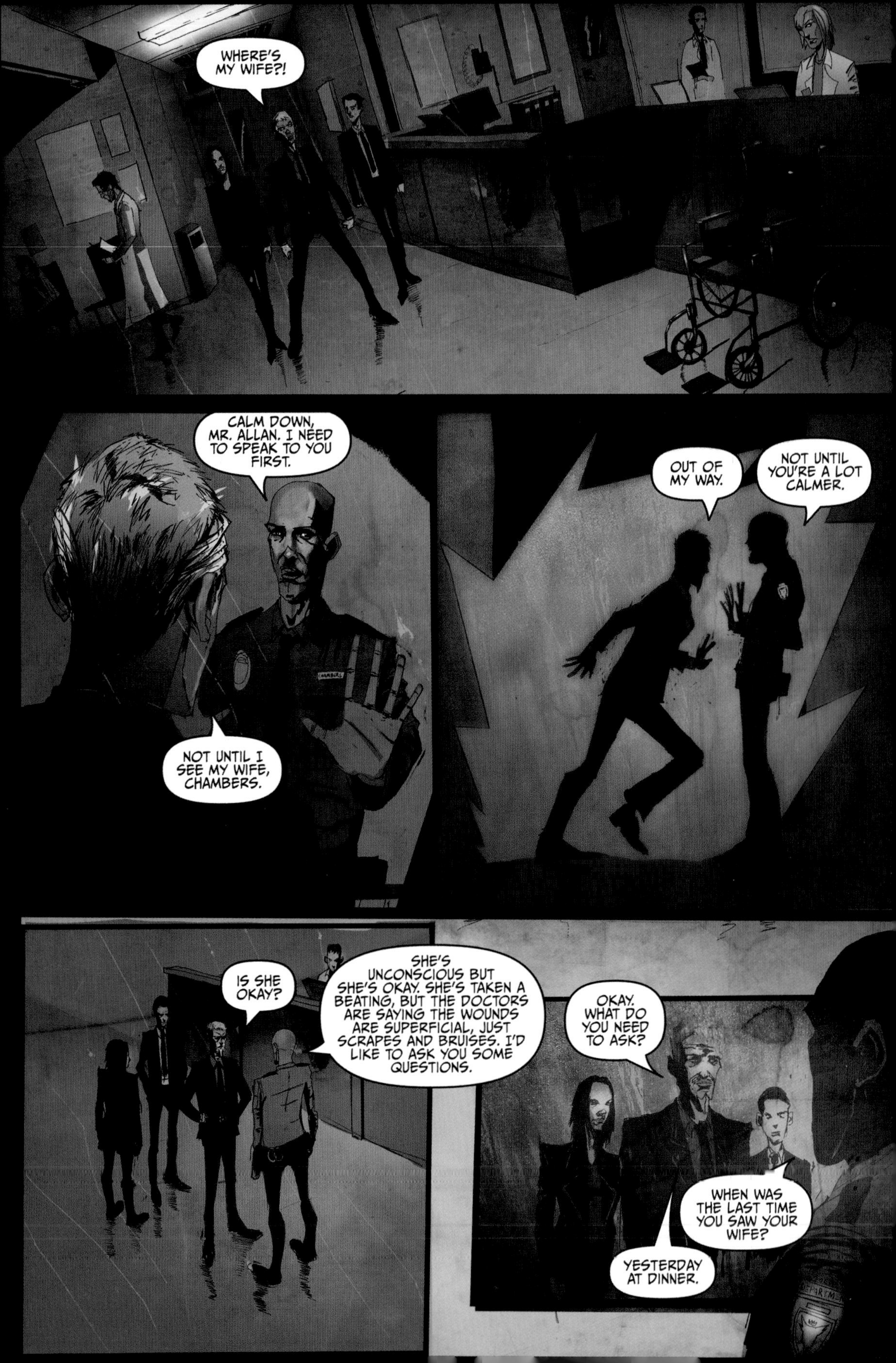
WHERE'S MY WIFE?!
CALM DOWN, MR. ALLAN. I NEED TO SPEAK TO YOU FIRST.
NOT UNTIL I SEE MY WIFE, CHAMBERS.
OUT OF MY WAY.
NOT UNTIL YOU'RE A LOT CALMER.
IS SHE OKAY?
SHE'S UNCONSCIOUS BUT SHE'S OKAY. SHE'S TAKEN A BEATING, BUT THE DOCTORS ARE SAYING THE WOUNDS ARE SUPERFICIAL, JUST SCRAPES AND BRUISES. I'D LIKE TO ASK YOU SOME QUESTIONS.
OKAY. WHAT DO YOU NEED TO ASK?
WHEN WAS THE LAST TIME YOU SAW YOUR WIFE?
YESTERDAY AT DINNER.

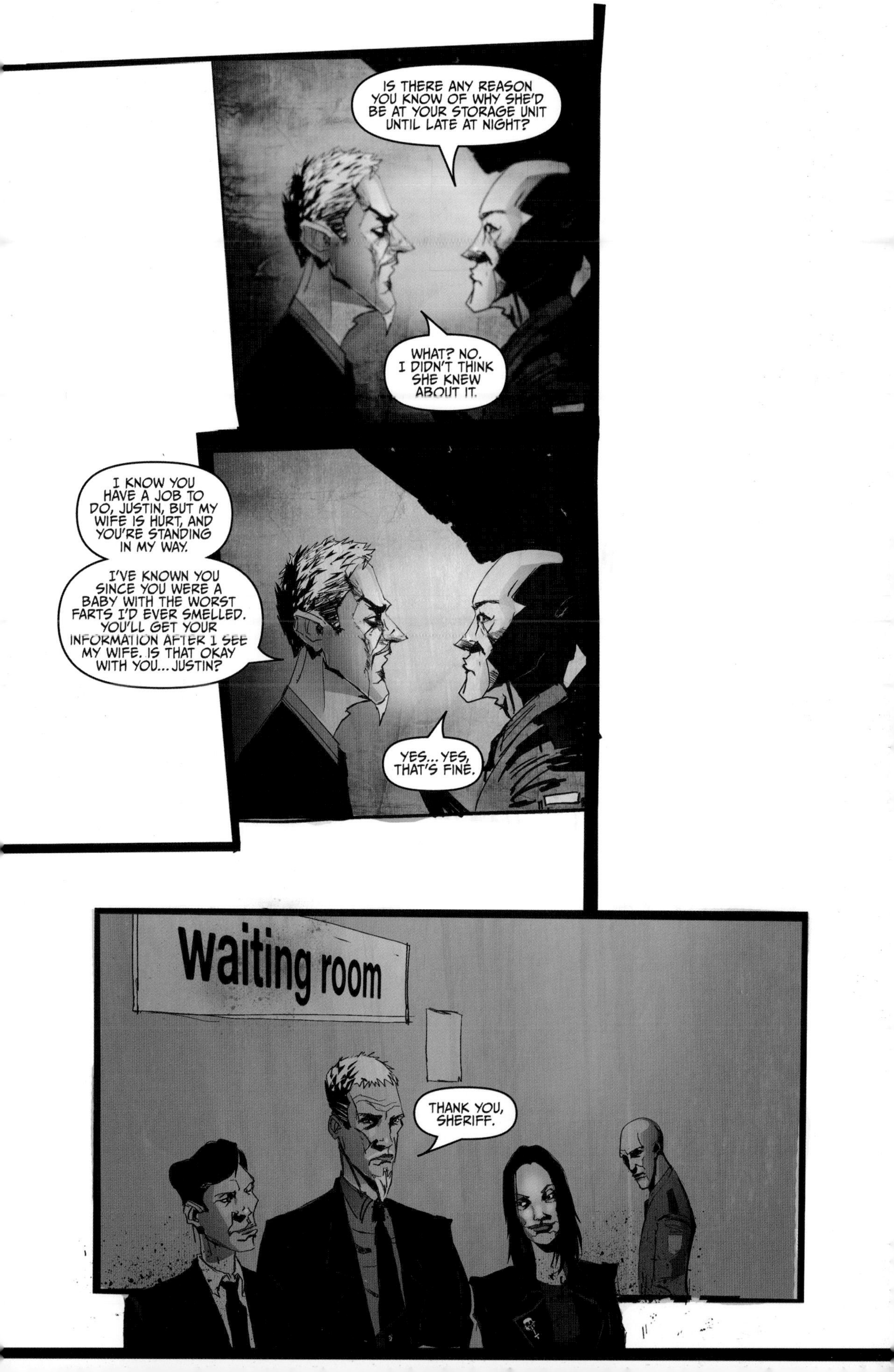
IS THERE ANY REASON YOU KNOW OF WHY SHE'D BE AT YOUR STORAGE UNIT UNTIL LATE AT NIGHT?
WHAT? NO. I DIDN'T THINK SHE KNEW ABOUT IT.
I KNOW YOU HAVE A JOB TO DO, JUSTIN, BUT MY WIFE IS HURT, AND YOU'RE STANDING IN MY WAY.
I'VE KNOWN YOU SINCE YOU WERE A BABY WITH THE WORST FARTS I'D EVER SMELLED. YOU'LL GET YOUR INFORMATION AFTER I SEE MY WIFE. IS THAT OKAY WITH YOU... JUSTIN?
YES... YES, THAT'S FINE.
waiting room
THANK YOU, SHERIFF.

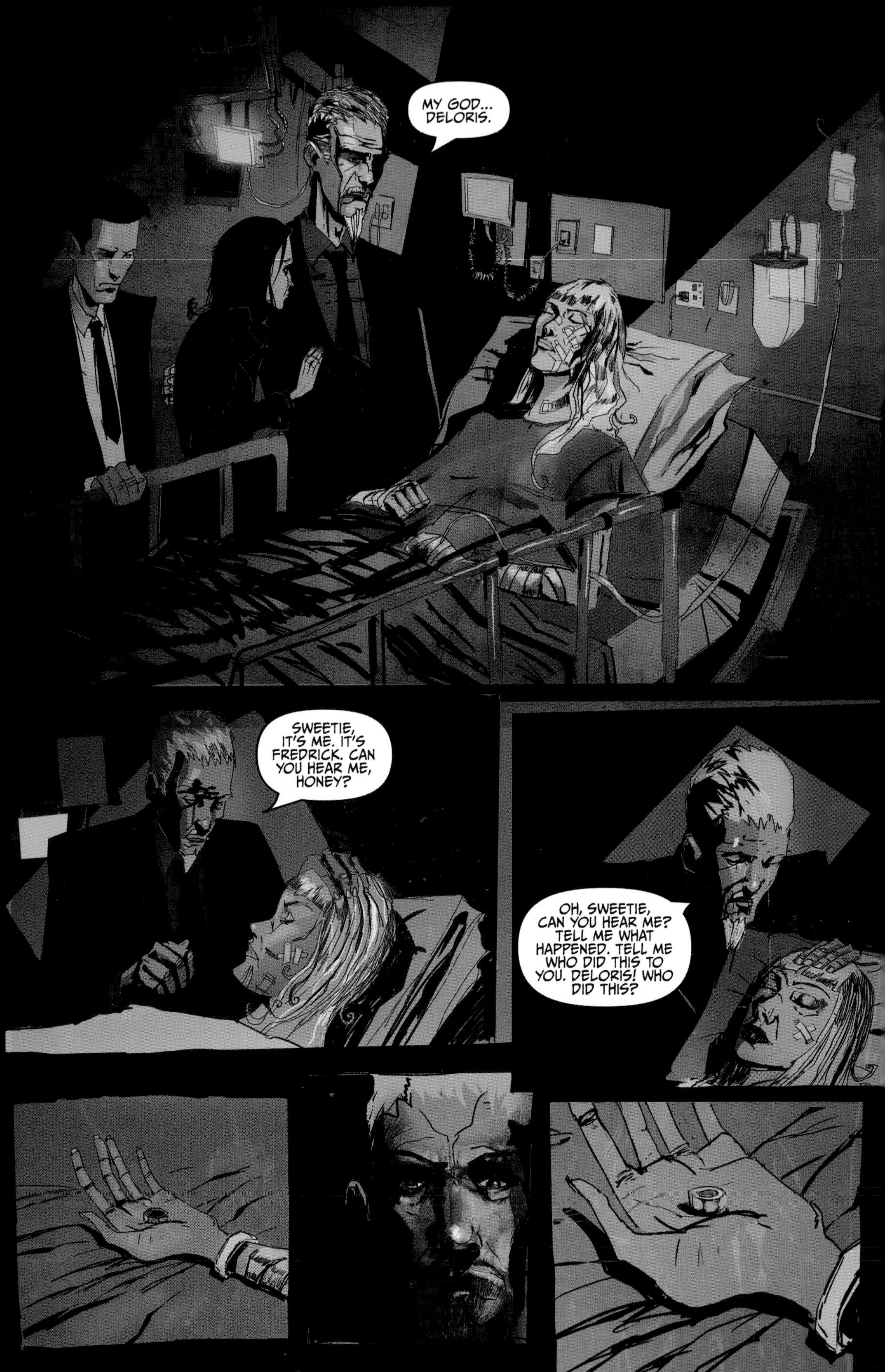
MY GOD... DELORIS.
SWEETIE, IT'S ME. IT'S FREDRICK. CAN YOU HEAR ME, HONEY?
OH, SWEETIE, CAN YOU HEAR ME? TELL ME WHAT HAPPENED. TELL ME WHO DID THIS TO YOU. DELORIS! WHO DID THIS?

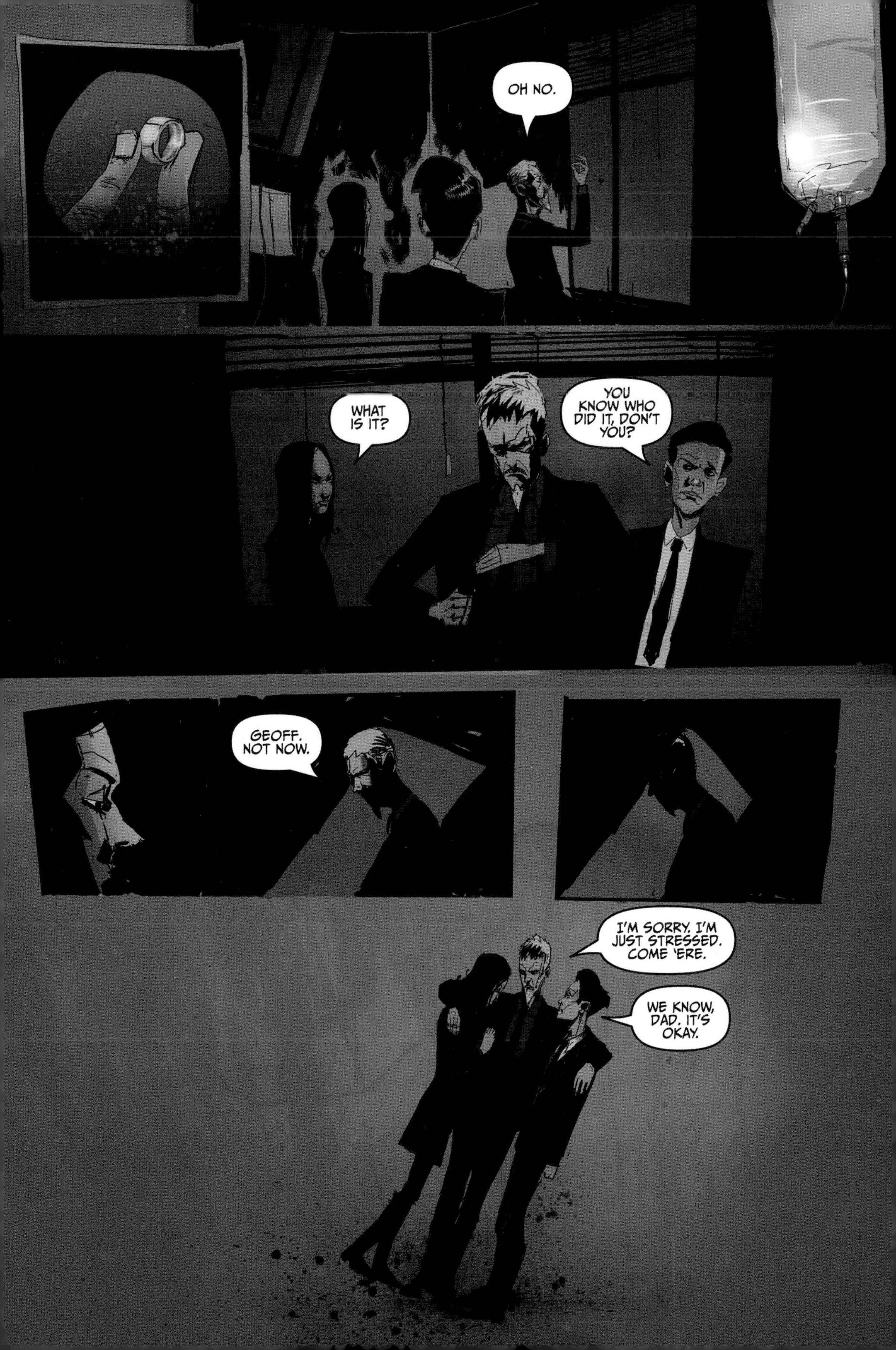
OH NO.
WHAT IS IT?
YOU KNOW WHO DID IT, DON'T YOU?
GEOFF. NOT NOW.
I'M SORRY. I'M JUST STRESSED. COME 'ERE.
WE KNOW, DAD. IT'S OKAY.

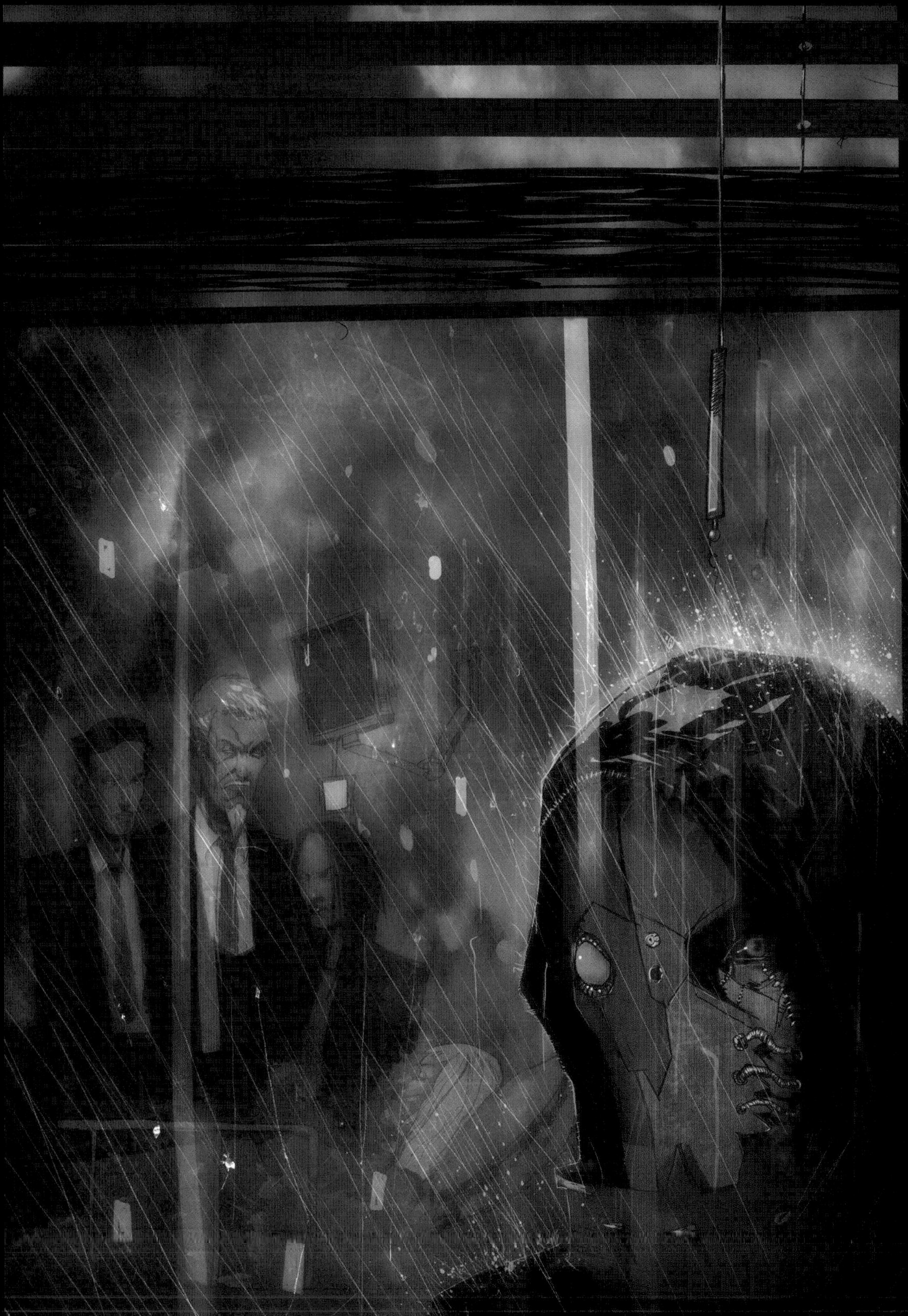

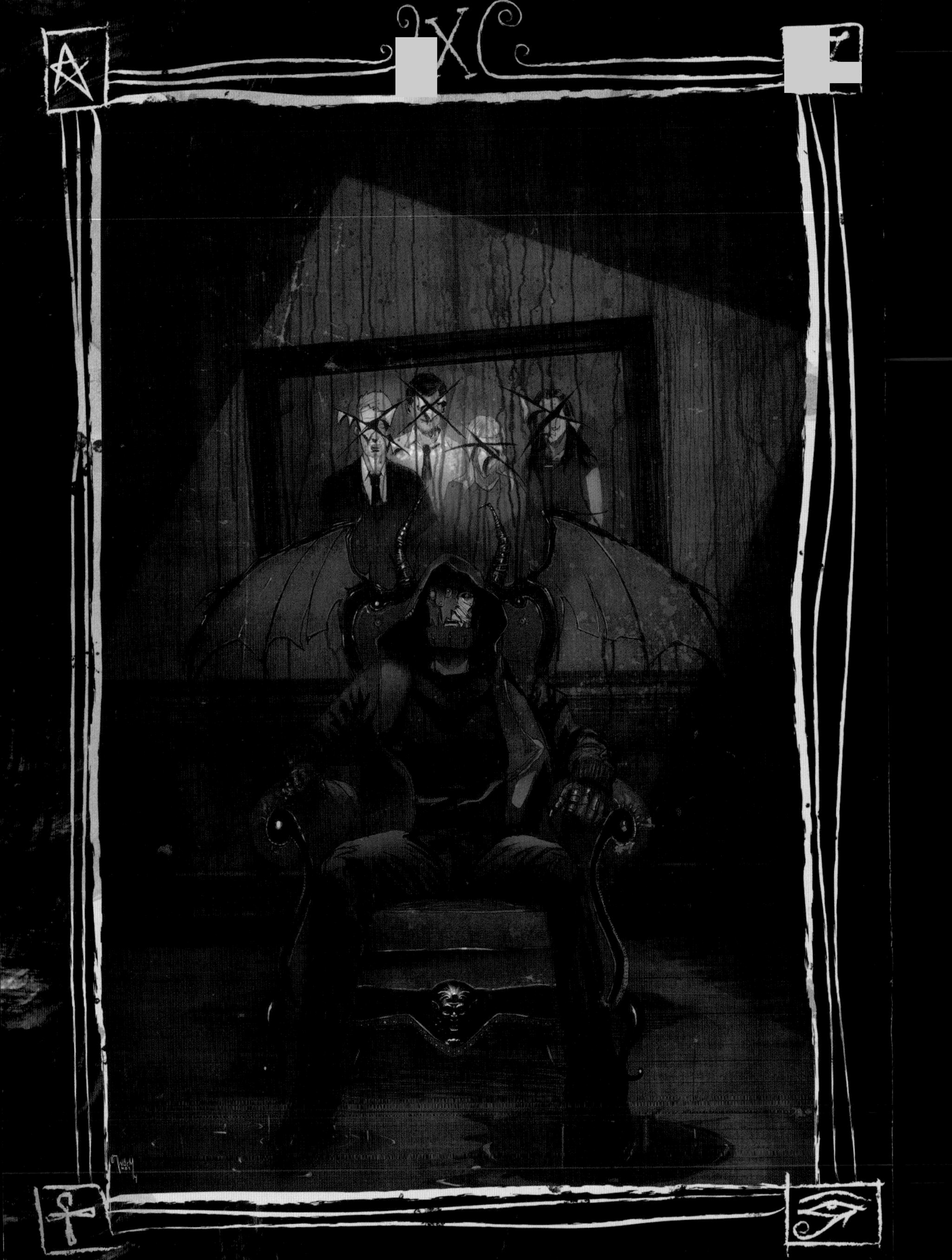

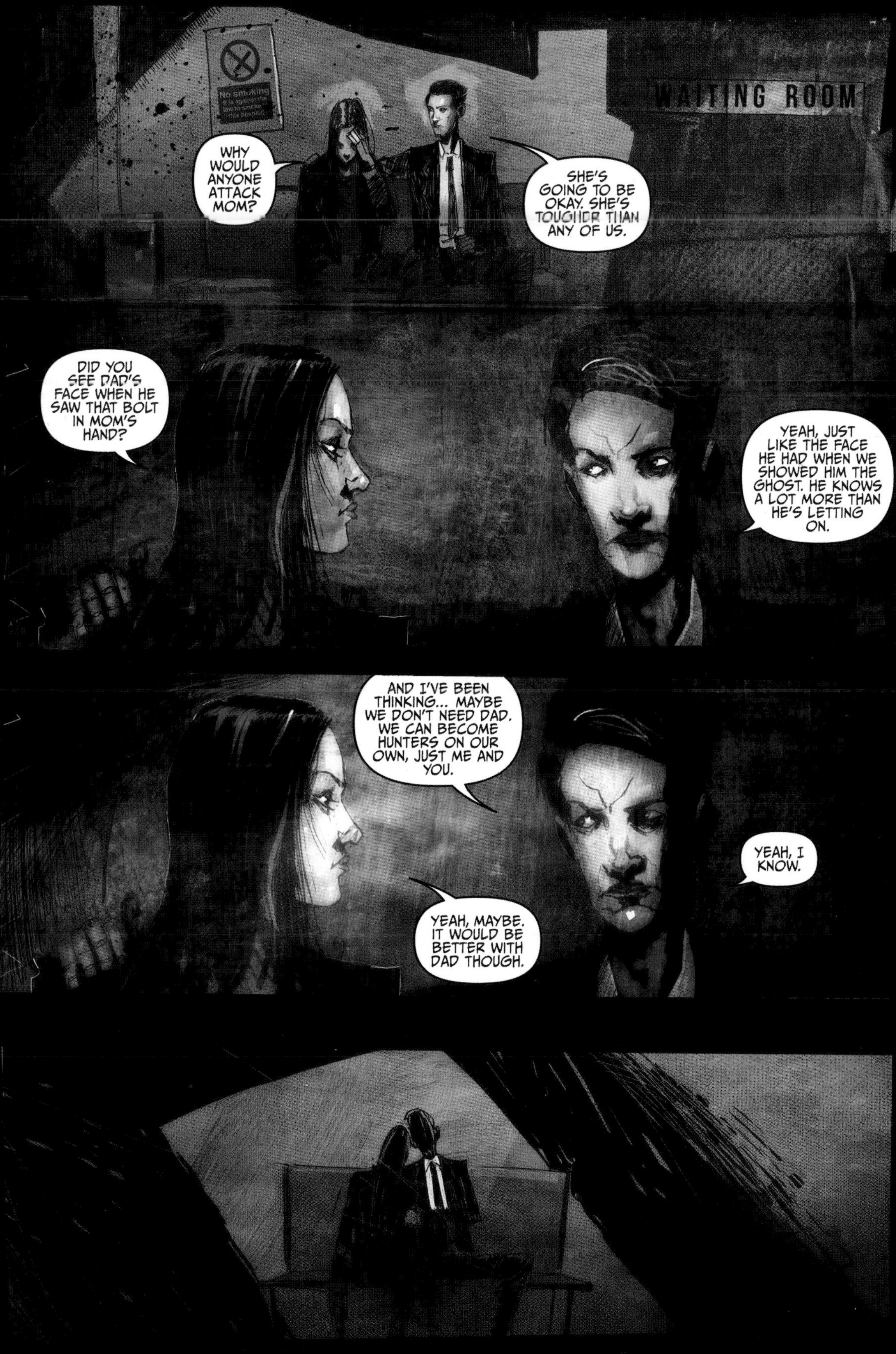
No smoking
WAITING ROOM
WHY WOULD ANYONE ATTACK MOM?
SHE'S GOING TO BE OKAY. SHE'S TOUGHER THAN ANY OF US.
DID YOU SEE DAD'S FACE WHEN HE SAW THAT BOLT IN MOM'S HAND?
YEAH, JUST LIKE THE FACE HE HAD WHEN WE SHOWED HIM THE GHOST. HE KNOWS A LOT MORE THAN HE'S LETTING ON.
AND I'VE BEEN THINKING... MAYBE WE DON'T NEED DAD. WE CAN BECOME HUNTERS ON OUR OWN, JUST ME AND YOU.
YEAH, MAYBE. IT WOULD BE BETTER WITH DAD THOUGH.
YEAH, I KNOW.

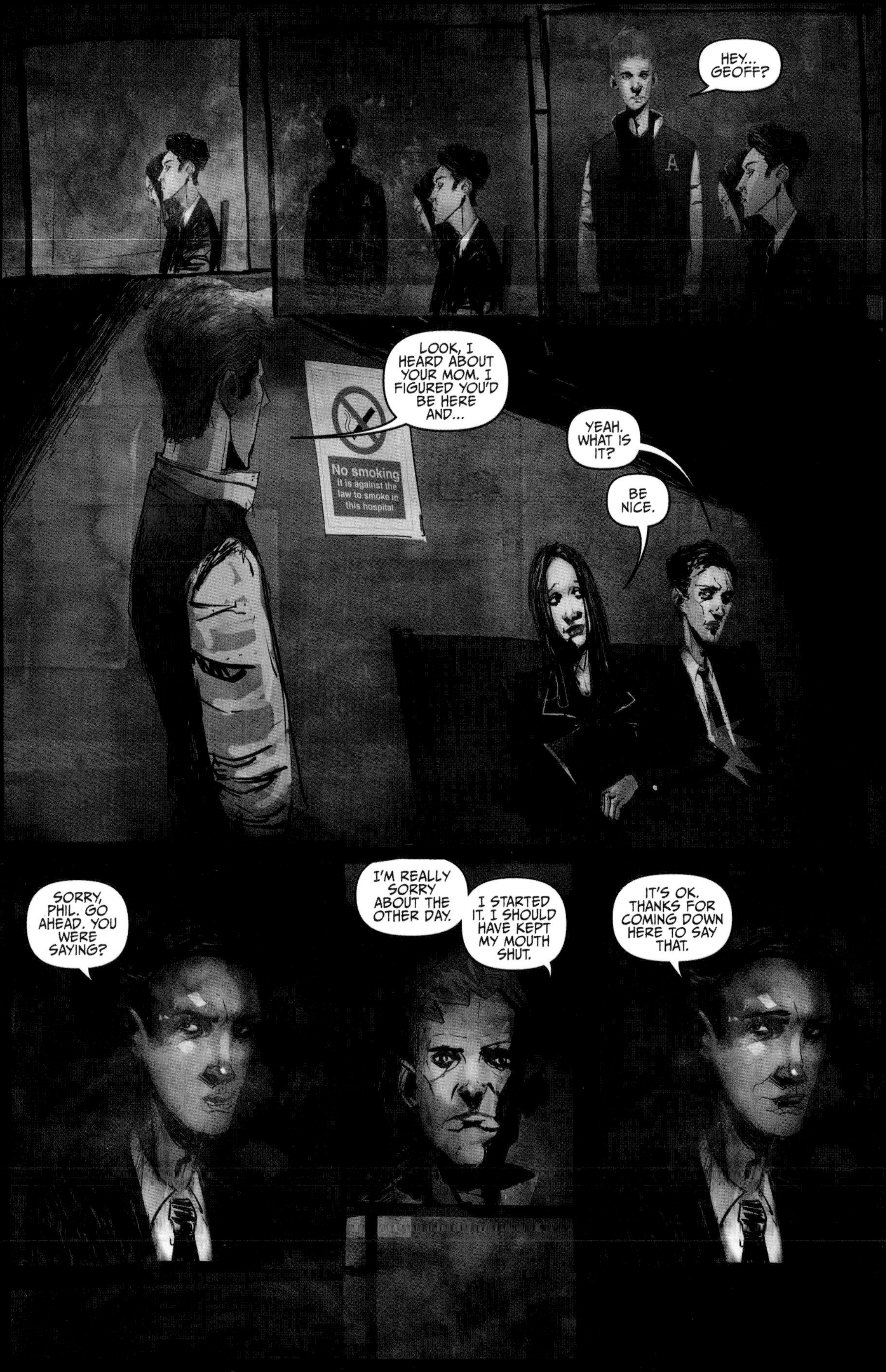
HEY... GEOFF?
LOOK, I HEARD ABOUT YOUR MOM. I FIGURED YOU'D BE HERE AND...
No smoking
It is against the law to smoke in this hospital
YEAH. WHAT IS IT?
BE NICE.
SORRY, PHIL. GO AHEAD. YOU WERE SAYING?
I'M REALLY SORRY ABOUT THE OTHER DAY.
I STARTED IT. I SHOULD HAVE KEPT MY MOUTH SHUT.
IT'S OK. THANKS FOR COMING DOWN HERE TO SAY THAT.

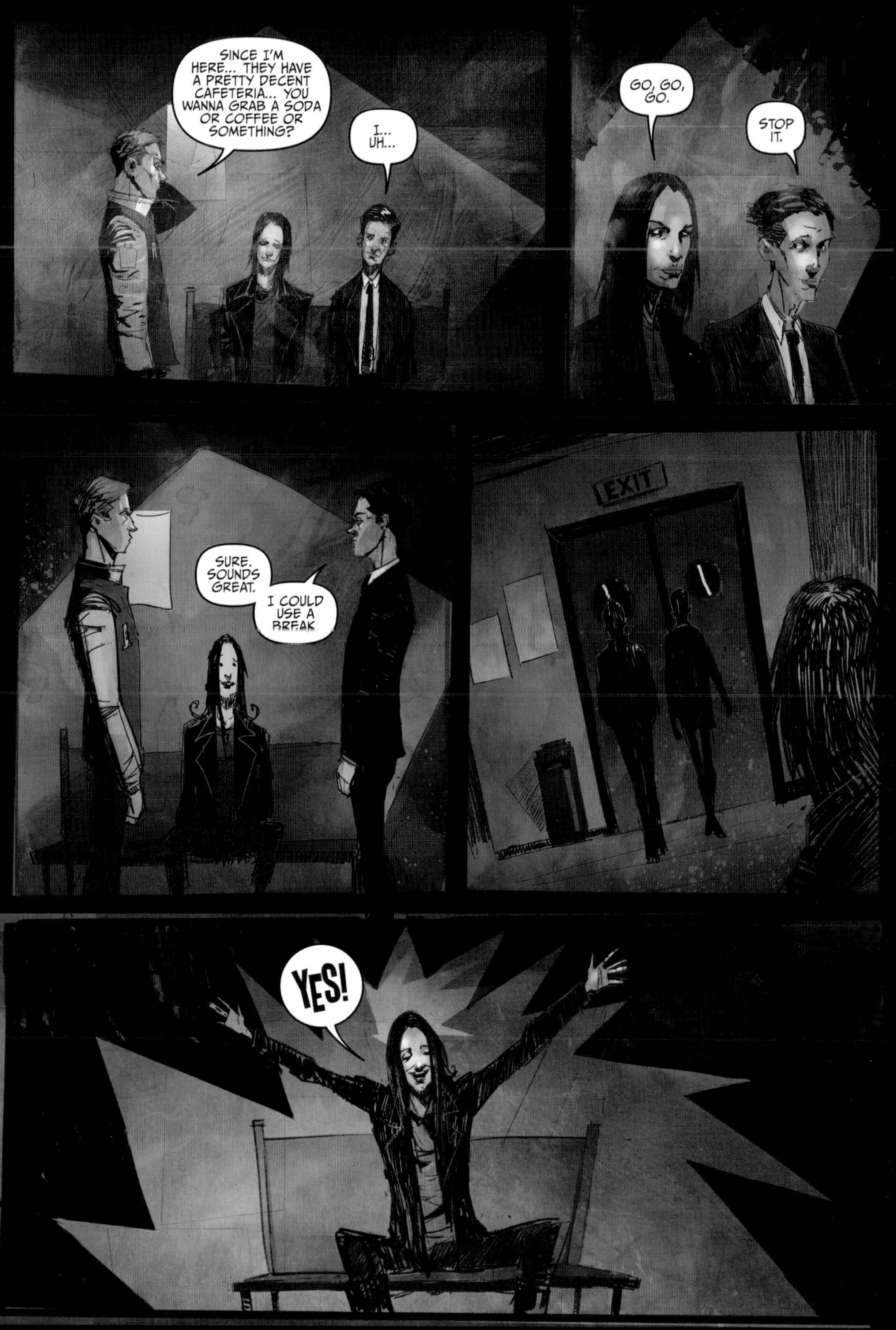
SINCE I'M HERE... THEY HAVE A PRETTY DECENT CAFETERIA... YOU WANNA GRAB A SODA OR COFFEE OR SOMETHING?
I... UH...
GO, GO, GO.
STOP IT.
SURE. SOUNDS GREAT.
I COULD USE A BREAK
EXIT
YES!

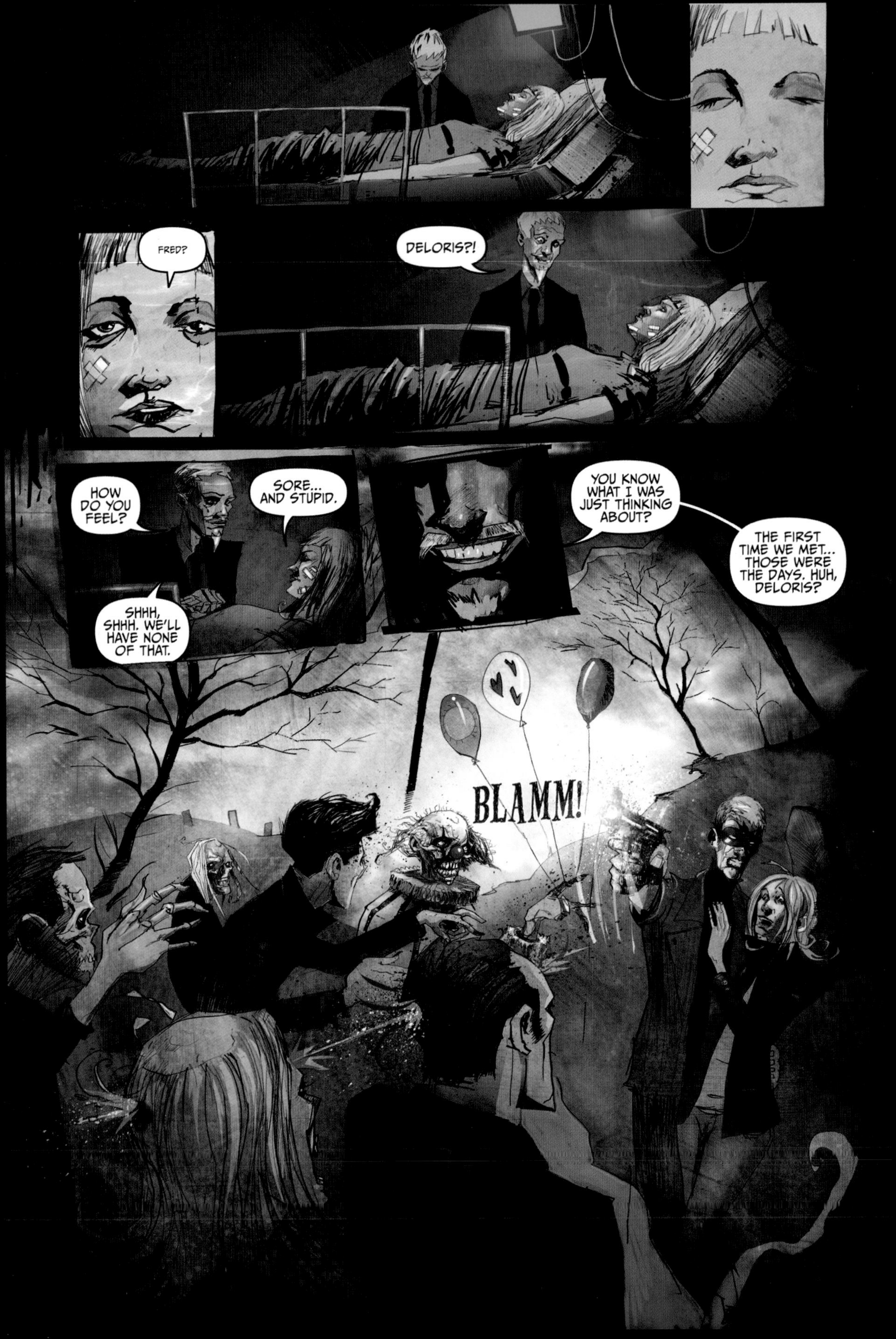
FRED?
DELORIS?!
HOW DO YOU FEEL?
SORE... AND STUPID.
SHHH, SHHH. WE'LL HAVE NONE OF THAT.
YOU KNOW WHAT I WAS JUST THINKING ABOUT?
THE FIRST TIME WE MET... THOSE WERE THE DAYS. HUH, DELORIS?
BLAMM!

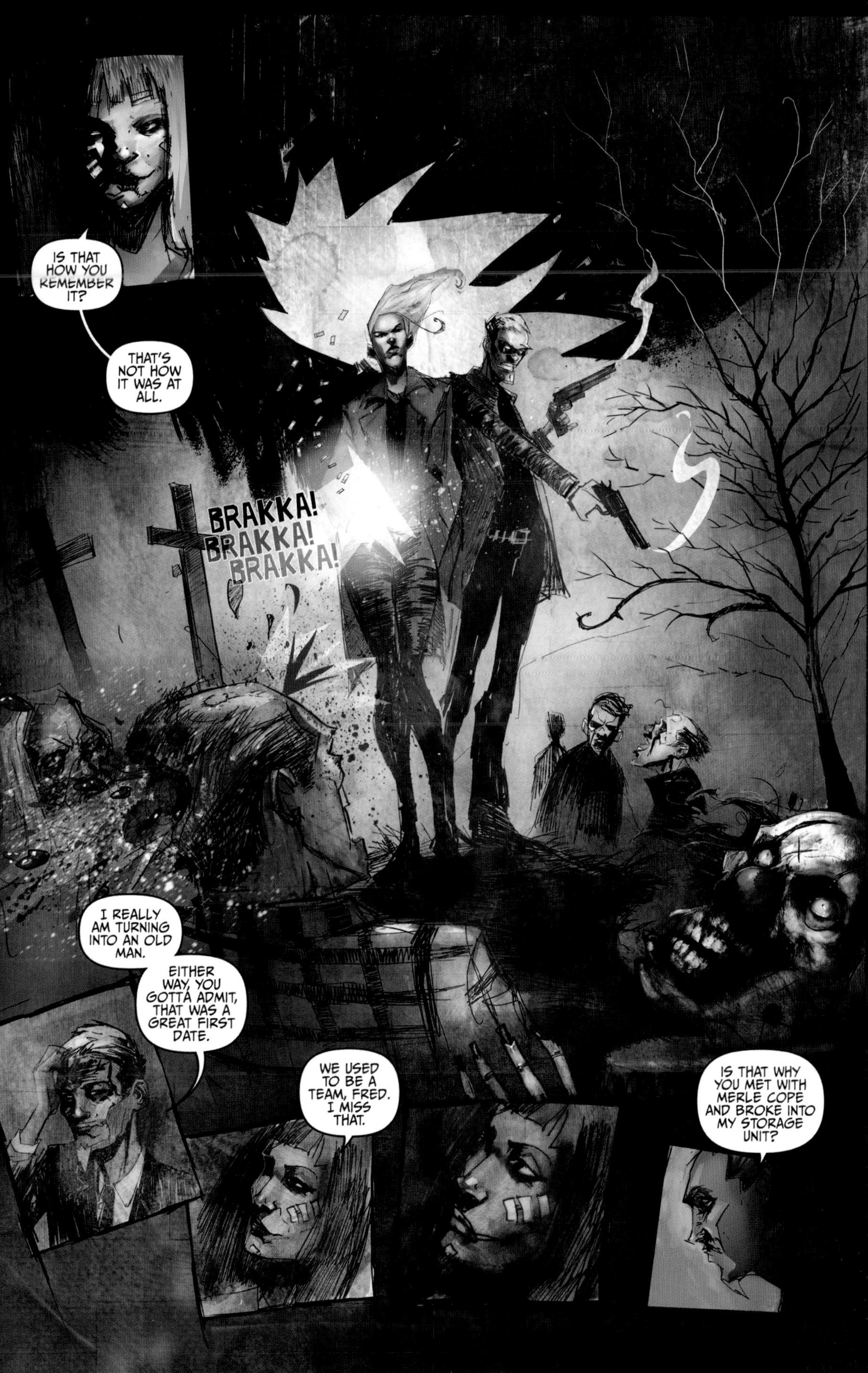
IS THAT HOW YOU REMEMBER IT?
THAT'S NOT HOW IT WAS AT ALL.
BRAKKA! BRAKKA! BRAKKA!
I REALLY AM TURNING INTO AN OLD MAN.
EITHER WAY, YOU GOTTA ADMIT, THAT WAS A GREAT FIRST DATE.
WE USED TO BE A TEAM, FRED. I MISS THAT.
IS THAT WHY YOU MET WITH MERLE COPE AND BROKE INTO MY STORAGE UNIT?

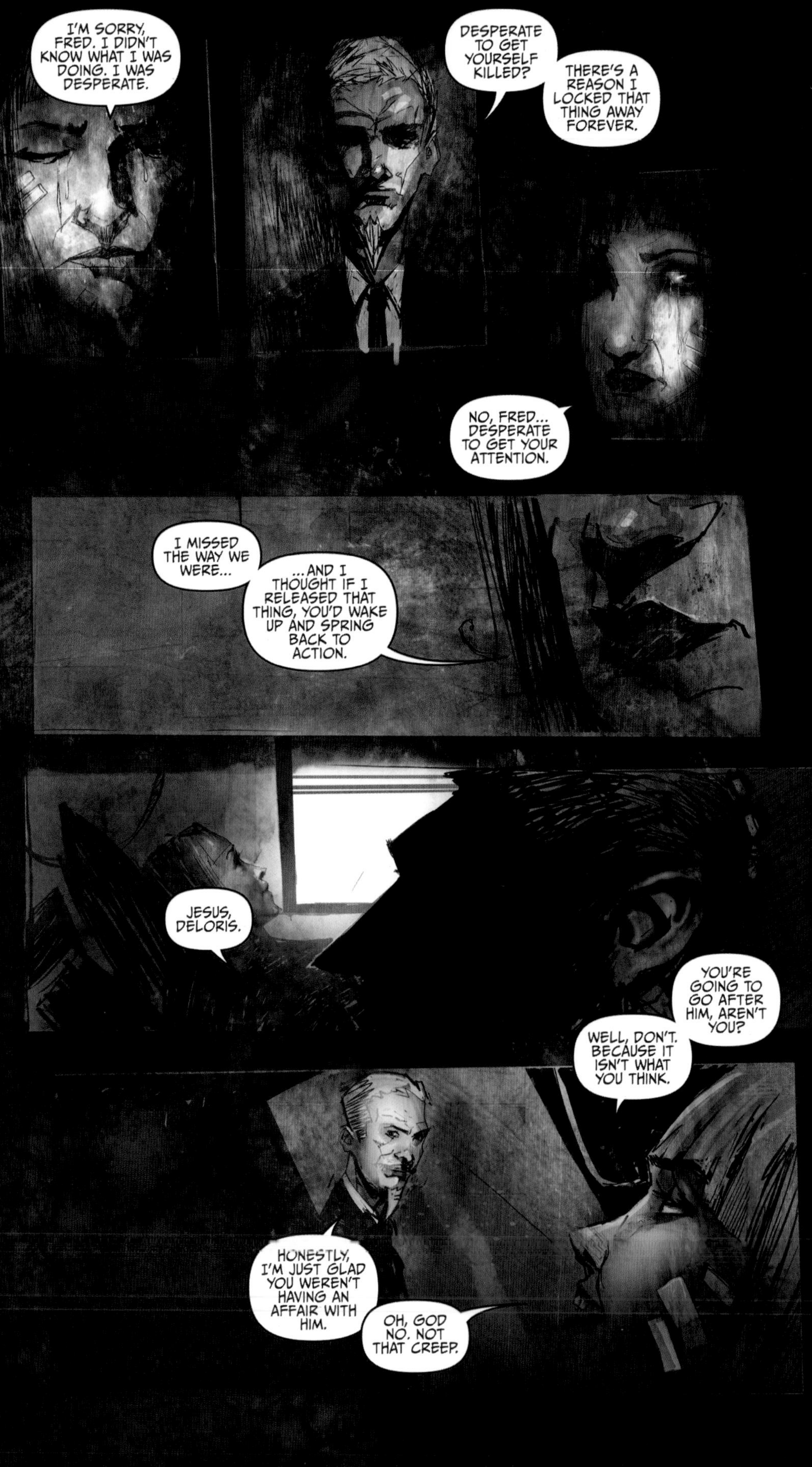
I'M SORRY, FRED. I DIDN'T KNOW WHAT I WAS DOING. I WAS DESPERATE.
DESPERATE TO GET YOURSELF KILLED?
THERE'S A REASON I LOCKED THAT THING AWAY FOREVER.
NO, FRED... DESPERATE TO GET YOUR ATTENTION.
I MISSED THE WAY WE WERE...
...AND I THOUGHT IF I RELEASED THAT THING, YOU'D WAKE UP AND SPRING BACK TO ACTION.
JESUS, DELORIS.
YOU'RE GOING TO GO AFTER HIM, AREN'T YOU?
WELL, DON'T. BECAUSE IT ISN'T WHAT YOU THINK.
HONESTLY, I'M JUST GLAD YOU WEREN'T HAVING AN AFFAIR WITH HIM.
OH, GOD NO. NOT THAT CREEP.

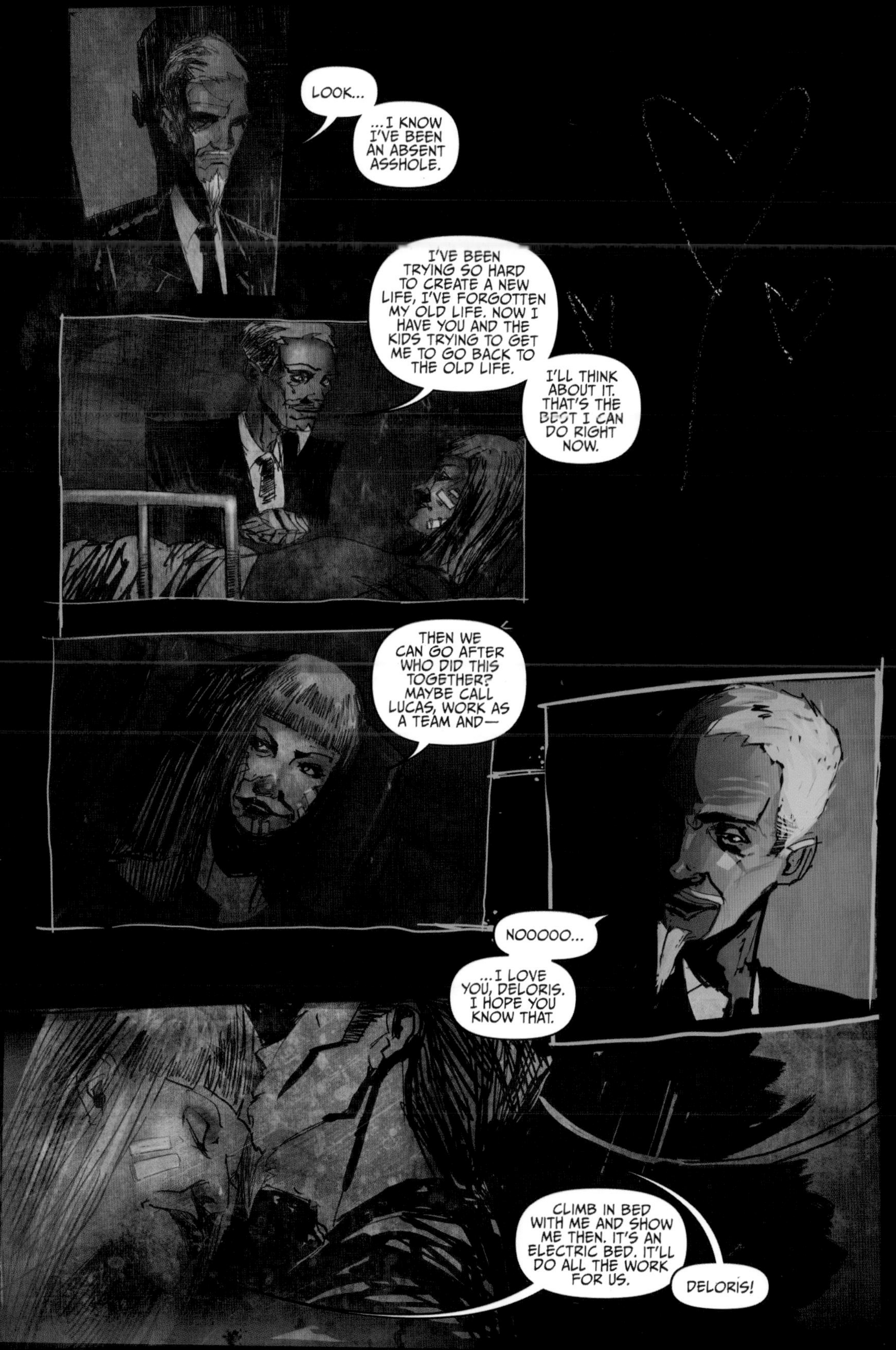
LOOK...
...I KNOW I'VE BEEN AN ABSENT ASSHOLE.
I'VE BEEN TRYING SO HARD TO CREATE A NEW LIFE, I'VE FORGOTTEN MY OLD LIFE. NOW I HAVE YOU AND THE KIDS TRYING TO GET ME TO GO BACK TO THE OLD LIFE.
I'LL THINK ABOUT IT. THAT'S THE BEST I CAN DO RIGHT NOW.
THEN WE CAN GO AFTER WHO DID THIS TOGETHER? MAYBE CALL LUCAS, WORK AS A TEAM AND—
NOOOOO...
...I LOVE YOU, DELORIS. I HOPE YOU KNOW THAT.
CLIMB IN BED WITH ME AND SHOW ME THEN. IT'S AN ELECTRIC BED. IT'LL DO ALL THE WORK FOR US.
DELORIS!

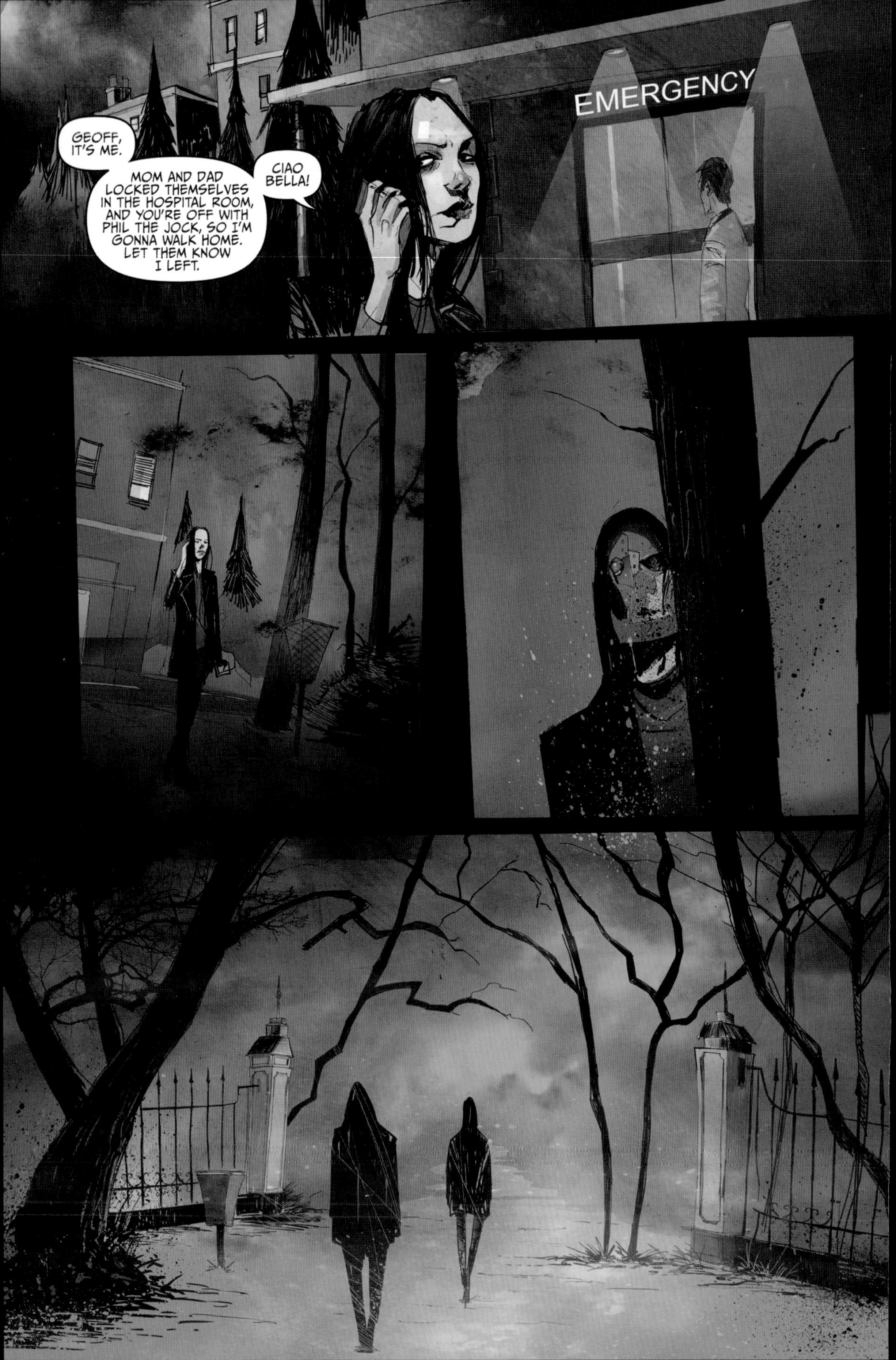
EMERGENCY
GEOFF, IT'S ME.
MOM AND DAD LOCKED THEMSELVES IN THE HOSPITAL ROOM, AND YOU'RE OFF WITH PHIL THE JOCK, SO I'M GONNA WALK HOME. LET THEM KNOW I LEFT.
CIAO BELLA!

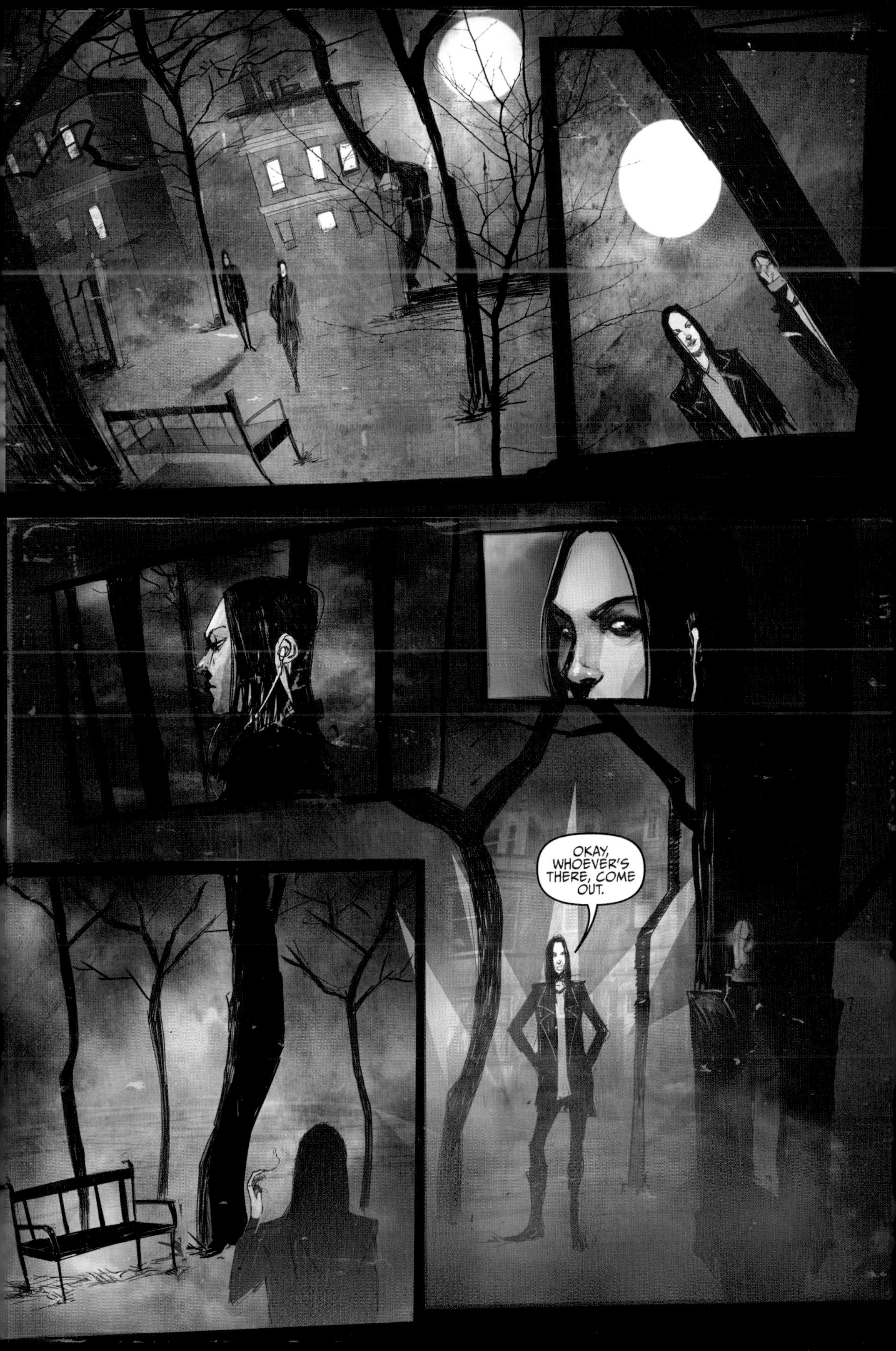
OKAY, WHOEVER'S THERE, COME OUT.

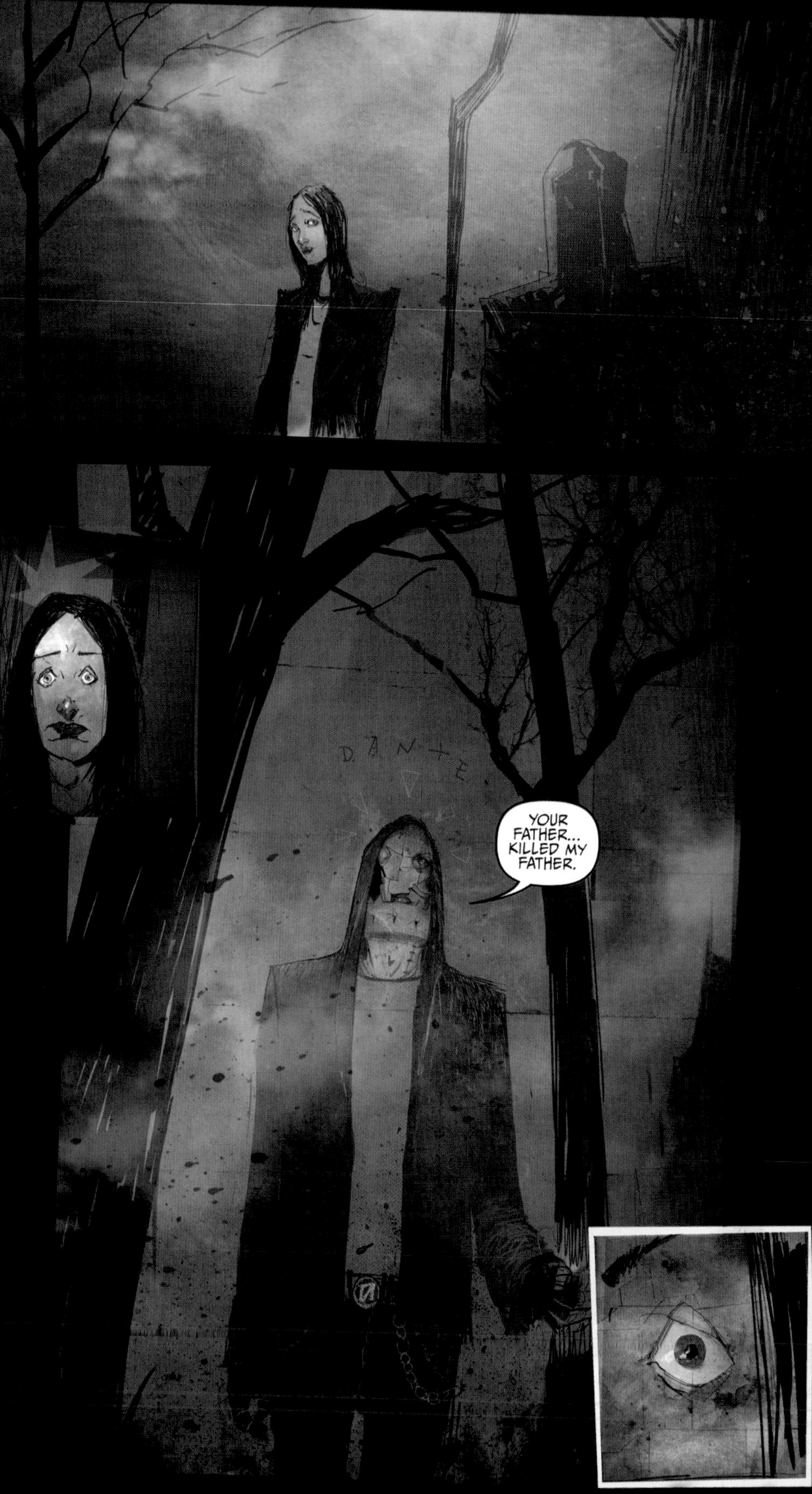
D.A.N.T.E.
YOUR FATHER... KILLED MY FATHER.

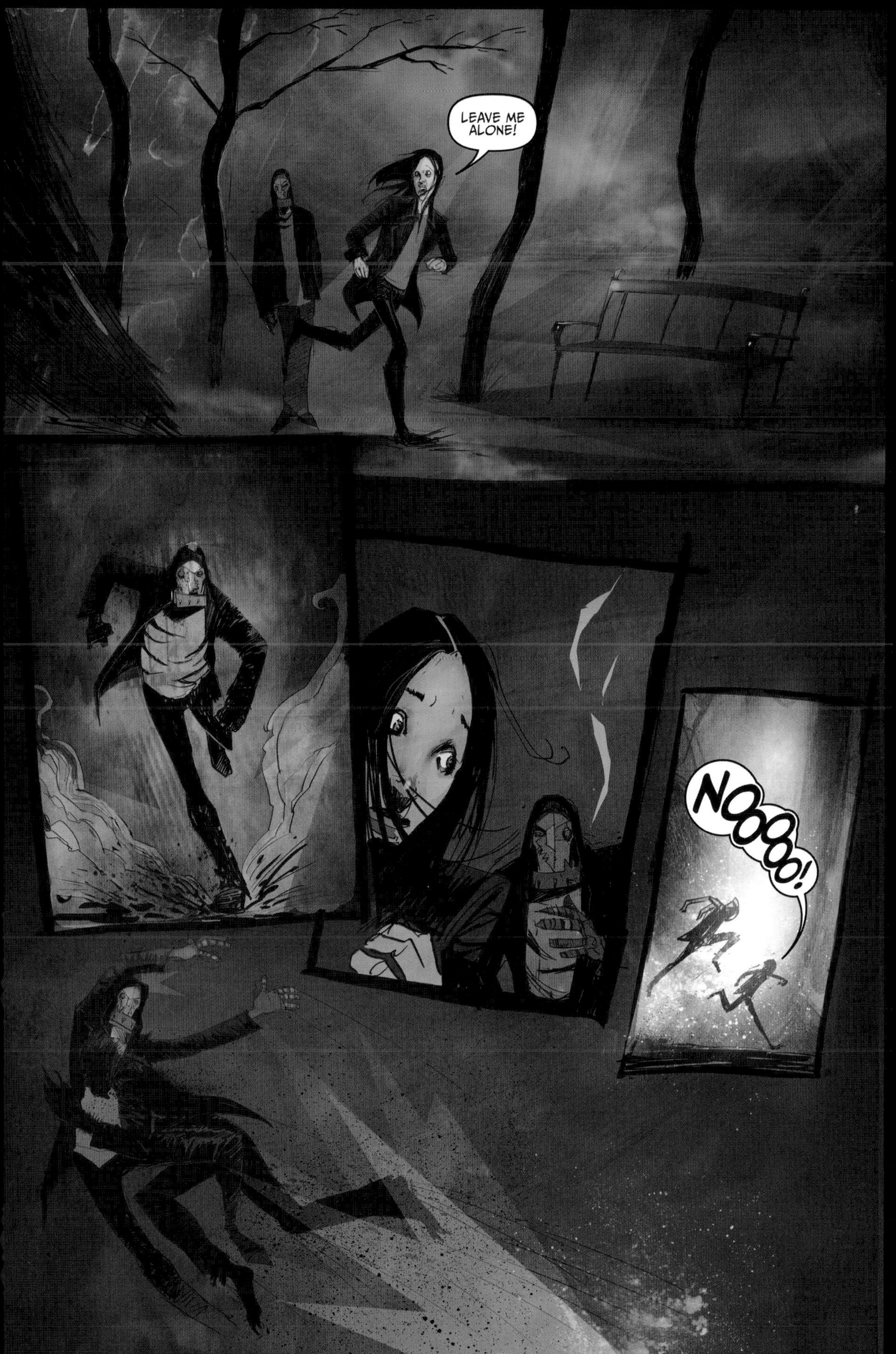
LEAVE ME ALONE!
NOOOOO!

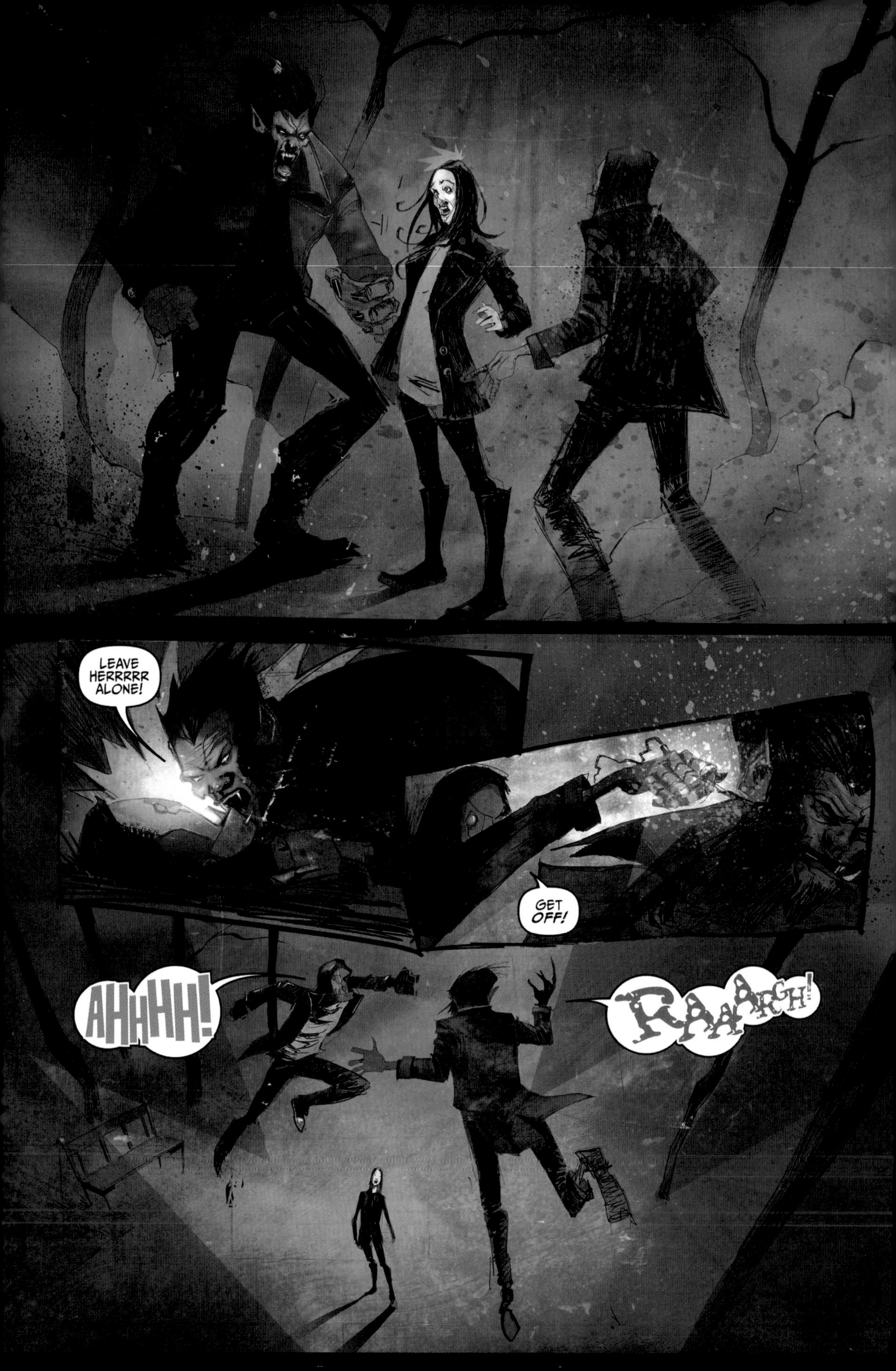
LEAVE HERRRRR ALONE!
GET OFF!
AHHHH!
RAAAARGH!

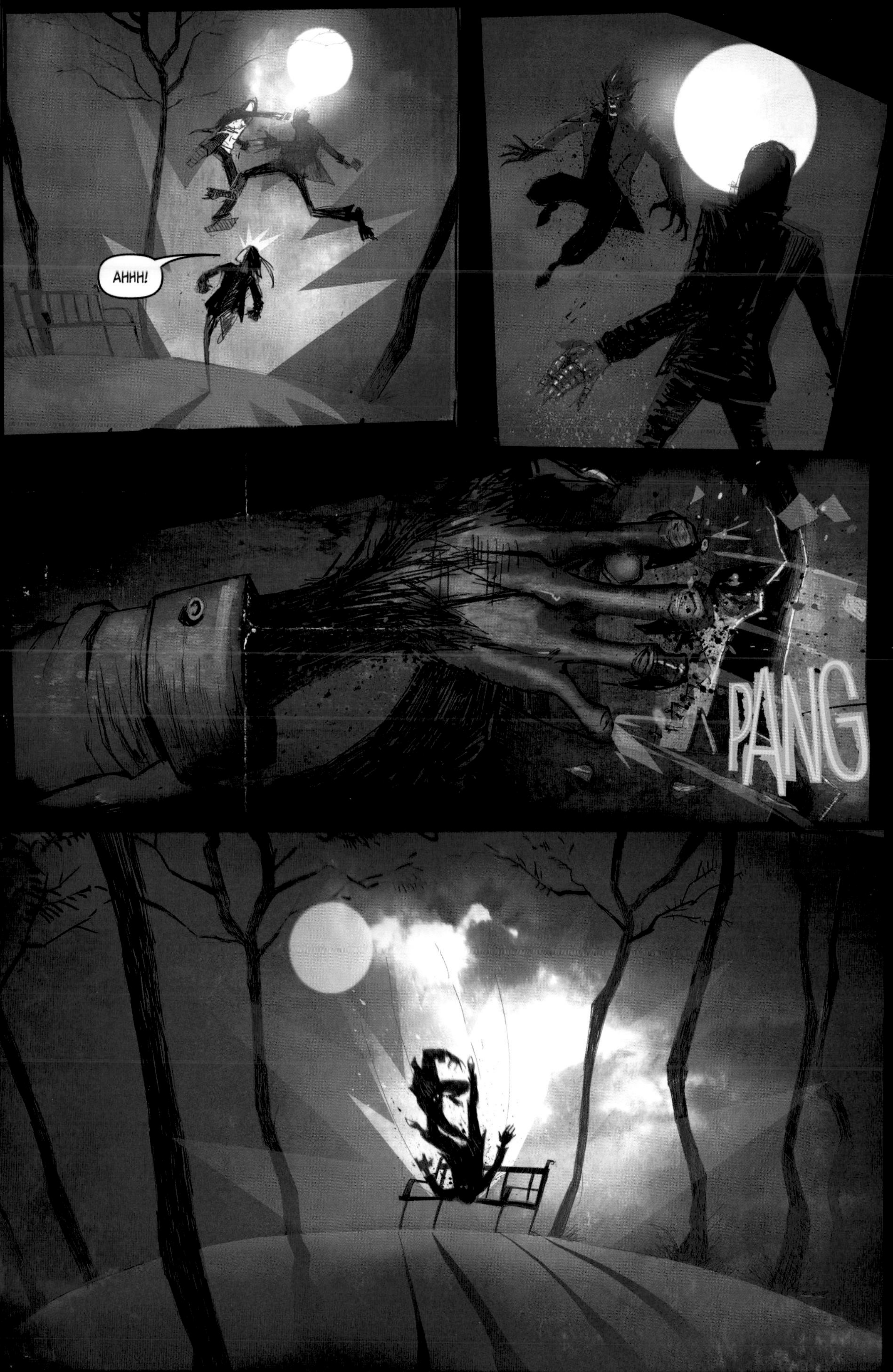
AHHH!
PANG

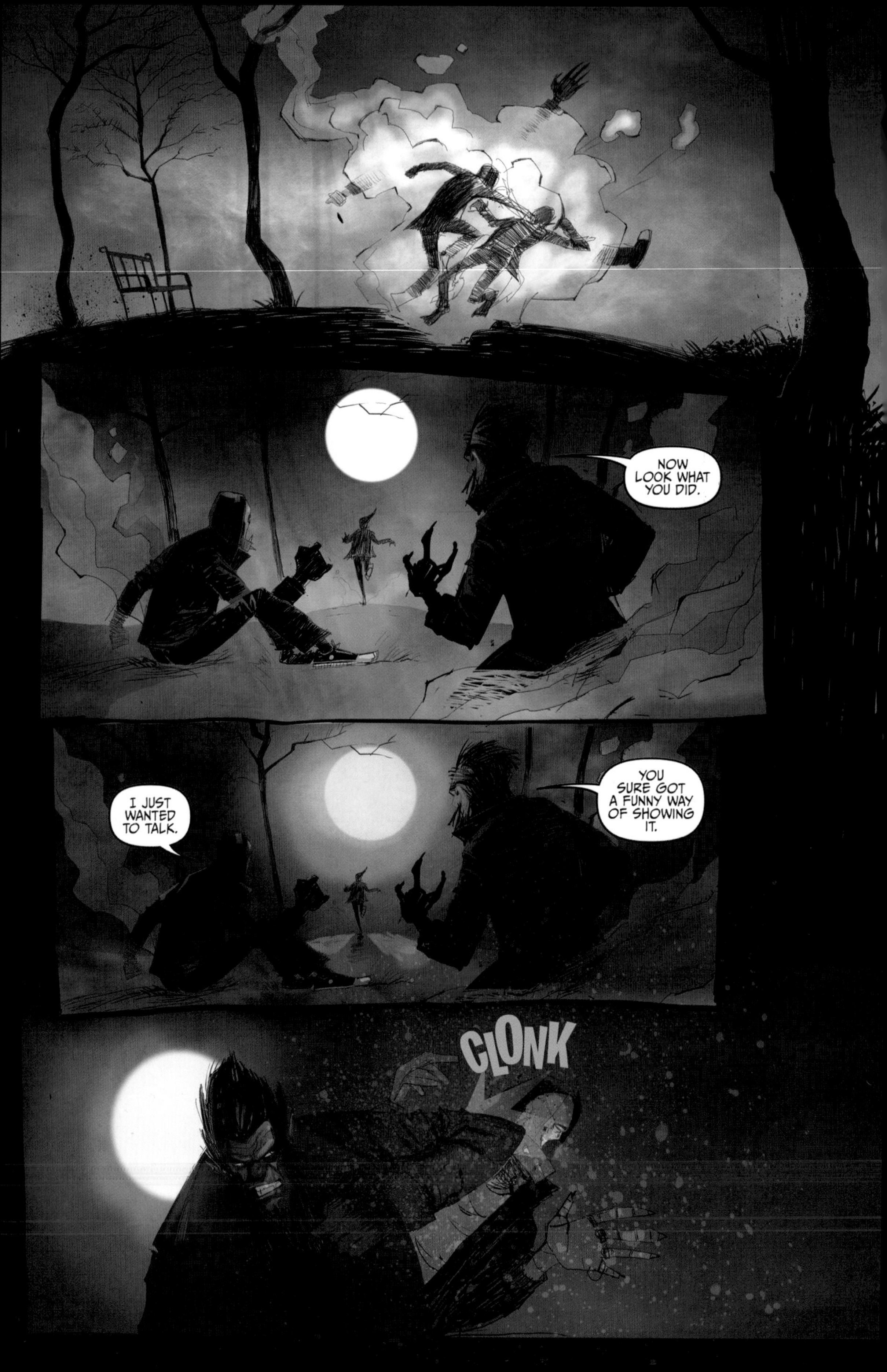
NOW LOOK WHAT YOU DID.
I JUST WANTED TO TALK.
YOU SURE GOT A FUNNY WAY OF SHOWING IT.
CLONK

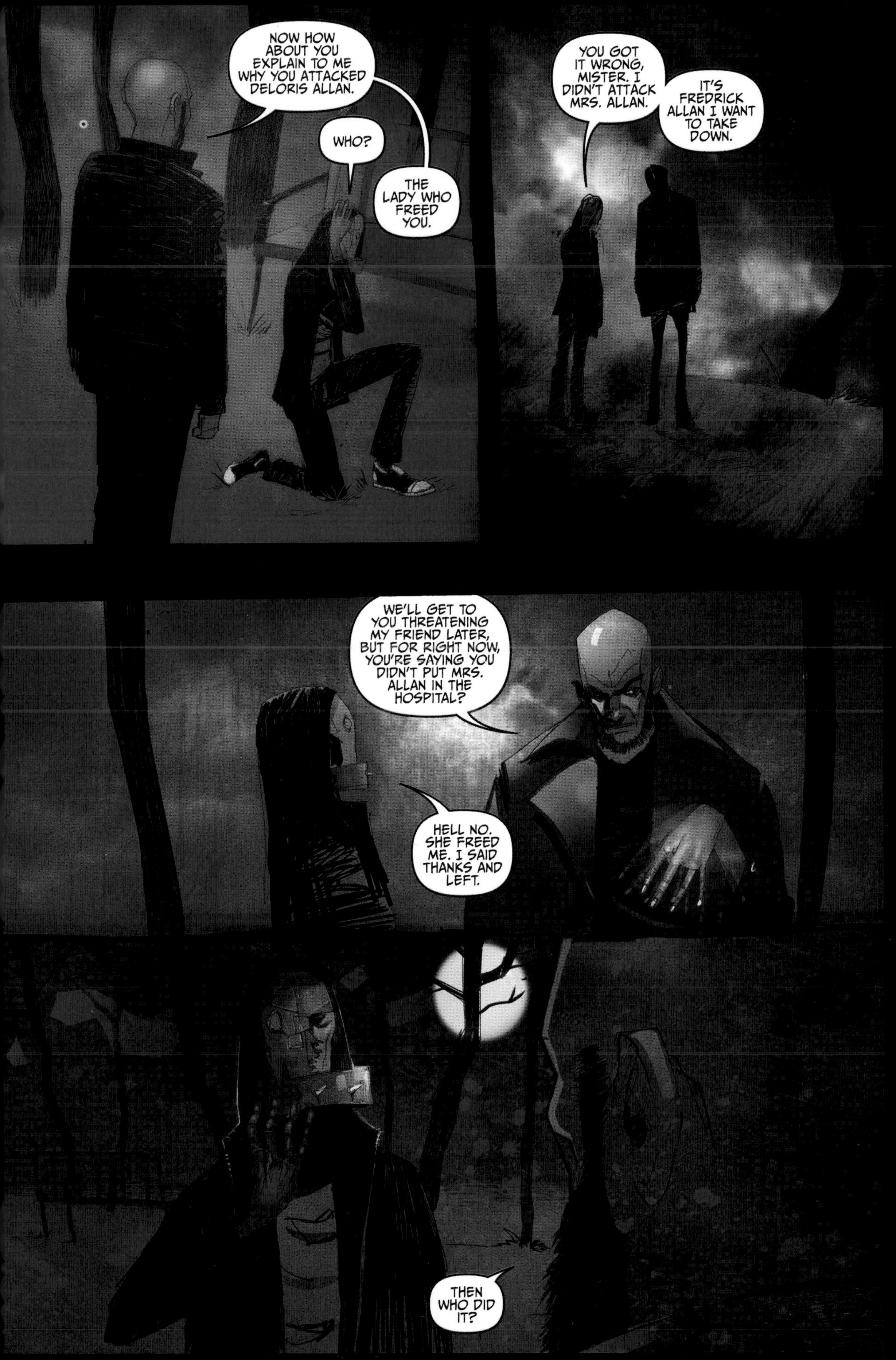
NOW HOW ABOUT YOU EXPLAIN TO ME WHY YOU ATTACKED DELORIS ALLAN.
WHO?
THE LADY WHO FREED YOU.
YOU GOT IT WRONG, MISTER. I DIDN'T ATTACK MRS. ALLAN.
IT'S FREDRICK ALLAN I WANT TO TAKE DOWN.
WE'LL GET TO YOU THREATENING MY FRIEND LATER, BUT FOR RIGHT NOW, YOU'RE SAYING YOU DIDN'T PUT MRS. ALLAN IN THE HOSPITAL?
HELL NO. SHE FREED ME. I SAID THANKS AND LEFT.
THEN WHO DID IT?

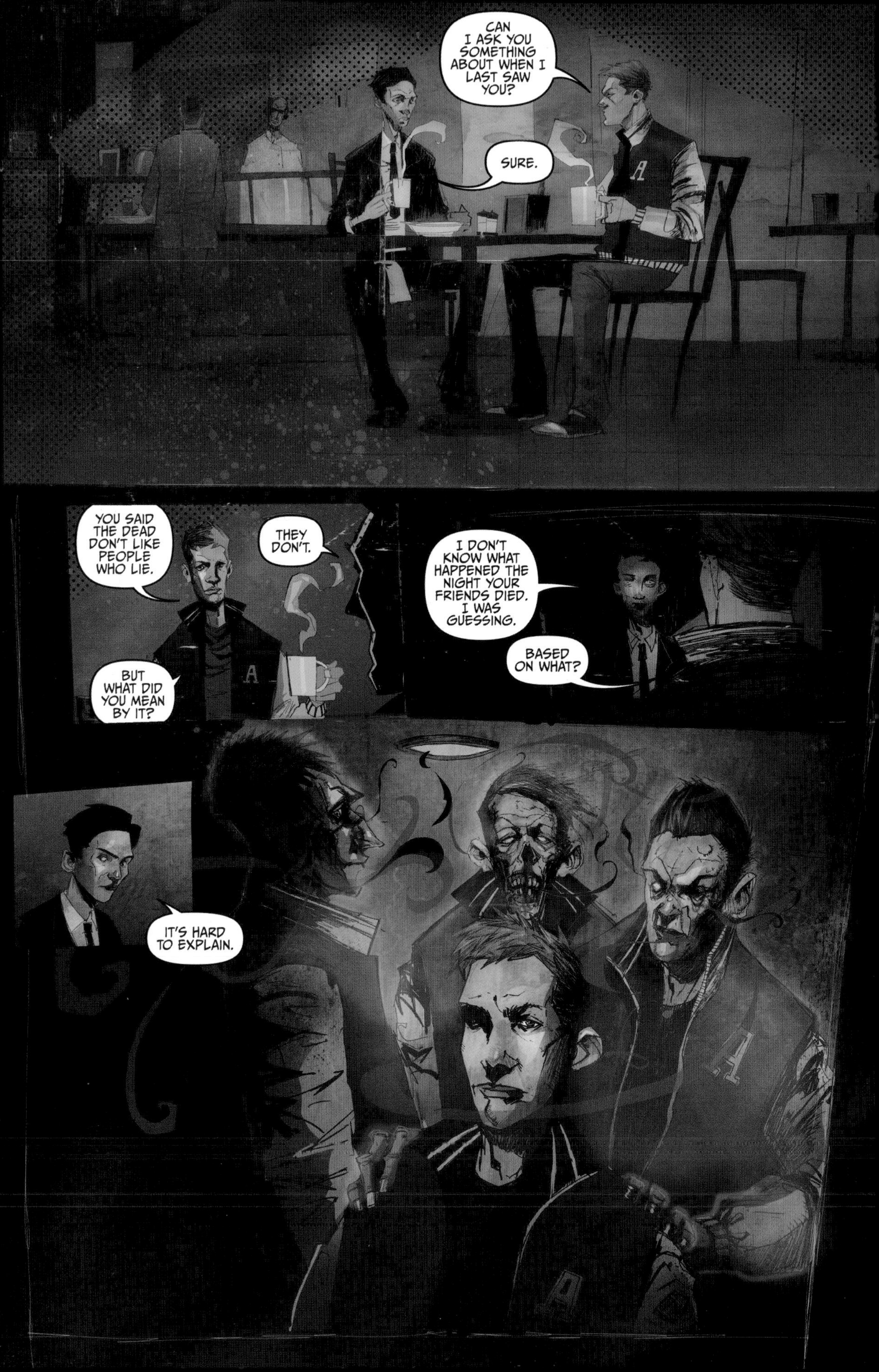
CAN I ASK YOU SOMETHING ABOUT WHEN I LAST SAW YOU?
SURE.
YOU SAID THE DEAD DON'T LIKE PEOPLE WHO LIE.
THEY DON'T.
BUT WHAT DID YOU MEAN BY IT?
I DON'T KNOW WHAT HAPPENED THE NIGHT YOUR FRIENDS DIED. I WAS GUESSING.
BASED ON WHAT?
IT'S HARD TO EXPLAIN.

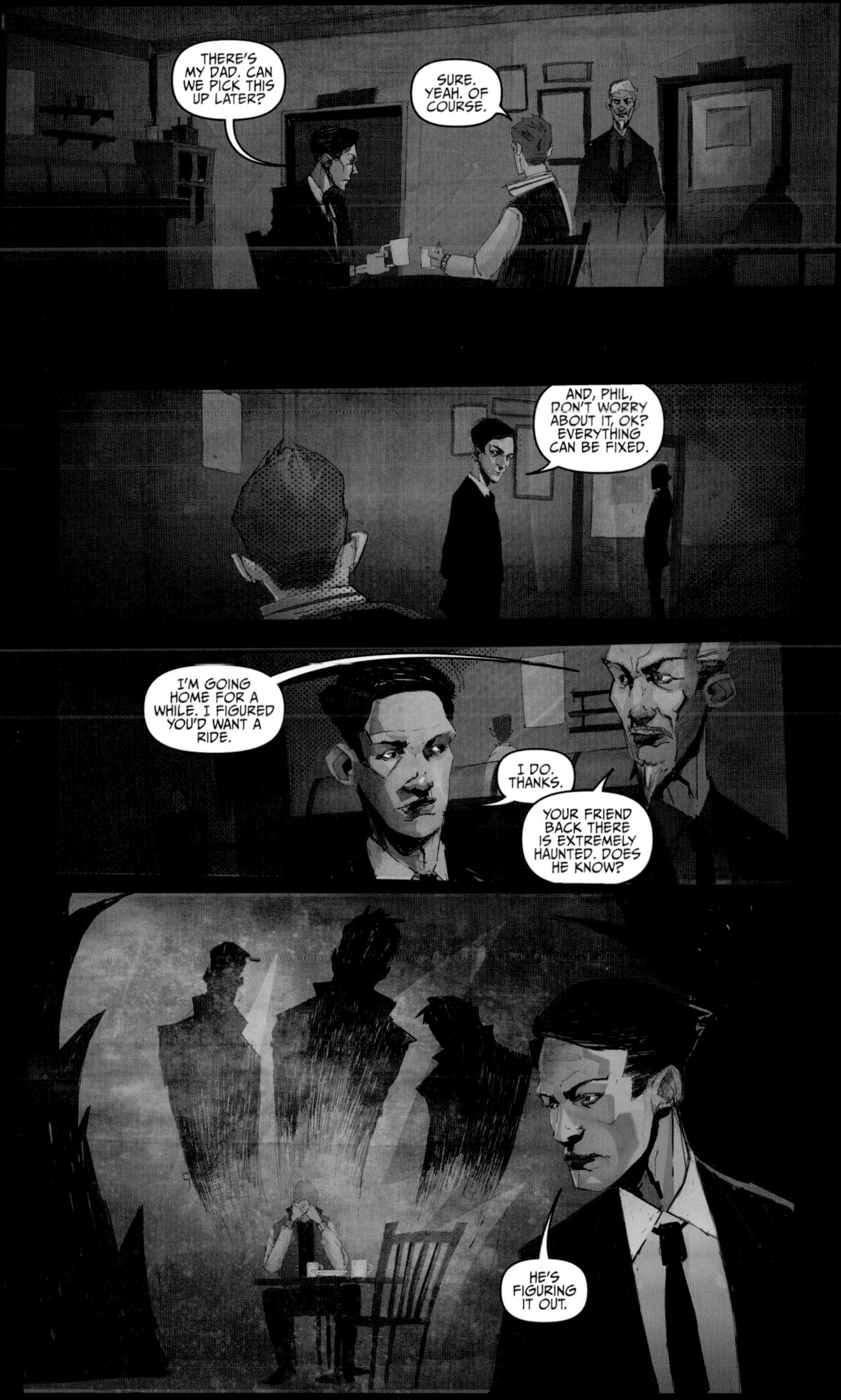
THERE'S MY DAD. CAN WE PICK THIS UP LATER?
SURE. YEAH. OF COURSE.
AND, PHIL, DON'T WORRY ABOUT IT, OK? EVERYTHING CAN BE FIXED.
I'M GOING HOME FOR A WHILE. I FIGURED YOU'D WANT A RIDE.
I DO. THANKS.
YOUR FRIEND BACK THERE IS EXTREMELY HAUNTED. DOES HE KNOW?
HE'S FIGURING IT OUT.

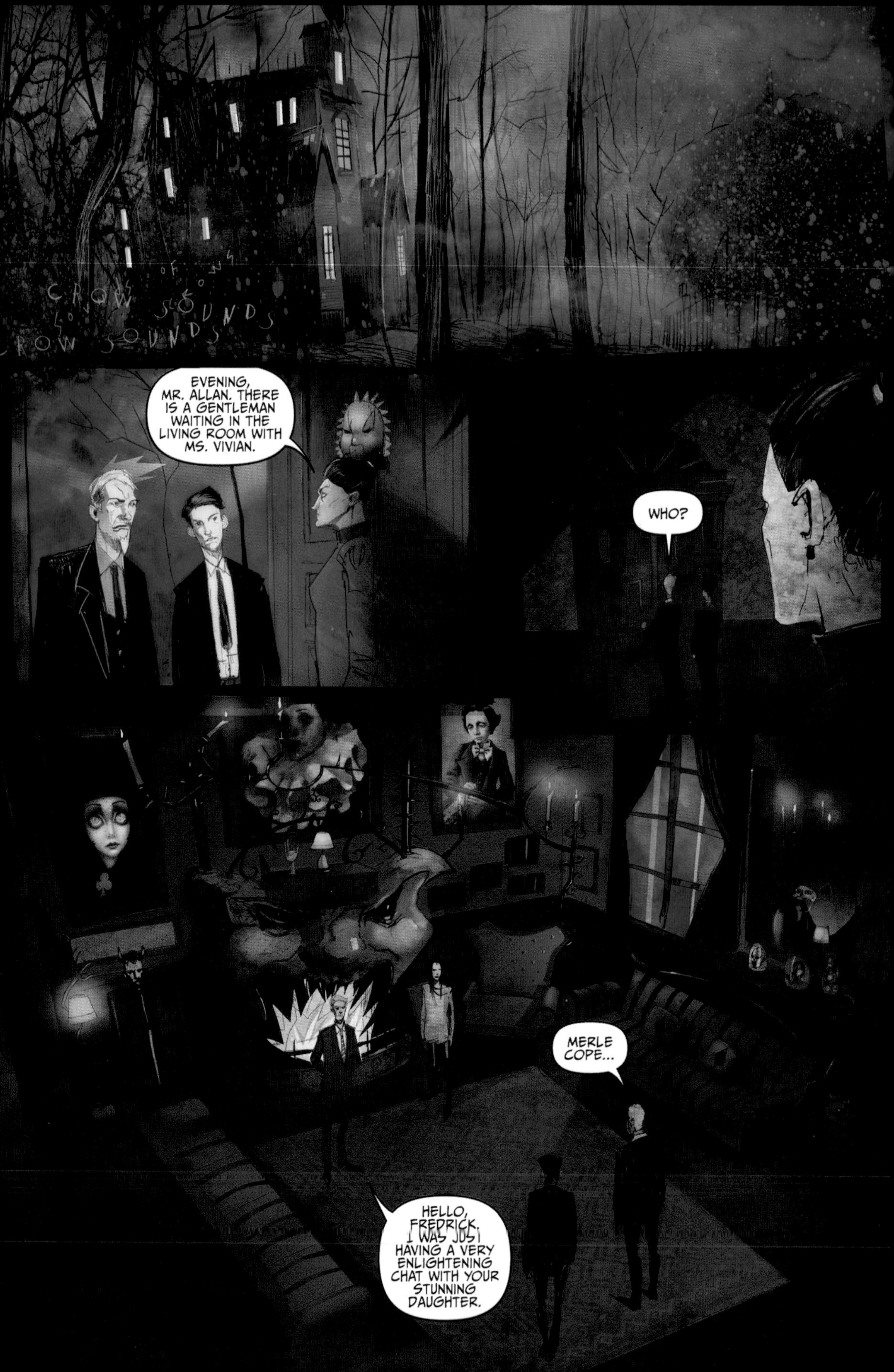
CROW SOUNDS
EVENING, MR. ALLAN. THERE IS A GENTLEMAN WAITING IN THE LIVING ROOM WITH MS. VIVIAN.
WHO?
MERLE COPE...
HELLO, FREDRICK. I WAS JUST HAVING A VERY ENLIGHTENING CHAT WITH YOUR STUNNING DAUGHTER.

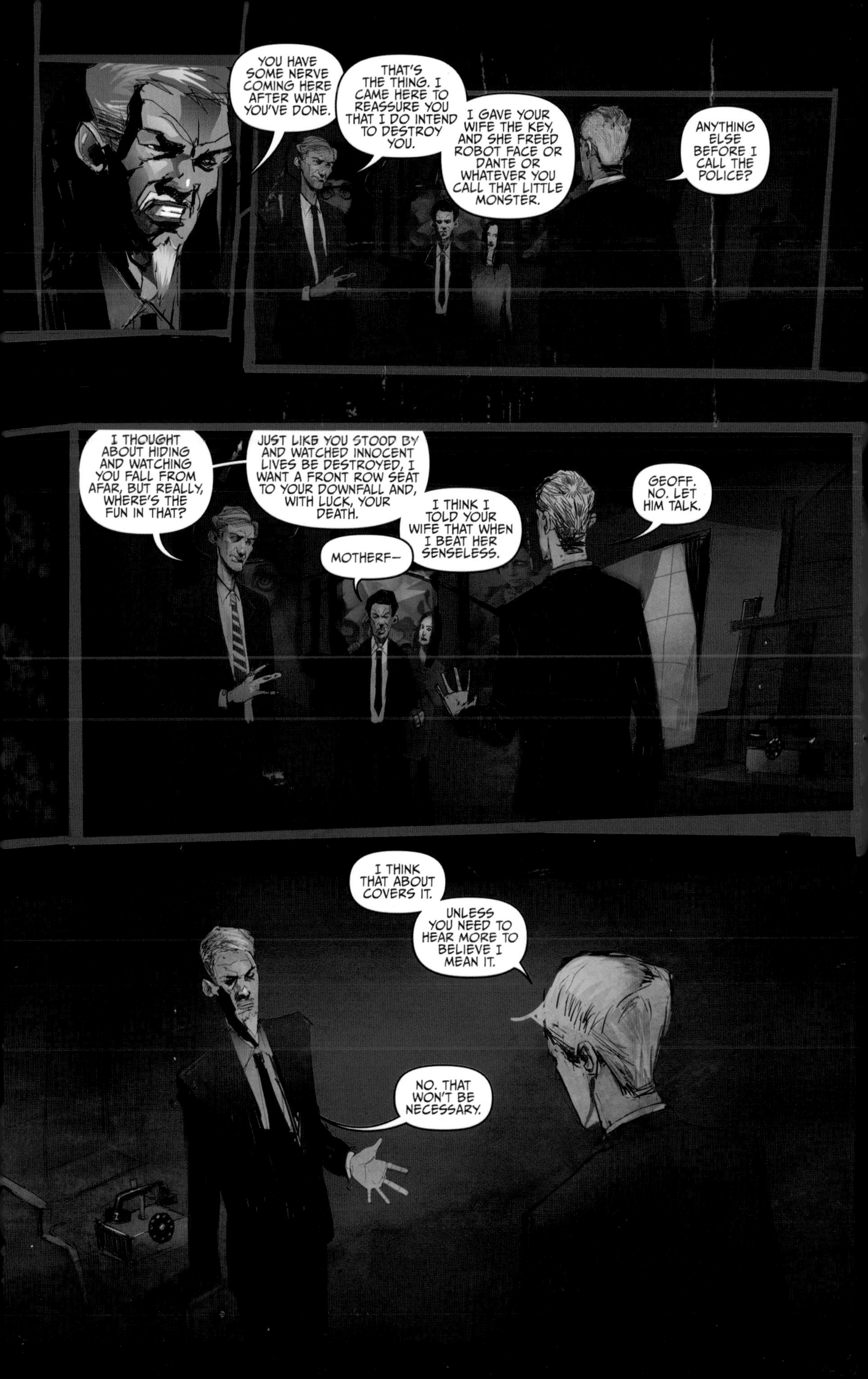
YOU HAVE SOME NERVE COMING HERE AFTER WHAT YOU'VE DONE.
THAT'S THE THING. I CAME HERE TO REASSURE YOU THAT I DO INTEND TO DESTROY YOU.
I GAVE YOUR WIFE THE KEY, AND SHE FREED ROBOT FACE OR DANTE OR WHATEVER YOU CALL THAT LITTLE MONSTER.
ANYTHING ELSE BEFORE I CALL THE POLICE?
I THOUGHT ABOUT HIDING AND WATCHING YOU FALL FROM AFAR, BUT REALLY, WHERE'S THE FUN IN THAT?
JUST LIKE YOU STOOD BY AND WATCHED INNOCENT LIVES BE DESTROYED, I WANT A FRONT ROW SEAT TO YOUR DOWNFALL AND, WITH LUCK, YOUR DEATH.
I THINK I TOLD YOUR WIFE THAT WHEN I BEAT HER SENSELESS.
MOTHERF—
GEOFF. NO. LET HIM TALK.
I THINK THAT ABOUT COVERS IT.
UNLESS YOU NEED TO HEAR MORE TO BELIEVE I MEAN IT.
NO. THAT WON'T BE NECESSARY.

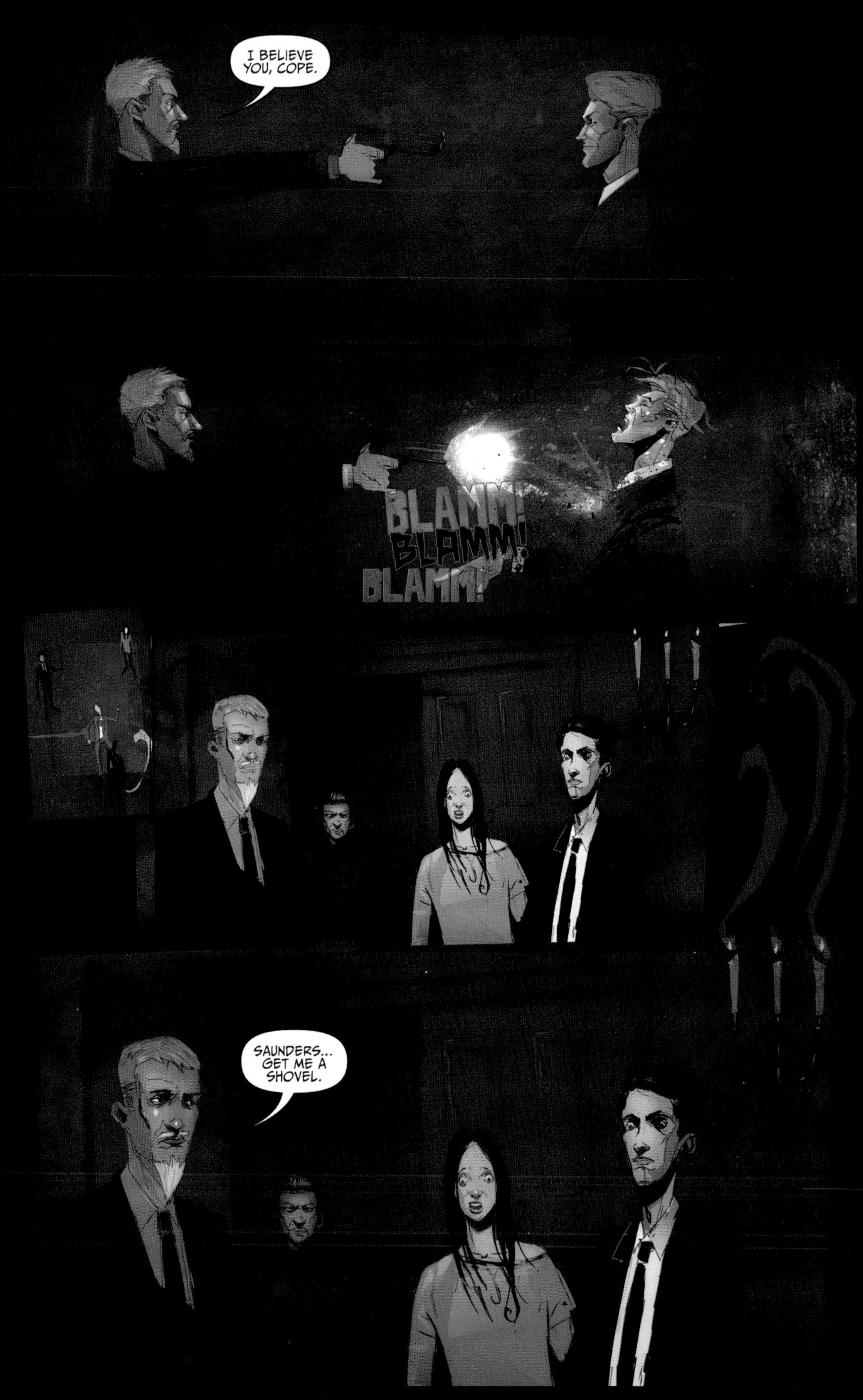
I BELIEVE YOU, COPE.
BLAMM!
BLAMM!
BLAMM!
SAUNDERS... GET ME A SHOVEL.

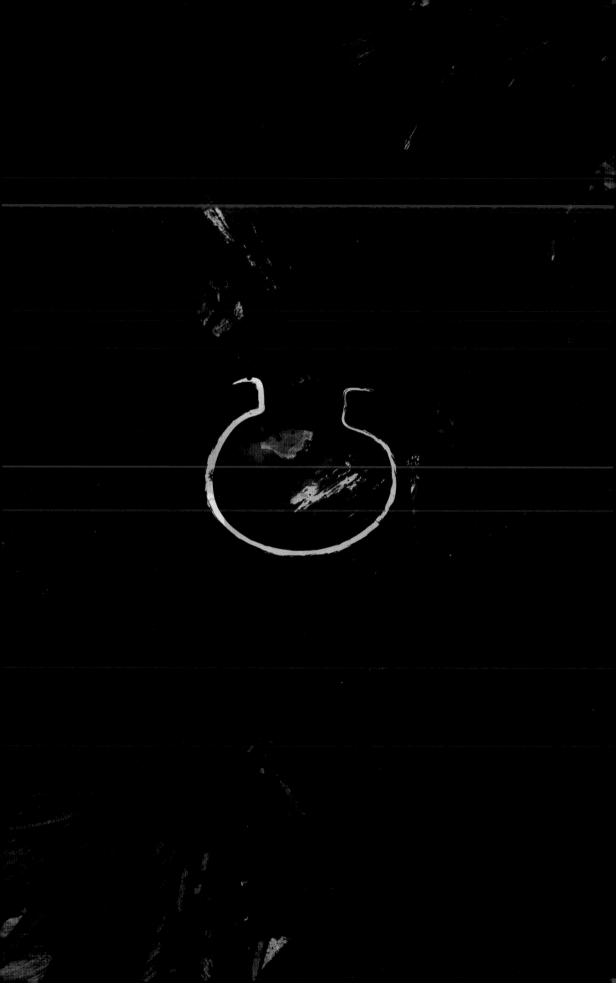

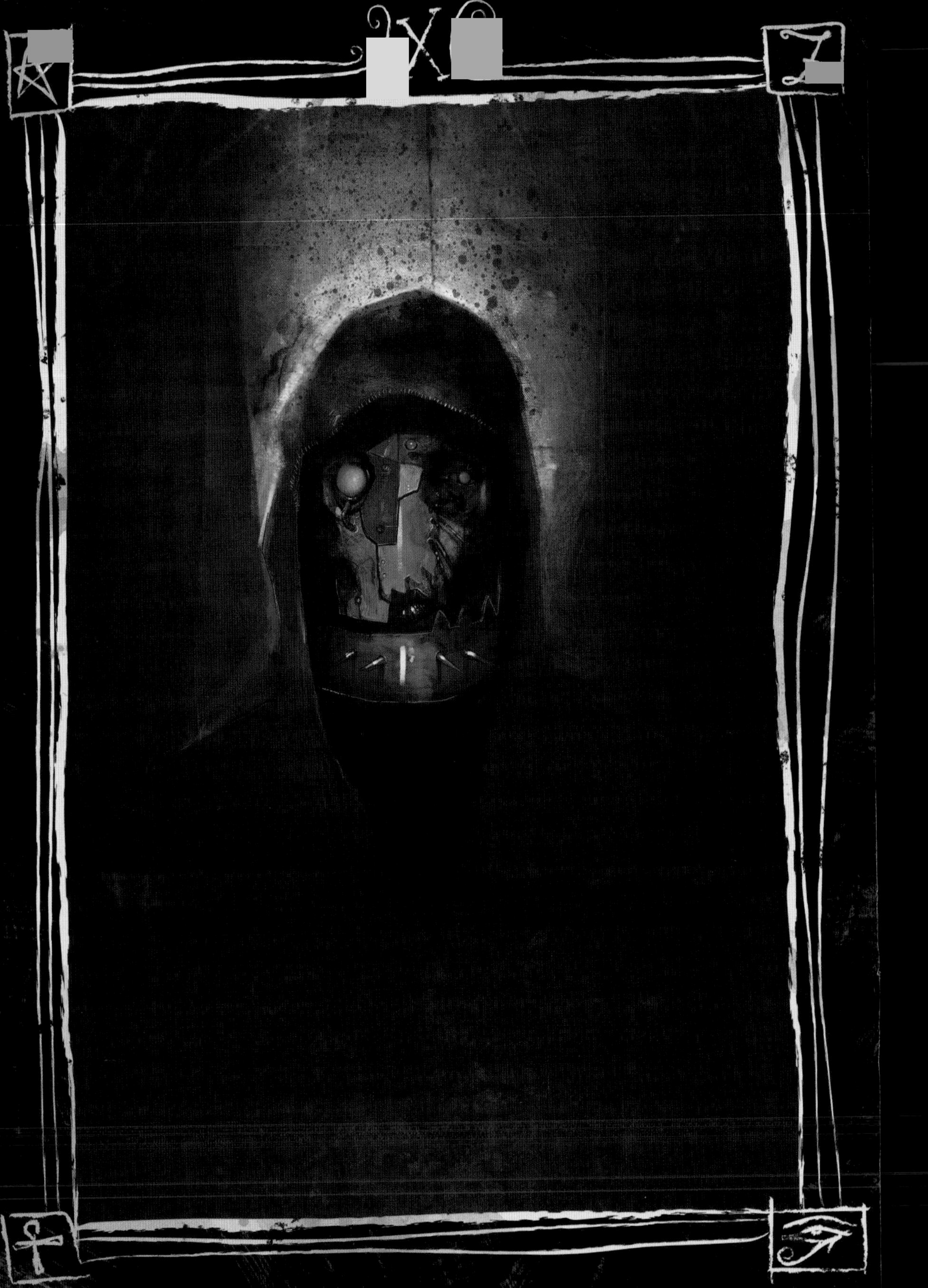

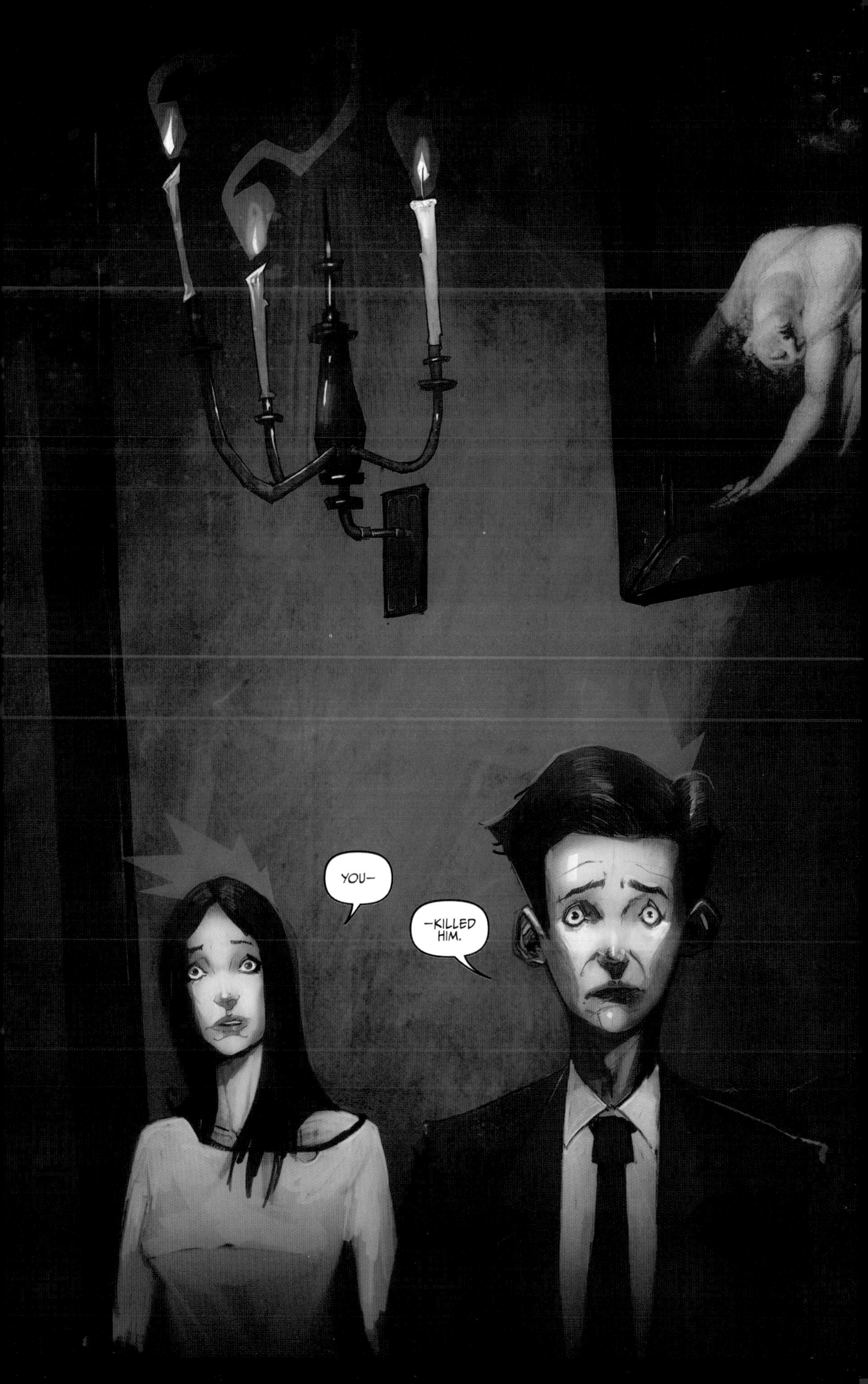
YOU–
–KILLED HIM.

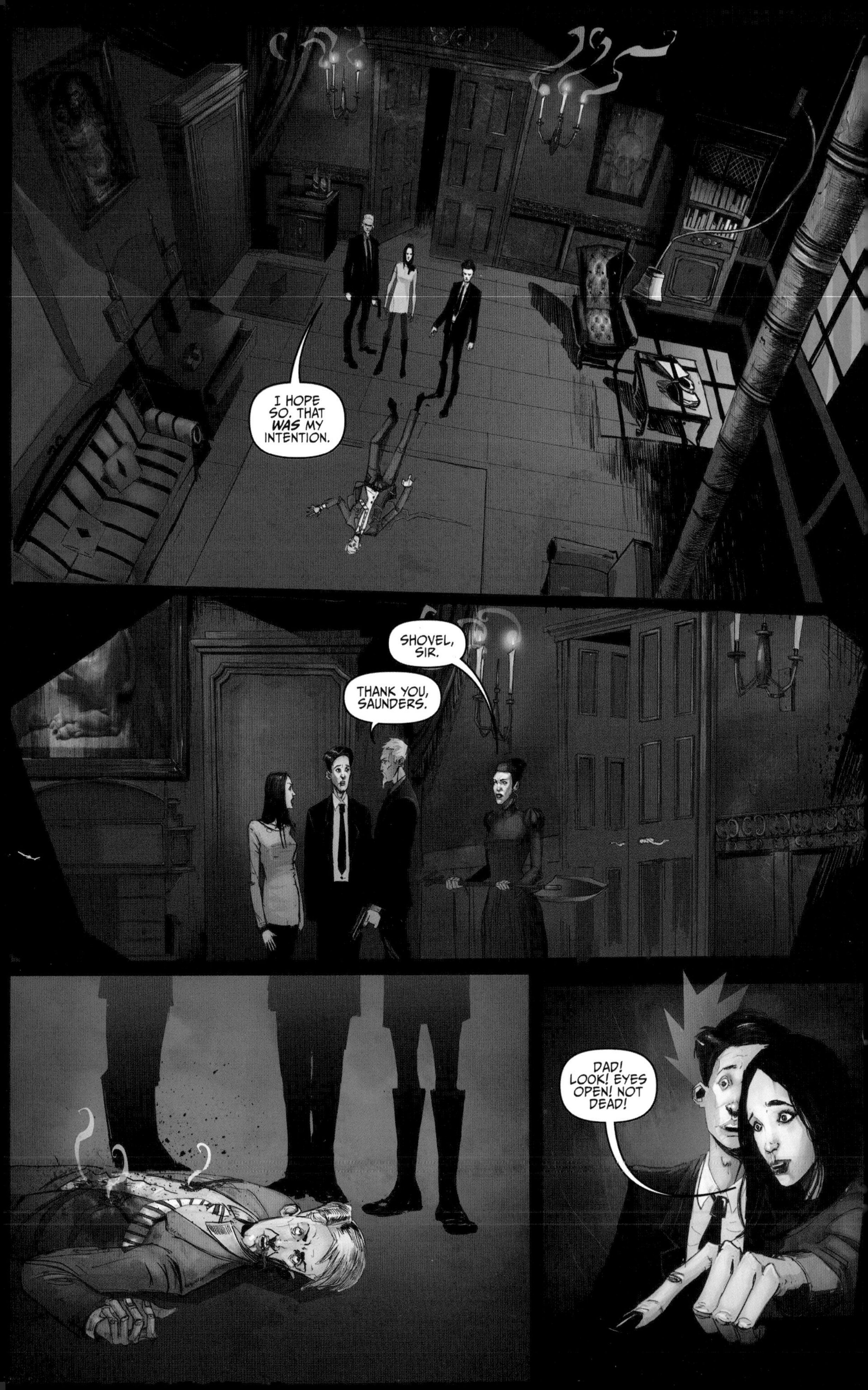
I HOPE SO. THAT WAS MY INTENTION.
SHOVEL, SIR.
THANK YOU, SAUNDERS.
DAD! LOOK! EYES OPEN! NOT DEAD!

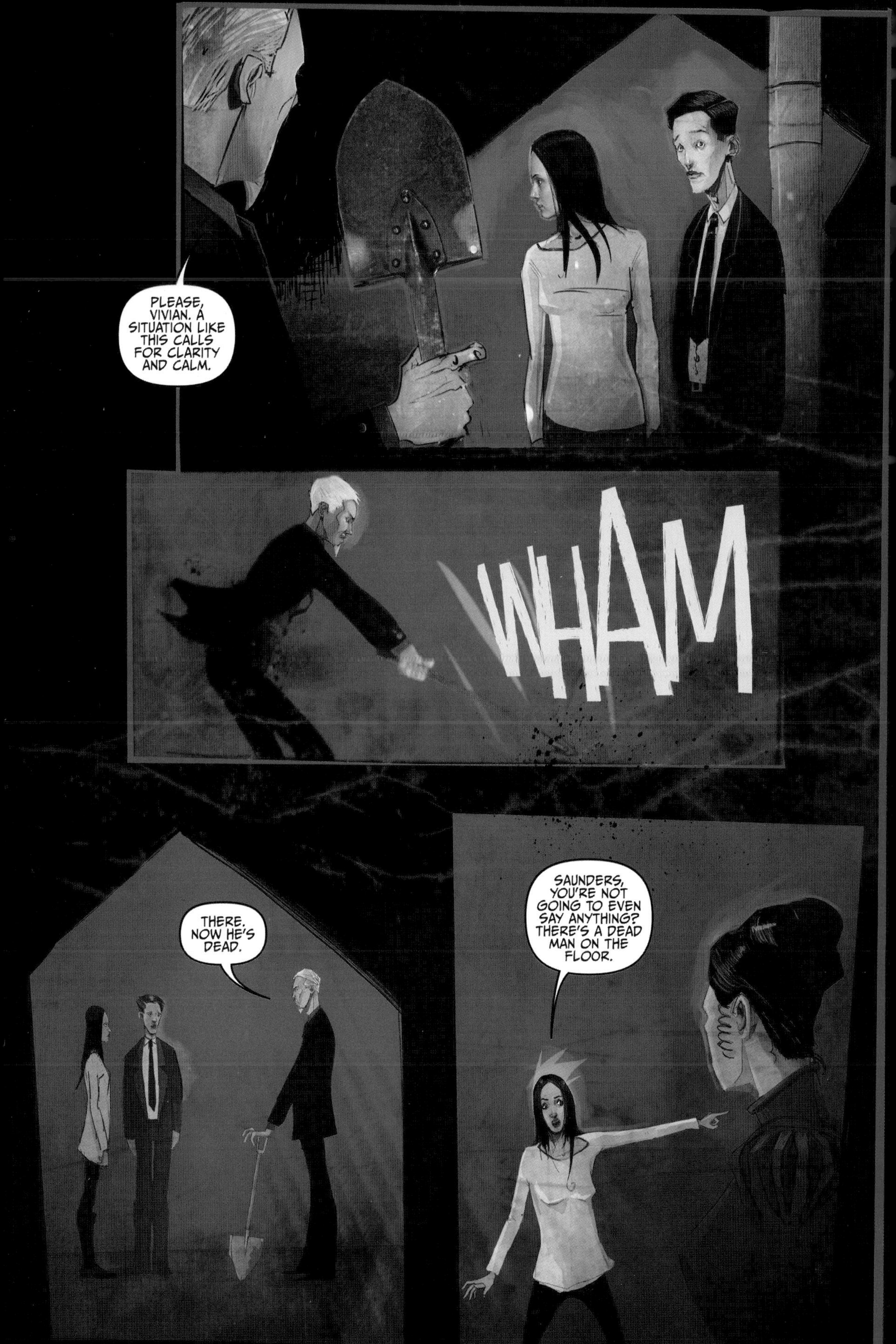
PLEASE, VIVIAN. A SITUATION LIKE THIS CALLS FOR CLARITY AND CALM.
WHAM
THERE. NOW HE'S DEAD.
SAUNDERS, YOU'RE NOT GOING TO EVEN SAY ANYTHING? THERE'S A DEAD MAN ON THE FLOOR.

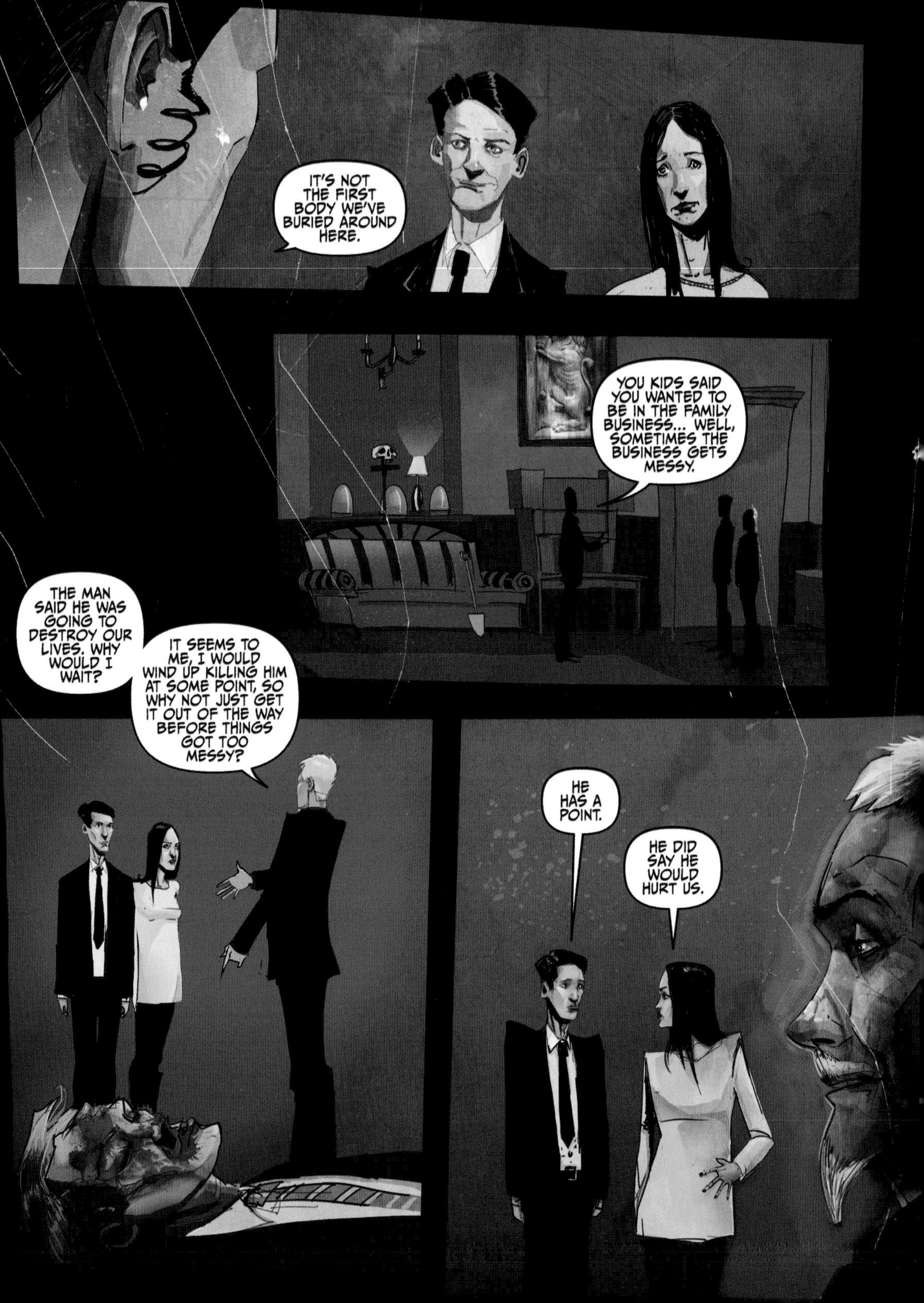
IT'S NOT THE FIRST BODY WE'VE BURIED AROUND HERE.
YOU KIDS SAID YOU WANTED TO BE IN THE FAMILY BUSINESS... WELL, SOMETIMES THE BUSINESS GETS MESSY.
THE MAN SAID HE WAS GOING TO DESTROY OUR LIVES. WHY WOULD I WAIT?
IT SEEMS TO ME, I WOULD WIND UP KILLING HIM AT SOME POINT, SO WHY NOT JUST GET IT OUT OF THE WAY BEFORE THINGS GOT TOO MESSY?
HE HAS A POINT.
HE DID SAY HE WOULD HURT US.

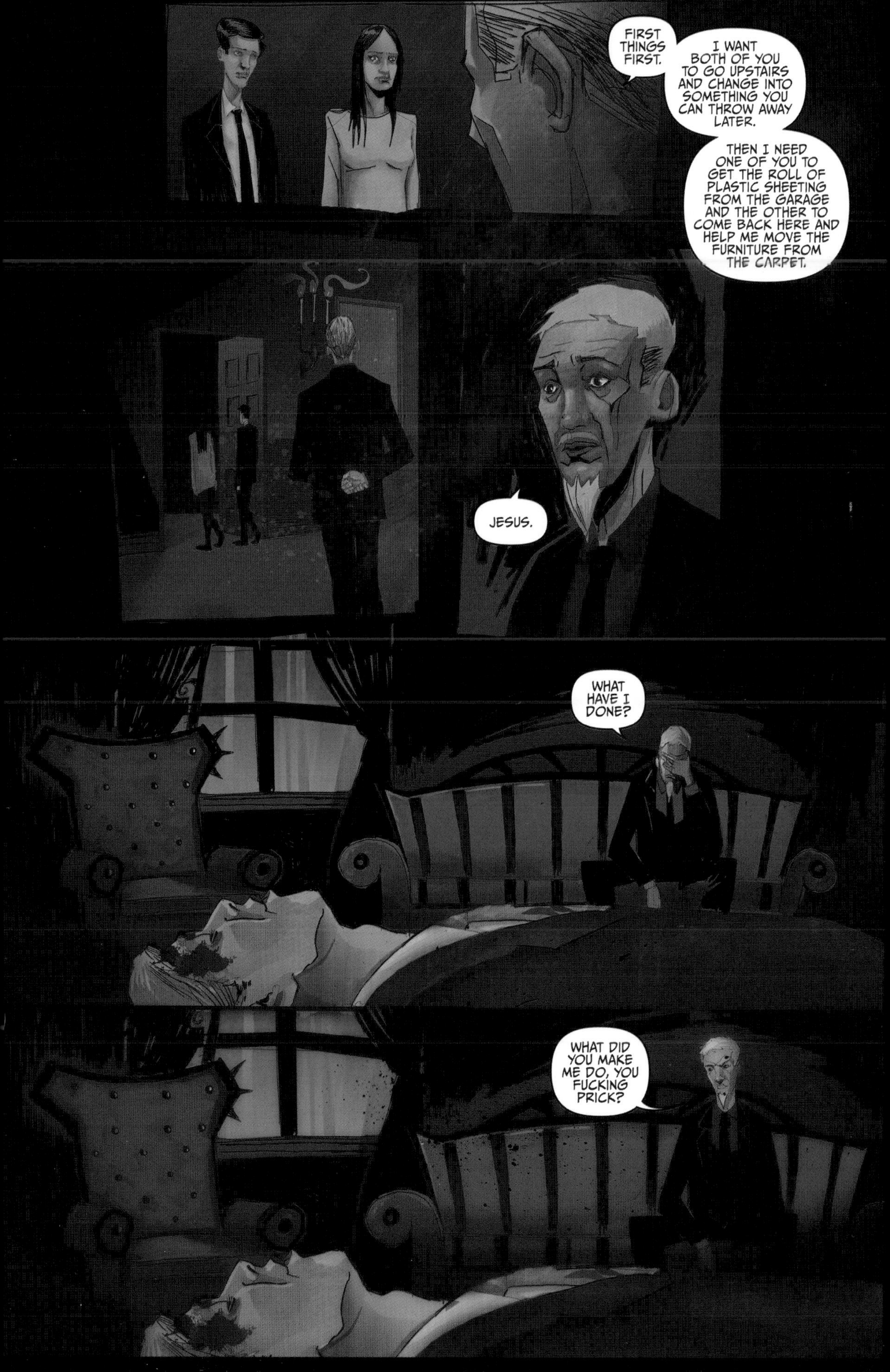
FIRST THINGS FIRST.
I WANT BOTH OF YOU TO GO UPSTAIRS AND CHANGE INTO SOMETHING YOU CAN THROW AWAY LATER.
THEN I NEED ONE OF YOU TO GET THE ROLL OF PLASTIC SHEETING FROM THE GARAGE AND THE OTHER TO COME BACK HERE AND HELP ME MOVE THE FURNITURE FROM THE CARPET.
JESUS.
WHAT HAVE I DONE?
WHAT DID YOU MAKE ME DO, YOU FUCKING PRICK?

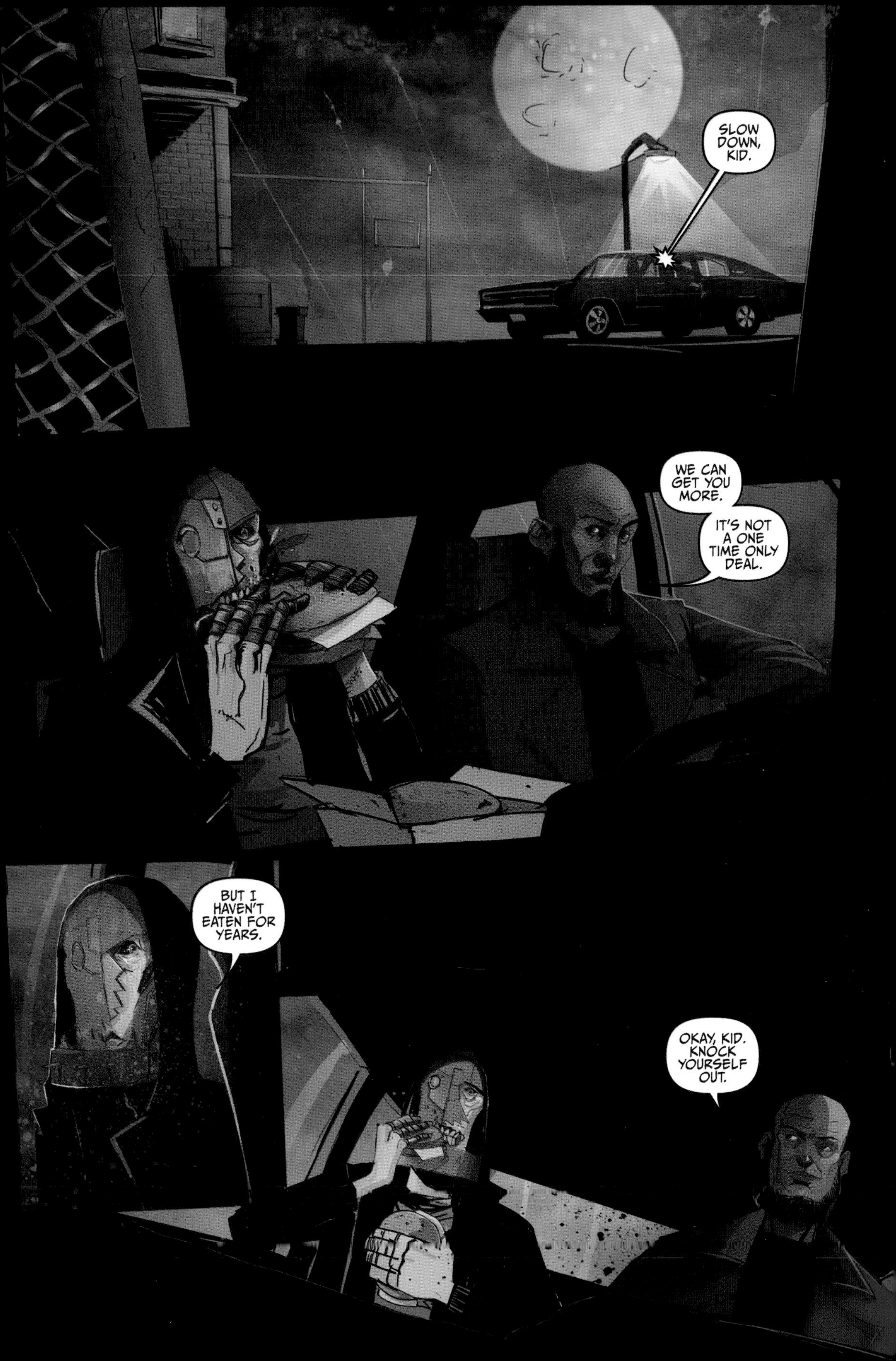
SLOW DOWN, KID.
WE CAN GET YOU MORE.
IT'S NOT A ONE TIME ONLY DEAL.
BUT I HAVEN'T EATEN FOR YEARS.
OKAY, KID. KNOCK YOURSELF OUT.

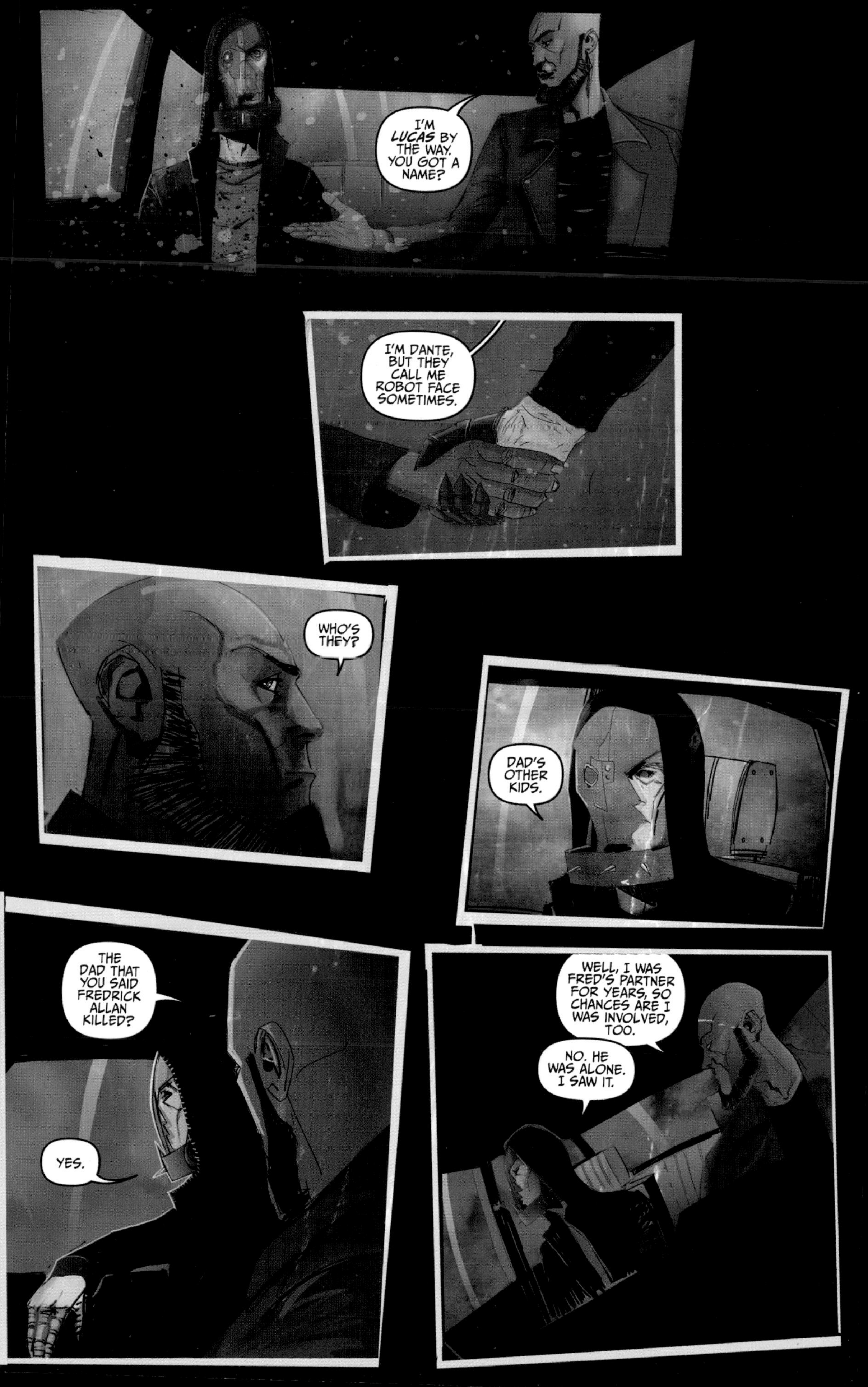
I'M LUCAS BY THE WAY. YOU GOT A NAME?
I'M DANTE, BUT THEY CALL ME ROBOT FACE SOMETIMES.
WHO'S THEY?
DAD'S OTHER KIDS.
THE DAD THAT YOU SAID FREDRICK ALLAN KILLED?
YES.
WELL, I WAS FRED'S PARTNER FOR YEARS, SO CHANCES ARE I WAS INVOLVED, TOO.
NO. HE WAS ALONE. I SAW IT.

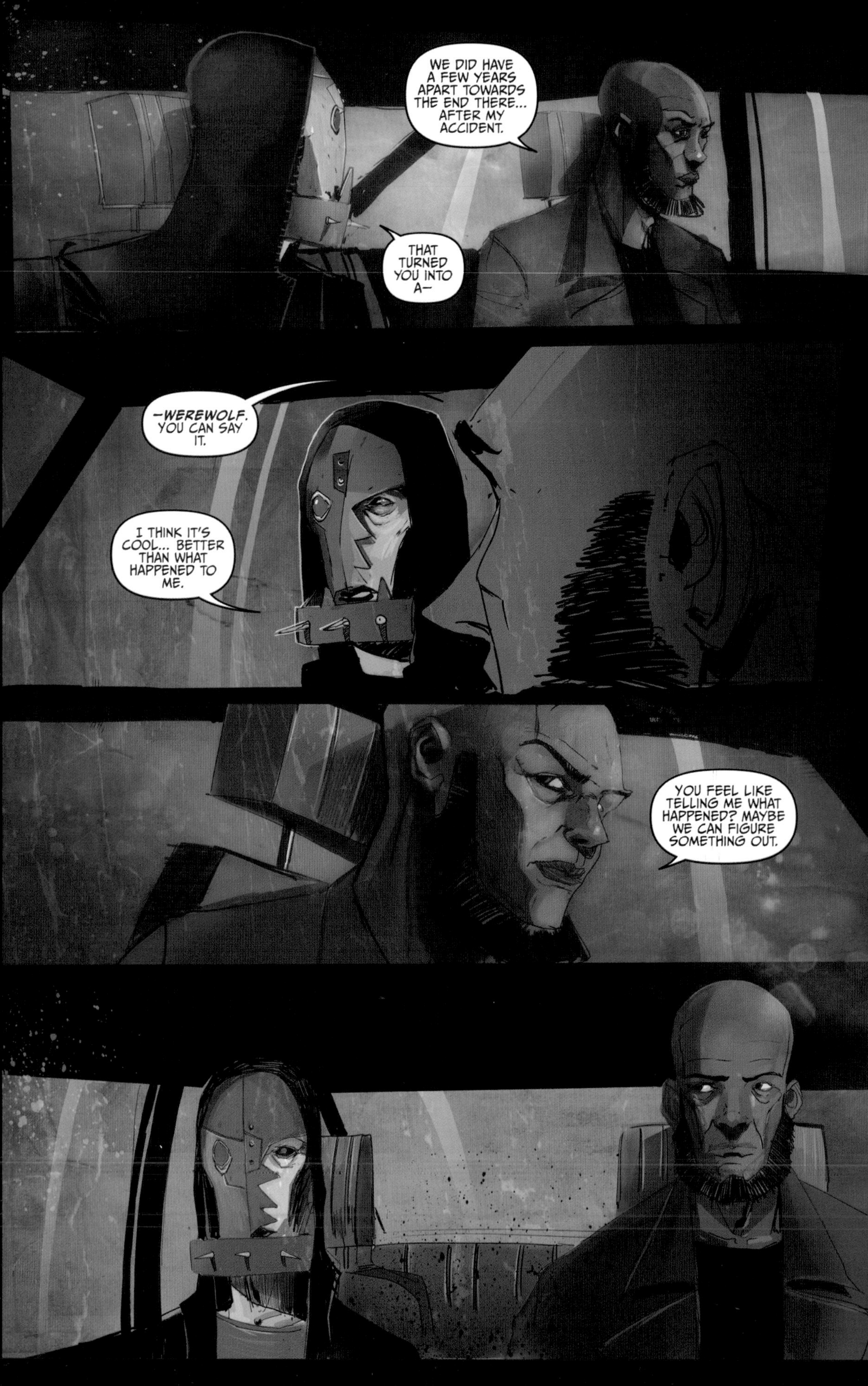
WE DID HAVE A FEW YEARS APART TOWARDS THE END THERE... AFTER MY ACCIDENT.
THAT TURNED YOU INTO A—
—WEREWOLF. YOU CAN SAY IT.
I THINK IT'S COOL... BETTER THAN WHAT HAPPENED TO ME.
YOU FEEL LIKE TELLING ME WHAT HAPPENED? MAYBE WE CAN FIGURE SOMETHING OUT.

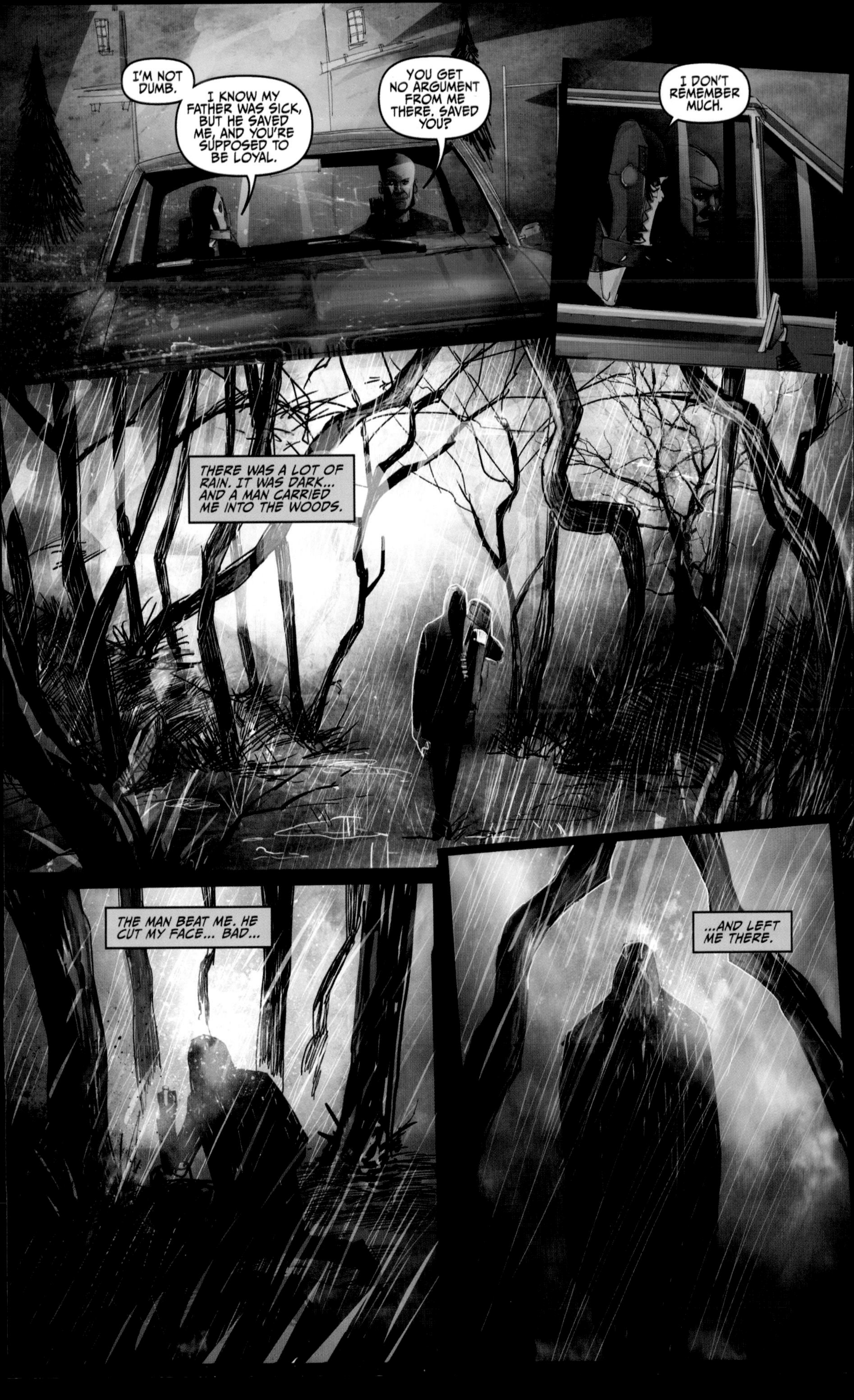
I'M NOT DUMB.
I KNOW MY FATHER WAS SICK, BUT HE SAVED ME, AND YOU'RE SUPPOSED TO BE LOYAL.
YOU GET NO ARGUMENT FROM ME THERE. SAVED YOU?
I DON'T REMEMBER MUCH.
THERE WAS A LOT OF RAIN. IT WAS DARK... AND A MAN CARRIED ME INTO THE WOODS.
THE MAN BEAT ME. HE CUT MY FACE... BAD...
...AND LEFT ME THERE.

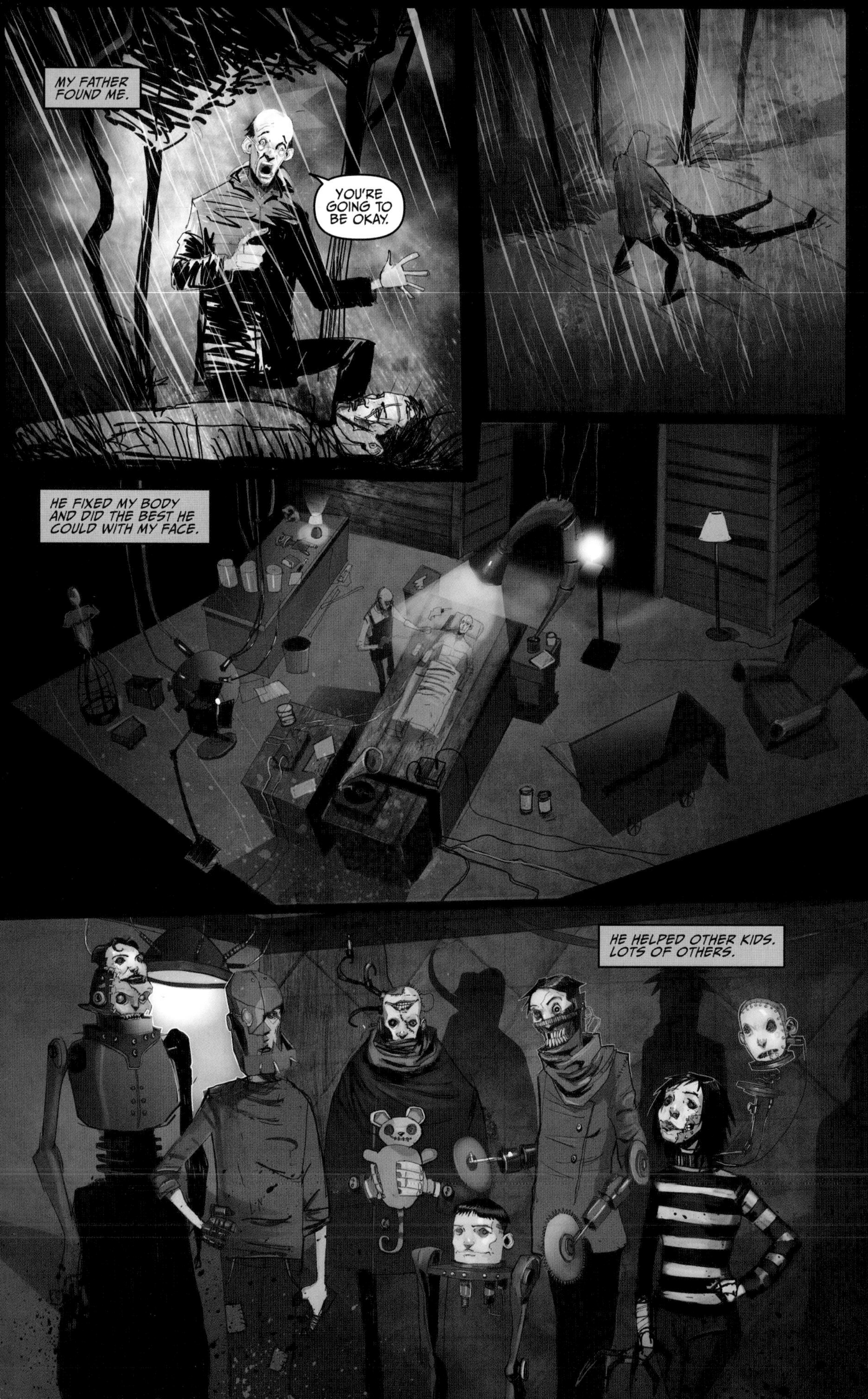
MY FATHER FOUND ME.
YOU'RE GOING TO BE OKAY.
HE FIXED MY BODY AND DID THE BEST HE COULD WITH MY FACE.
HE HELPED OTHER KIDS. LOTS OF OTHERS.

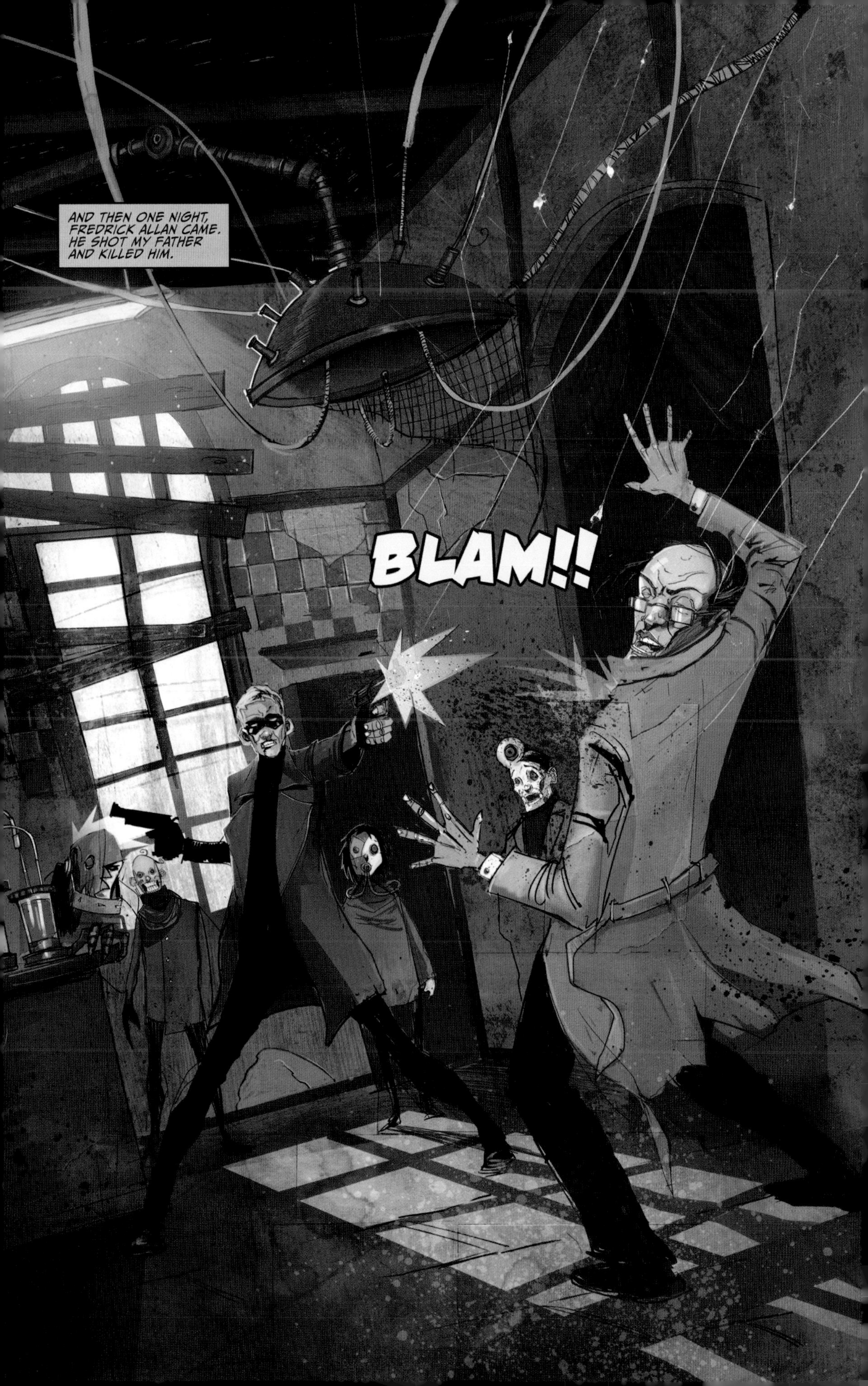
AND THEN ONE NIGHT, FREDRICK ALLAN CAME. HE SHOT MY FATHER AND KILLED HIM.
BLAM!!

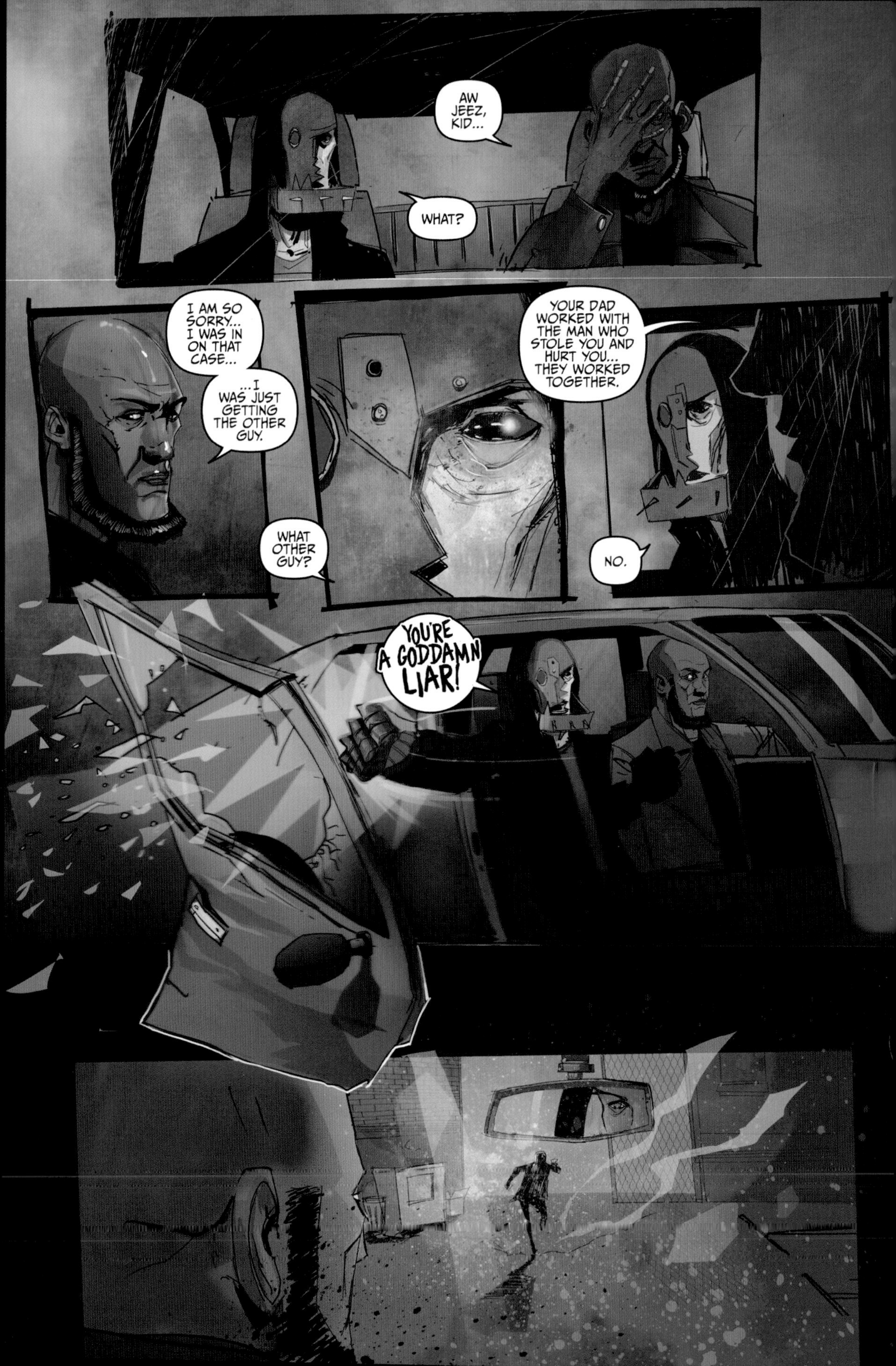
AW JEEZ, KID...
WHAT?
I AM SO SORRY... I WAS IN ON THAT CASE...
...I WAS JUST GETTING THE OTHER GUY.
WHAT OTHER GUY?
YOUR DAD WORKED WITH THE MAN WHO STOLE YOU AND HURT YOU... THEY WORKED TOGETHER.
NO.
YOU'RE A GODDAMN LIAR!

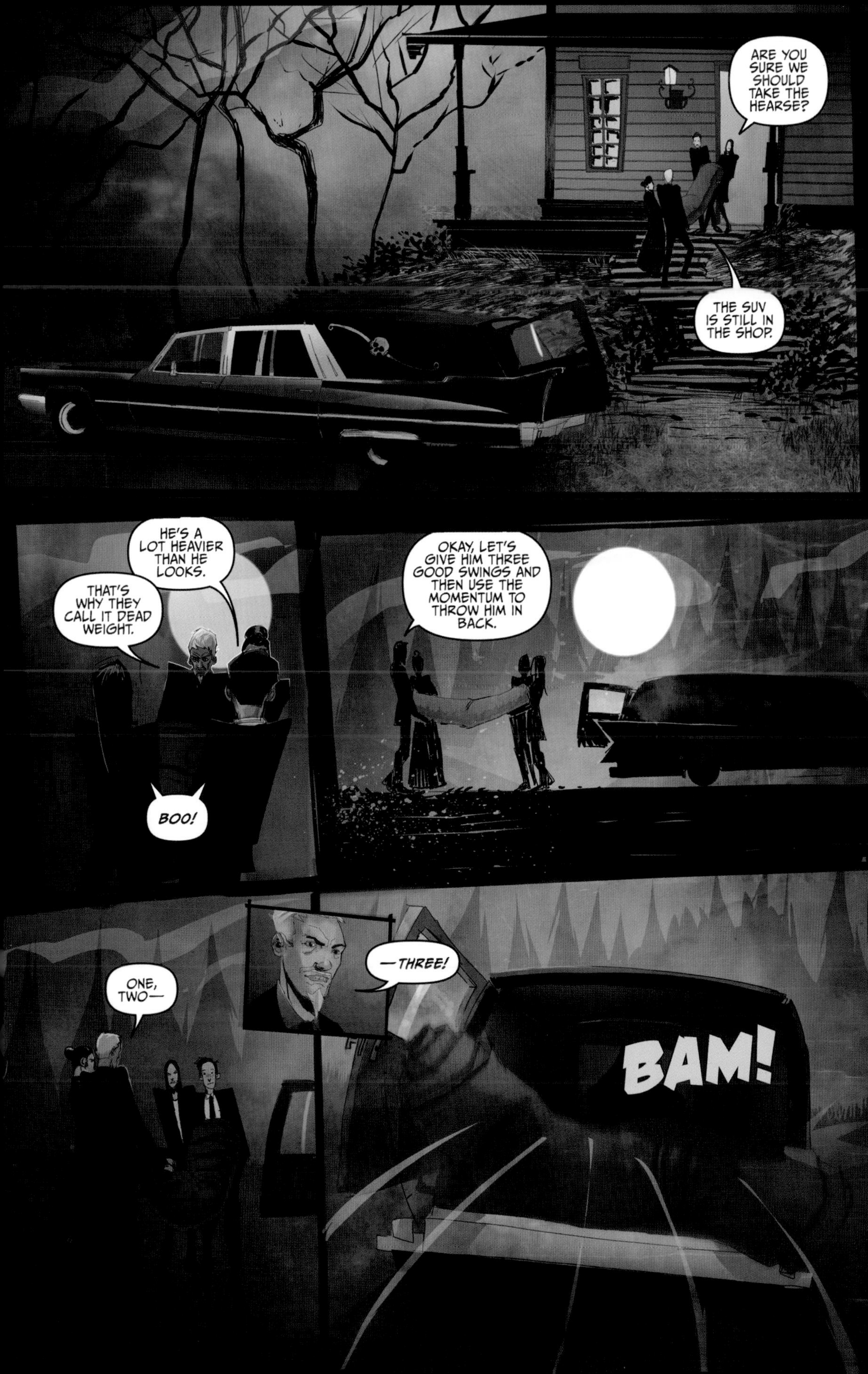
ARE YOU SURE WE SHOULD TAKE THE HEARSE?
THE SUV IS STILL IN THE SHOP.
HE'S A LOT HEAVIER THAN HE LOOKS.
THAT'S WHY THEY CALL IT DEAD WEIGHT.
BOO!
OKAY, LET'S GIVE HIM THREE GOOD SWINGS AND THEN USE THE MOMENTUM TO THROW HIM IN BACK.
ONE, TWO—
—THREE!
BAM!

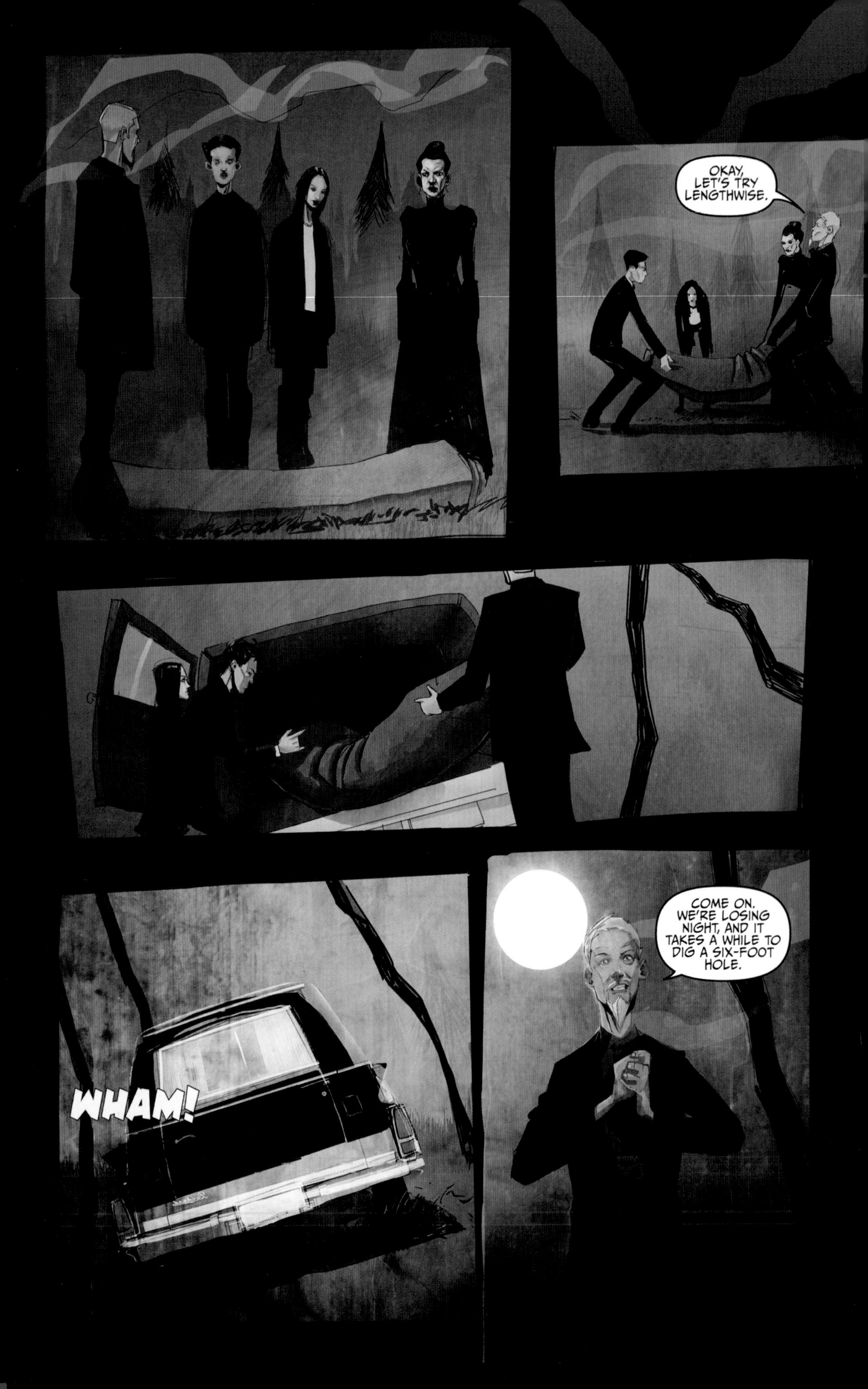
OKAY, LET'S TRY LENGTHWISE.
WHAM!
COME ON. WE'RE LOSING NIGHT, AND IT TAKES A WHILE TO DIG A SIX-FOOT HOLE.

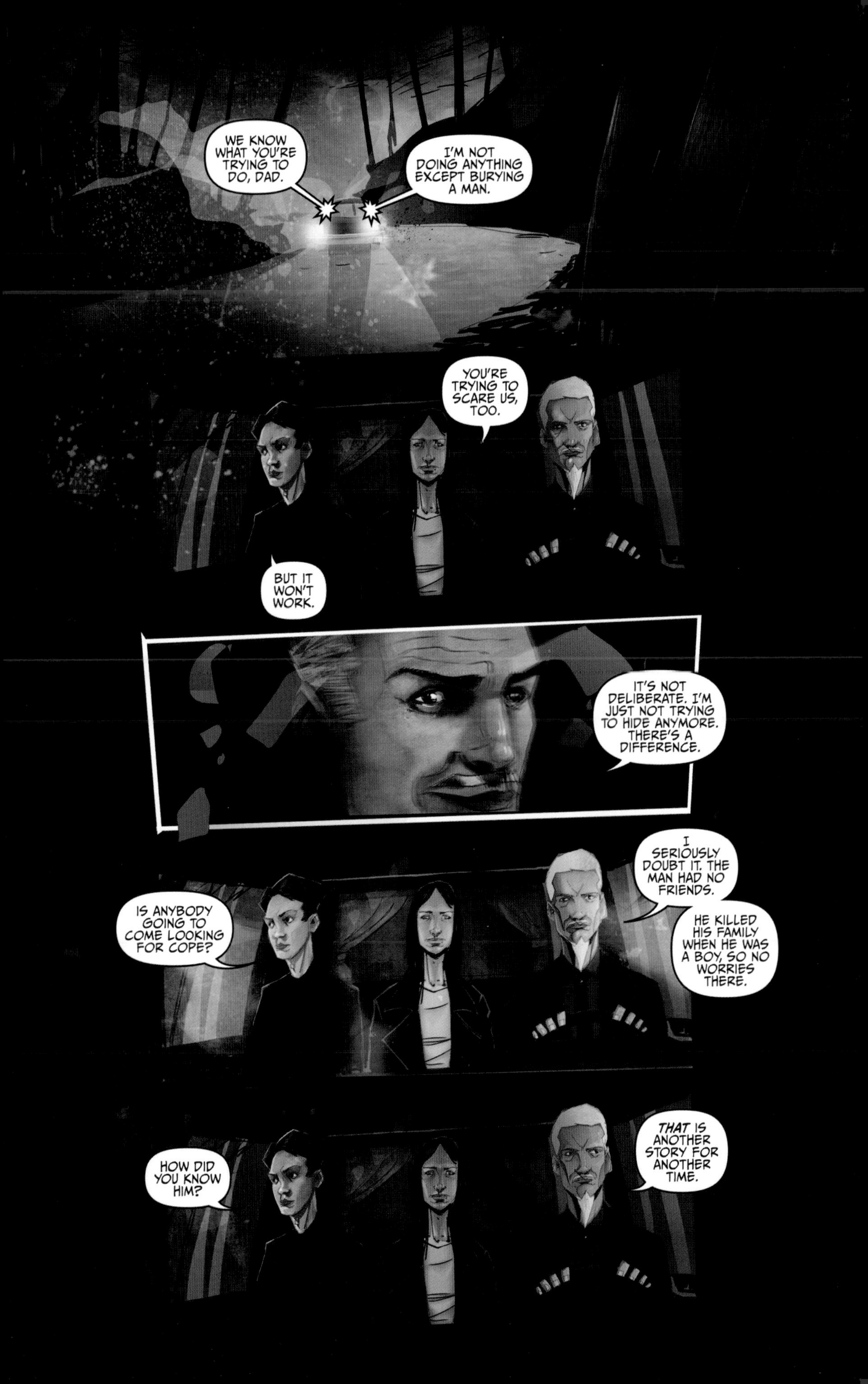
WE KNOW WHAT YOU'RE TRYING TO DO, DAD.
I'M NOT DOING ANYTHING EXCEPT BURYING A MAN.
YOU'RE TRYING TO SCARE US, TOO.
BUT IT WON'T WORK.
IT'S NOT DELIBERATE. I'M JUST NOT TRYING TO HIDE ANYMORE. THERE'S A DIFFERENCE.
IS ANYBODY GOING TO COME LOOKING FOR COPE?
I SERIOUSLY DOUBT IT. THE MAN HAD NO FRIENDS.
HE KILLED HIS FAMILY WHEN HE WAS A BOY, SO NO WORRIES THERE.
HOW DID YOU KNOW HIM?
THAT IS ANOTHER STORY FOR ANOTHER TIME.

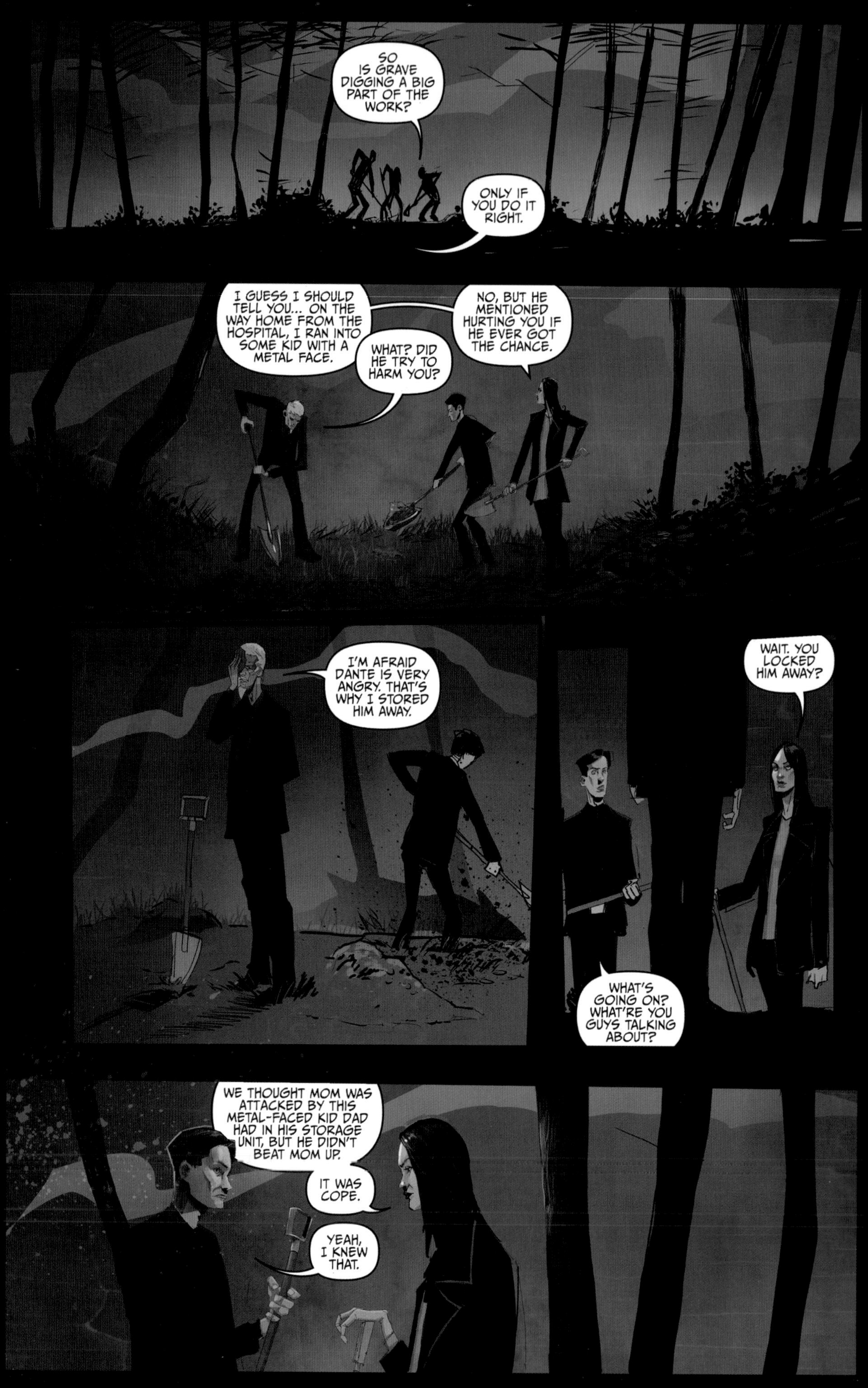
SO IS GRAVE DIGGING A BIG PART OF THE WORK?
ONLY IF YOU DO IT RIGHT.
I GUESS I SHOULD TELL YOU... ON THE WAY HOME FROM THE HOSPITAL, I RAN INTO SOME KID WITH A METAL FACE.
WHAT? DID HE TRY TO HARM YOU?
NO, BUT HE MENTIONED HURTING YOU IF HE EVER GOT THE CHANCE.
I'M AFRAID DANTE IS VERY ANGRY. THAT'S WHY I STORED HIM AWAY.
WAIT. YOU LOCKED HIM AWAY?
WHAT'S GOING ON? WHAT'RE YOU GUYS TALKING ABOUT?
WE THOUGHT MOM WAS ATTACKED BY THIS METAL-FACED KID DAD HAD IN HIS STORAGE UNIT, BUT HE DIDN'T BEAT MOM UP.
IT WAS COPE.
YEAH, I KNEW THAT.

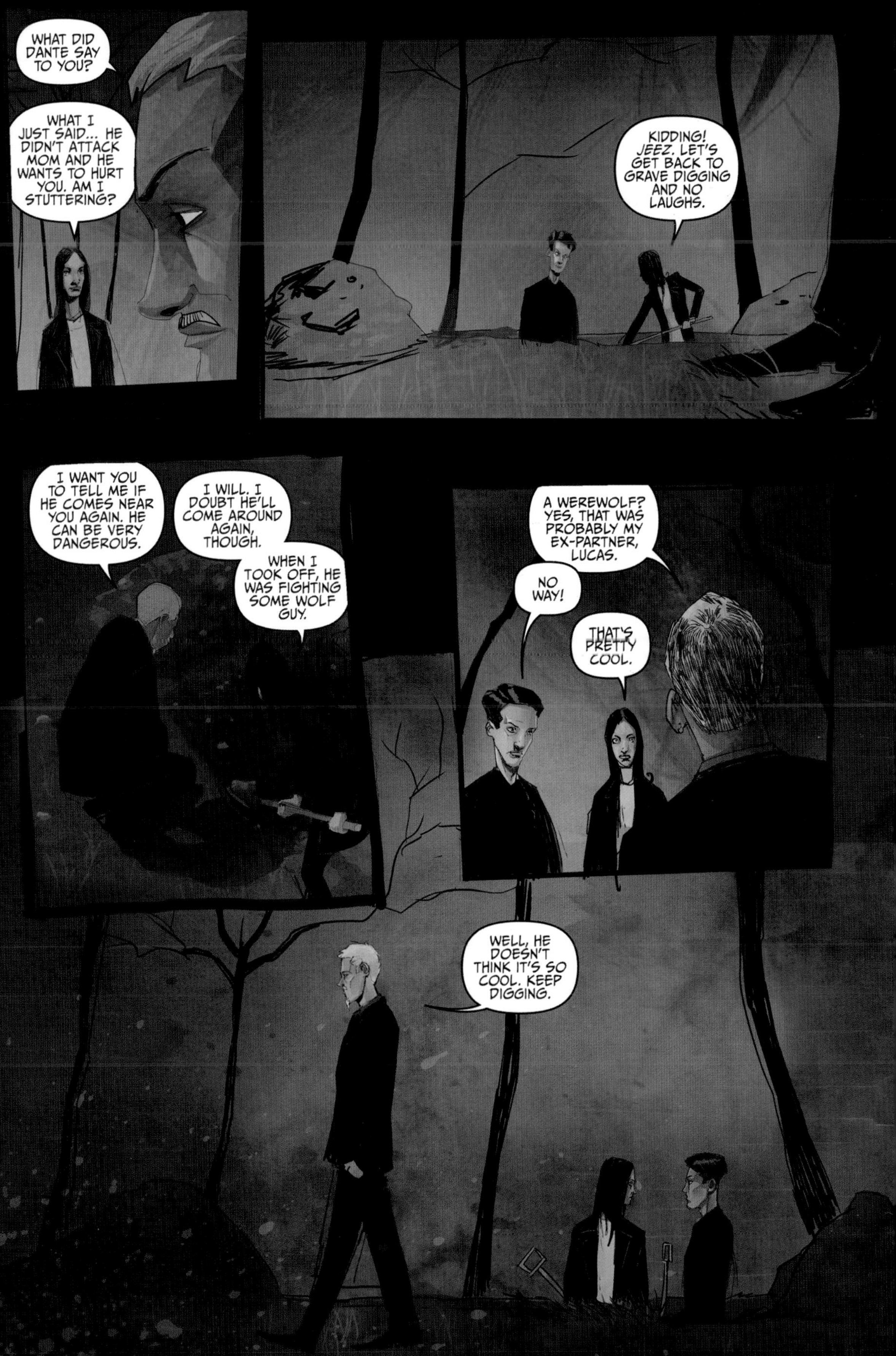
WHAT DID DANTE SAY TO YOU?
WHAT I JUST SAID... HE DIDN'T ATTACK MOM AND HE WANTS TO HURT YOU. AM I STUTTERING?
KIDDING! JEEZ. LET'S GET BACK TO GRAVE DIGGING AND NO LAUGHS.
I WANT YOU TO TELL ME IF HE COMES NEAR YOU AGAIN. HE CAN BE VERY DANGEROUS.
I WILL. I DOUBT HE'LL COME AROUND AGAIN, THOUGH.
WHEN I TOOK OFF, HE WAS FIGHTING SOME WOLF GUY.
A WEREWOLF? YES, THAT WAS PROBABLY MY EX-PARTNER, LUCAS.
NO WAY!
THAT'S PRETTY COOL.
WELL, HE DOESN'T THINK IT'S SO COOL. KEEP DIGGING.

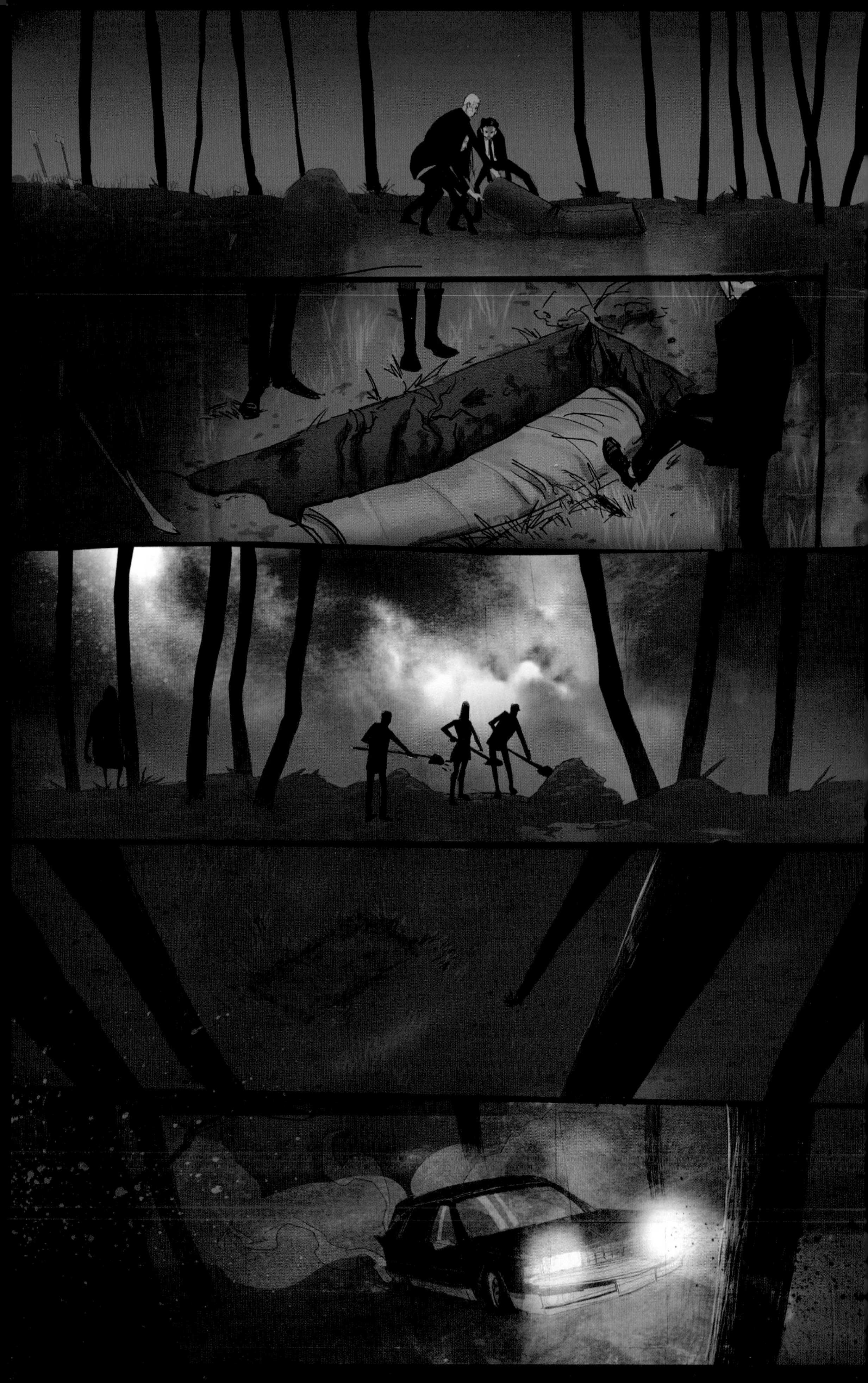

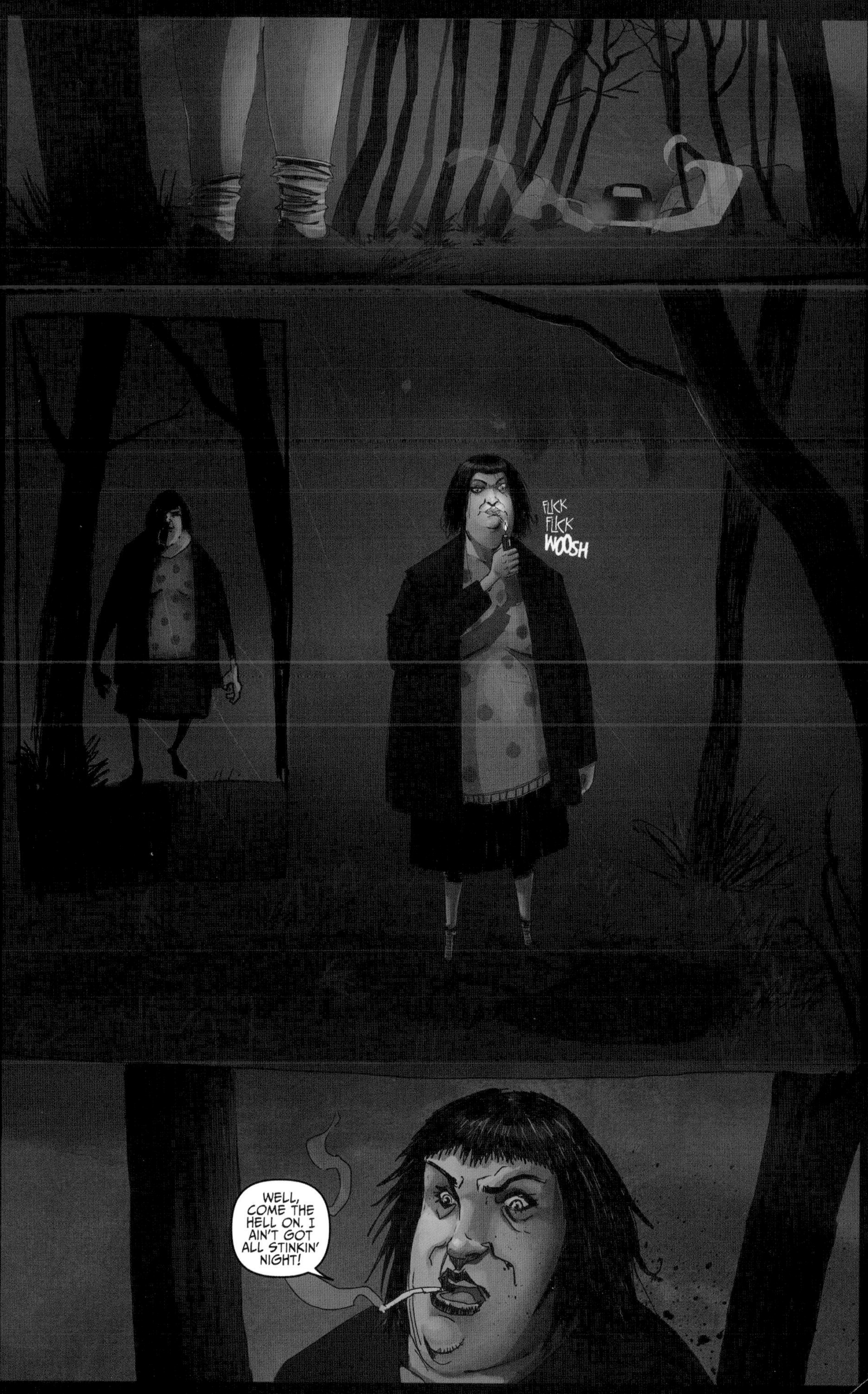
FLICK
FLICK
WOOSH
WELL, COME THE HELL ON. I AIN'T GOT ALL STINKIN' NIGHT!

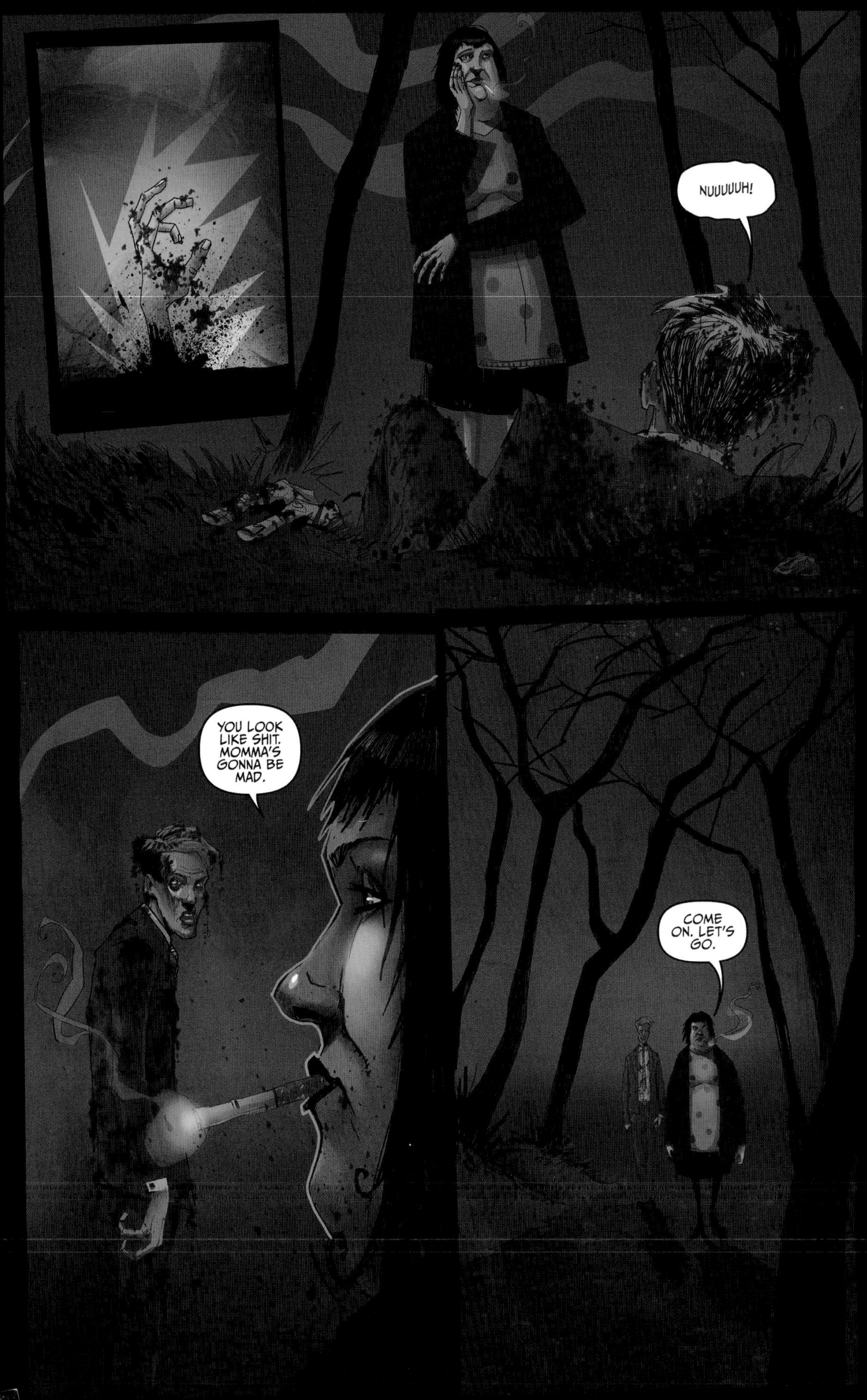
NUUUUUH!
YOU LOOK LIKE SHIT. MOMMA'S GONNA BE MAD.
COME ON. LET'S GO.

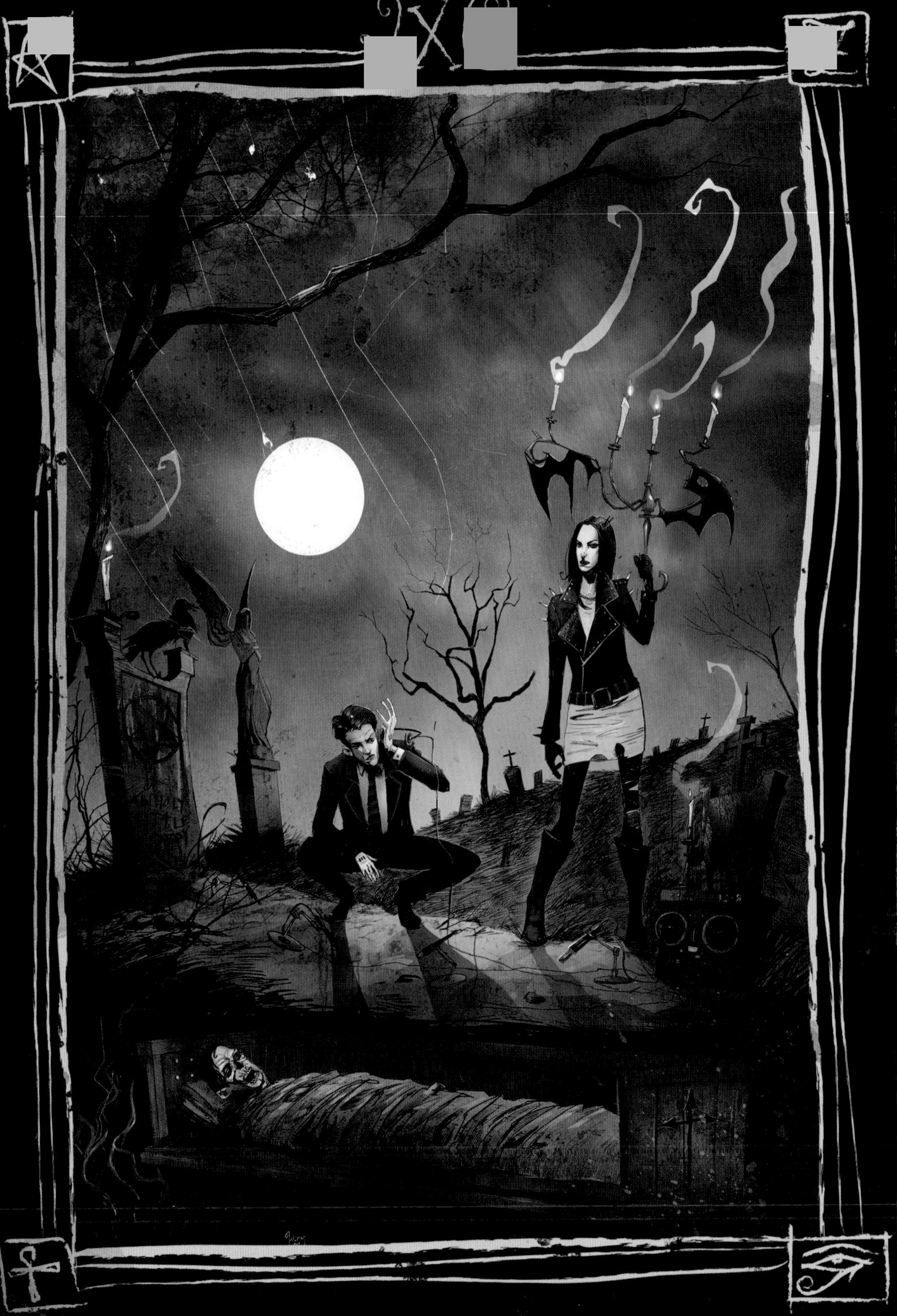

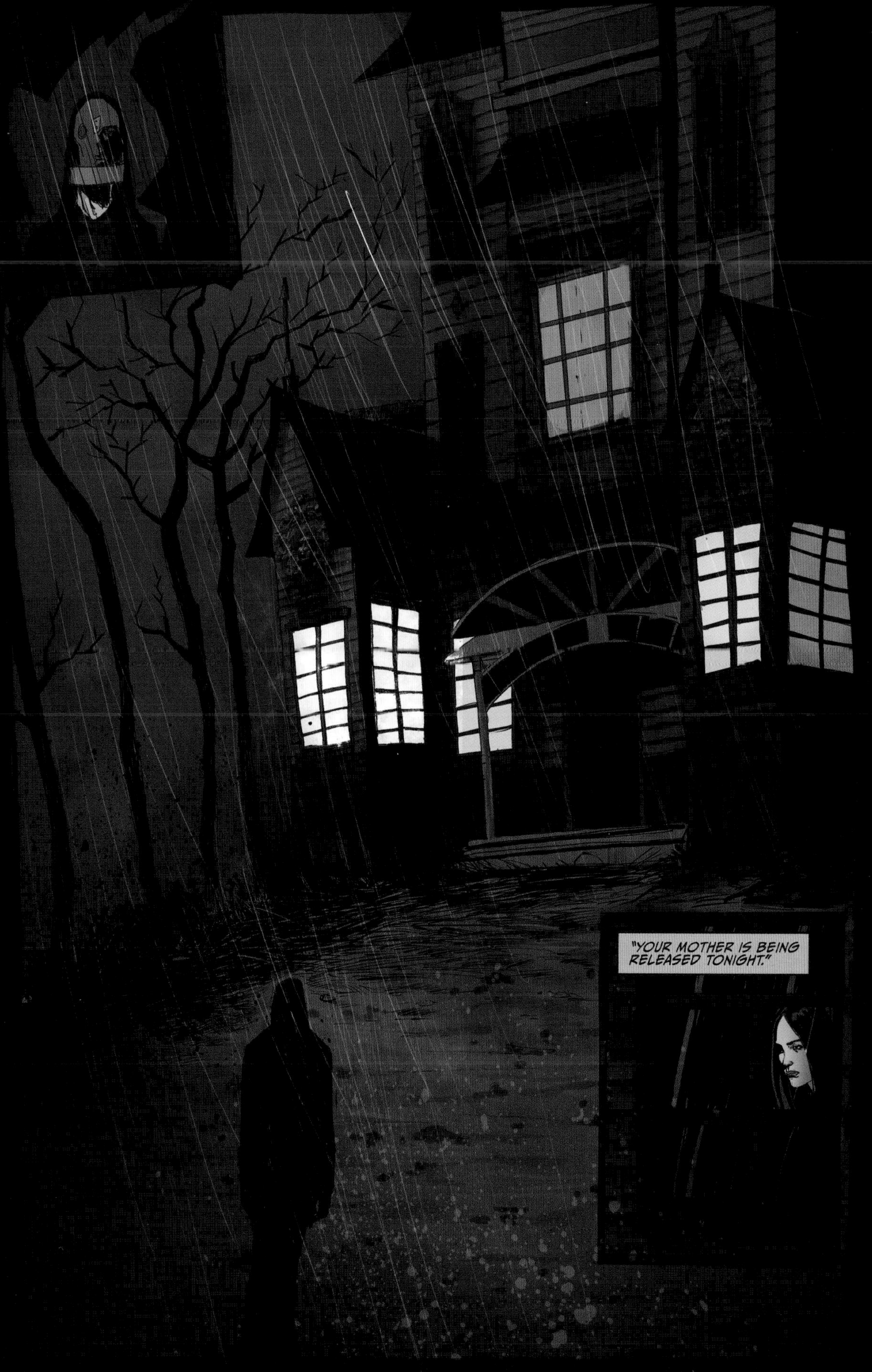
"YOUR MOTHER IS BEING RELEASED TONIGHT."

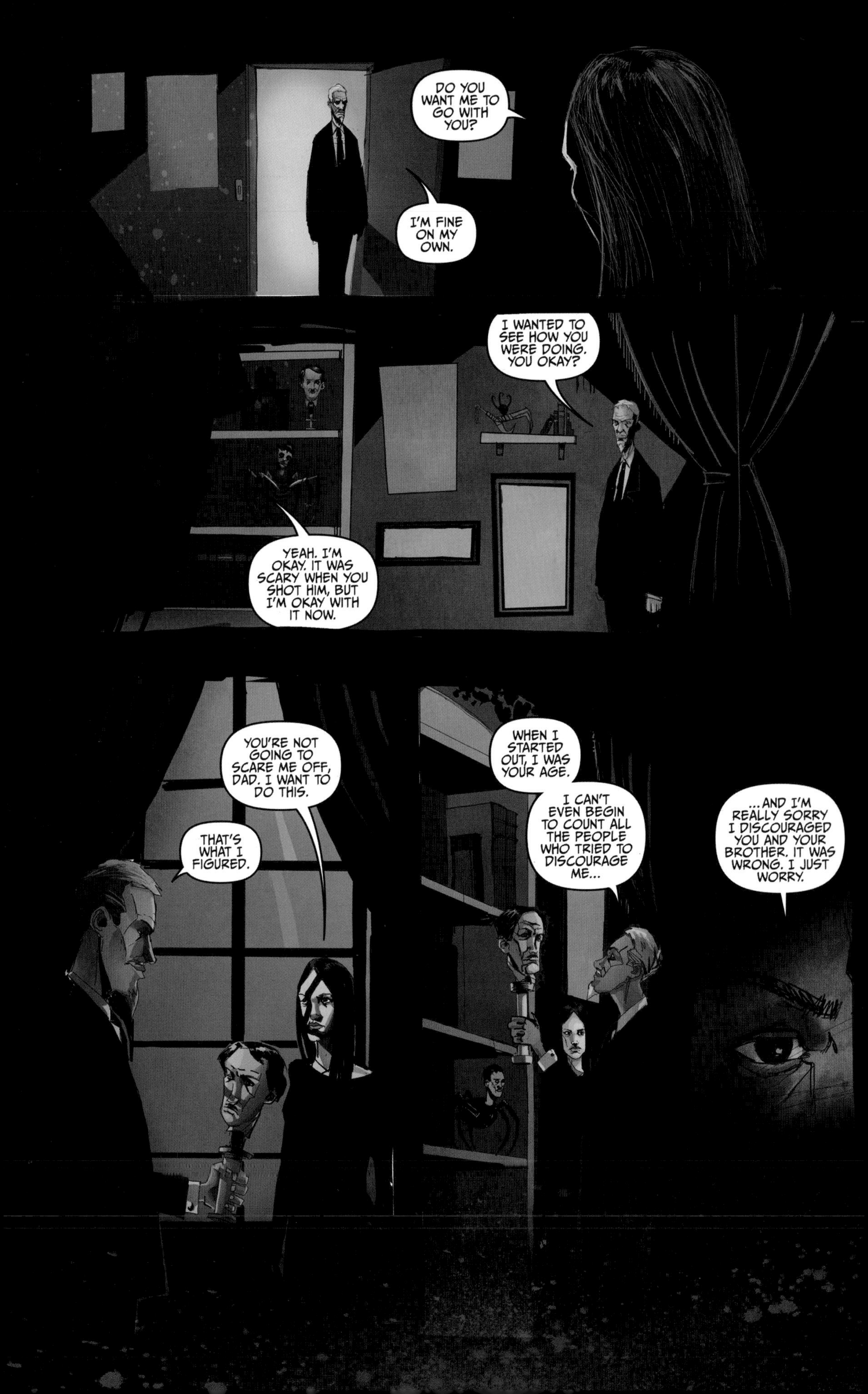
DO YOU WANT ME TO GO WITH YOU?
I'M FINE ON MY OWN.
I WANTED TO SEE HOW YOU WERE DOING. YOU OKAY?
YEAH. I'M OKAY. IT WAS SCARY WHEN YOU SHOT HIM, BUT I'M OKAY WITH IT NOW.
YOU'RE NOT GOING TO SCARE ME OFF, DAD. I WANT TO DO THIS.
THAT'S WHAT I FIGURED.
WHEN I STARTED OUT, I WAS YOUR AGE.
I CAN'T EVEN BEGIN TO COUNT ALL THE PEOPLE WHO TRIED TO DISCOURAGE ME...
...AND I'M REALLY SORRY I DISCOURAGED YOU AND YOUR BROTHER. IT WAS WRONG. I JUST WORRY.

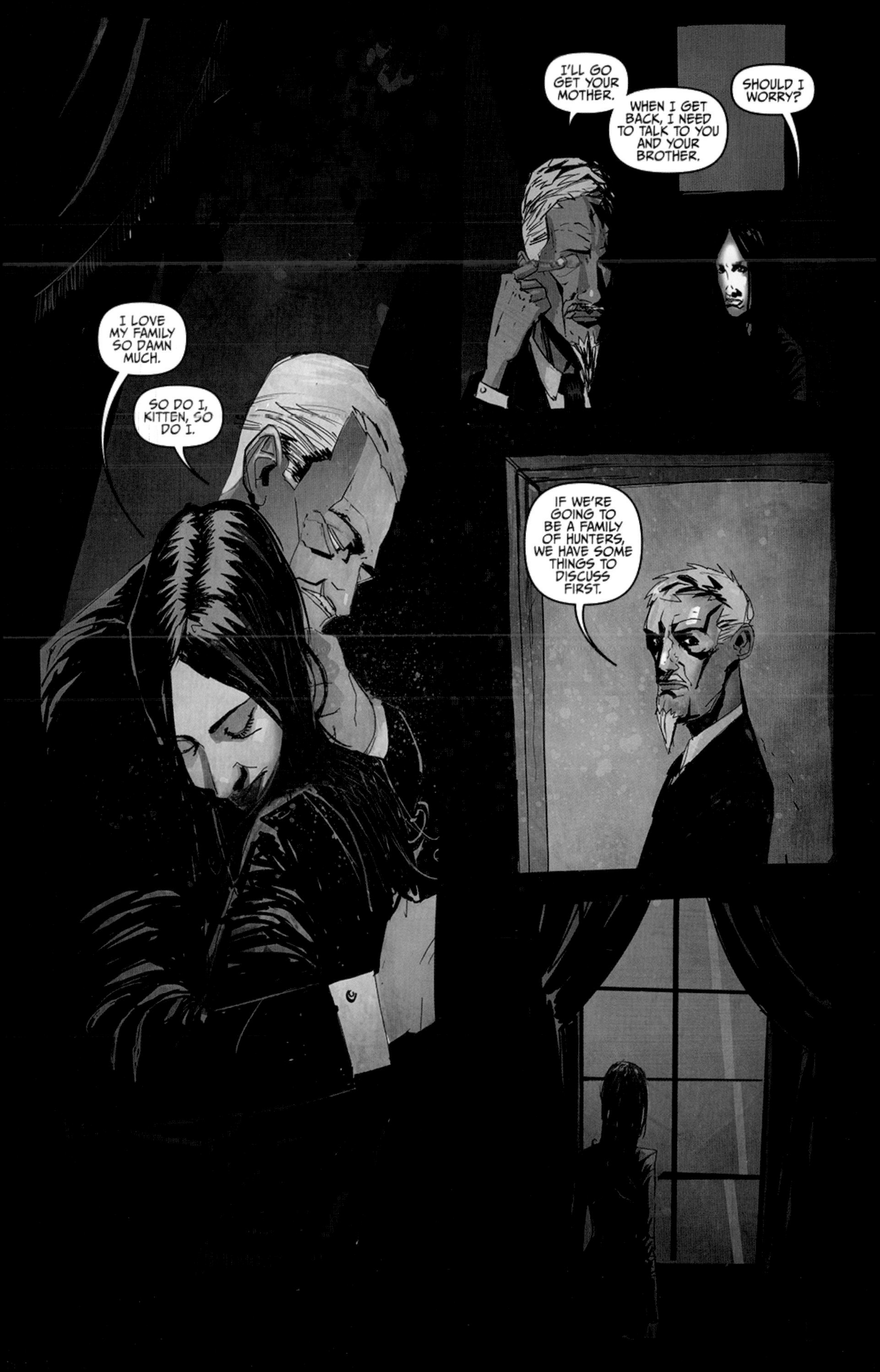
I'LL GO GET YOUR MOTHER.
WHEN I GET BACK, I NEED TO TALK TO YOU AND YOUR BROTHER.
SHOULD I WORRY?
I LOVE MY FAMILY SO DAMN MUCH.
SO DO I, KITTEN, SO DO I.
IF WE'RE GOING TO BE A FAMILY OF HUNTERS, WE HAVE SOME THINGS TO DISCUSS FIRST.

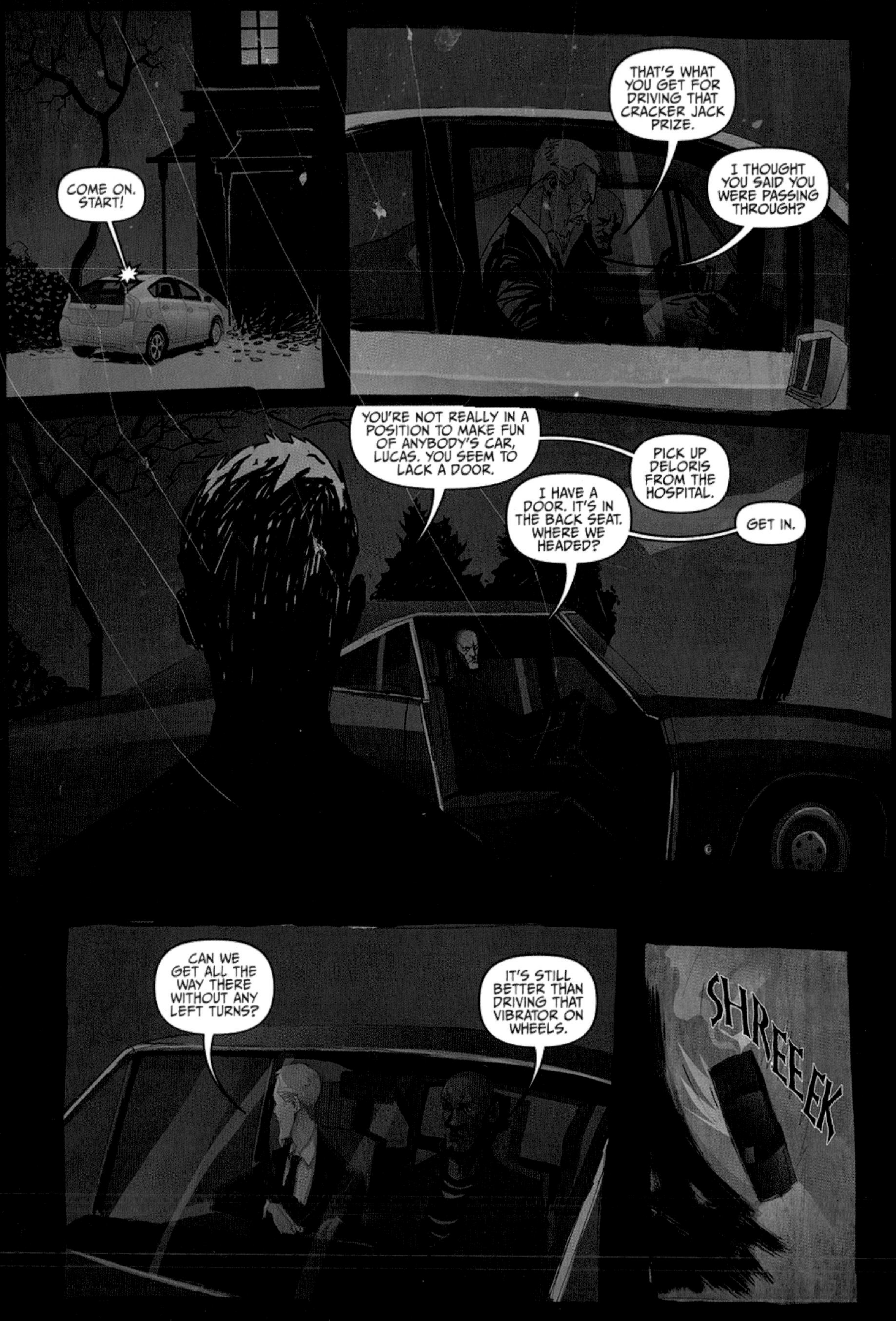
COME ON. START!
THAT'S WHAT YOU GET FOR DRIVING THAT CRACKER JACK PRIZE.
I THOUGHT YOU SAID YOU WERE PASSING THROUGH?
YOU'RE NOT REALLY IN A POSITION TO MAKE FUN OF ANYBODY'S CAR, LUCAS. YOU SEEM TO LACK A DOOR.
I HAVE A DOOR. IT'S IN THE BACK SEAT. WHERE WE HEADED?
PICK UP DELORIS FROM THE HOSPITAL.
GET IN.
CAN WE GET ALL THE WAY THERE WITHOUT ANY LEFT TURNS?
IT'S STILL BETTER THAN DRIVING THAT VIBRATOR ON WHEELS.
SHREEEK

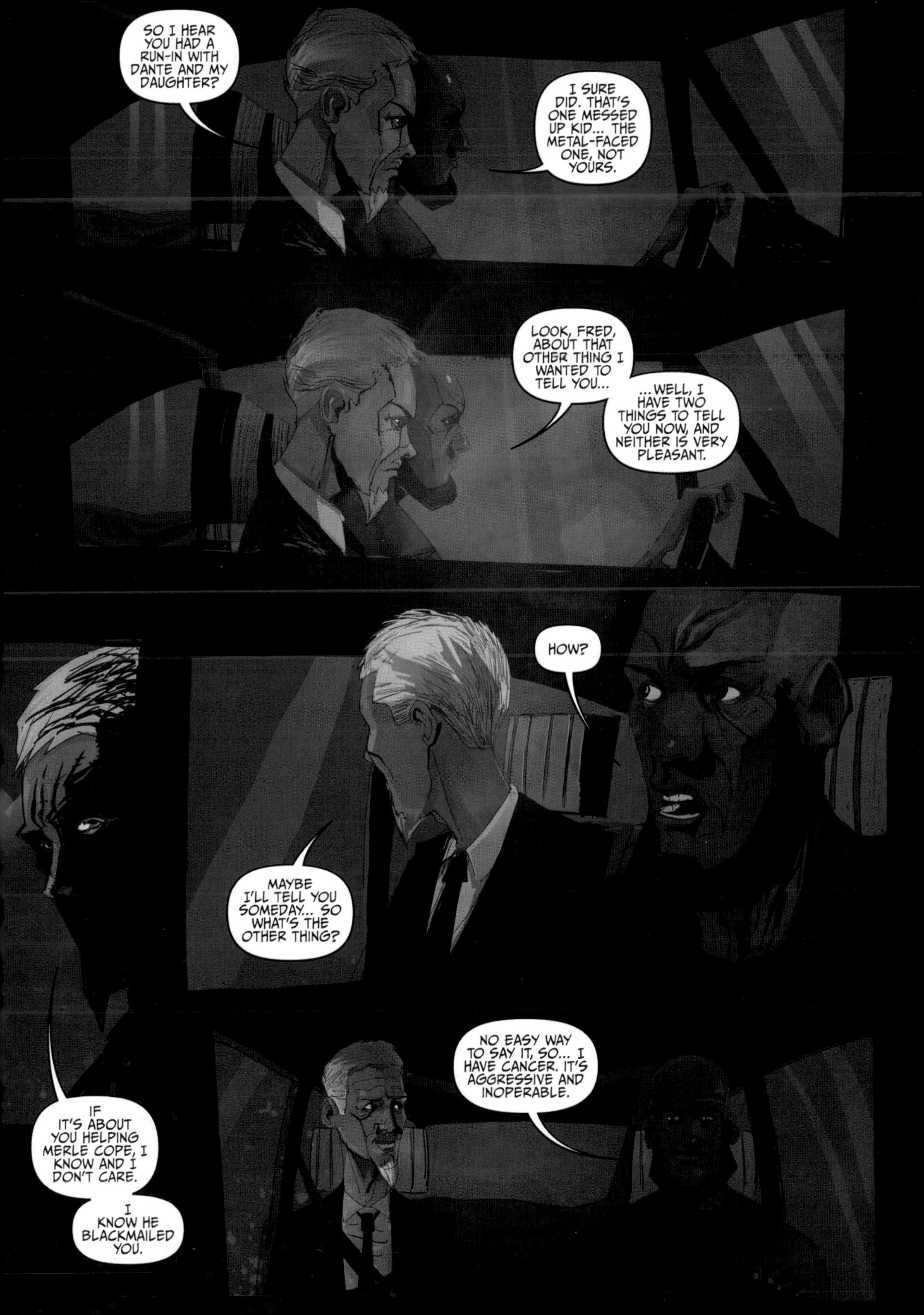
SO I HEAR YOU HAD A RUN-IN WITH DANTE AND MY DAUGHTER?
I SURE DID. THAT'S ONE MESSED UP KID... THE METAL-FACED ONE, NOT YOURS.
LOOK, FRED, ABOUT THAT OTHER THING I WANTED TO TELL YOU...
...WELL, I HAVE TWO THINGS TO TELL YOU NOW, AND NEITHER IS VERY PLEASANT.
IF IT'S ABOUT YOU HELPING MERLE COPE, I KNOW AND I DON'T CARE.
I KNOW HE BLACKMAILED YOU.
HOW?
MAYBE I'LL TELL YOU SOMEDAY... SO WHAT'S THE OTHER THING?
NO EASY WAY TO SAY IT, SO... I HAVE CANCER. IT'S AGGRESSIVE AND INOPERABLE.

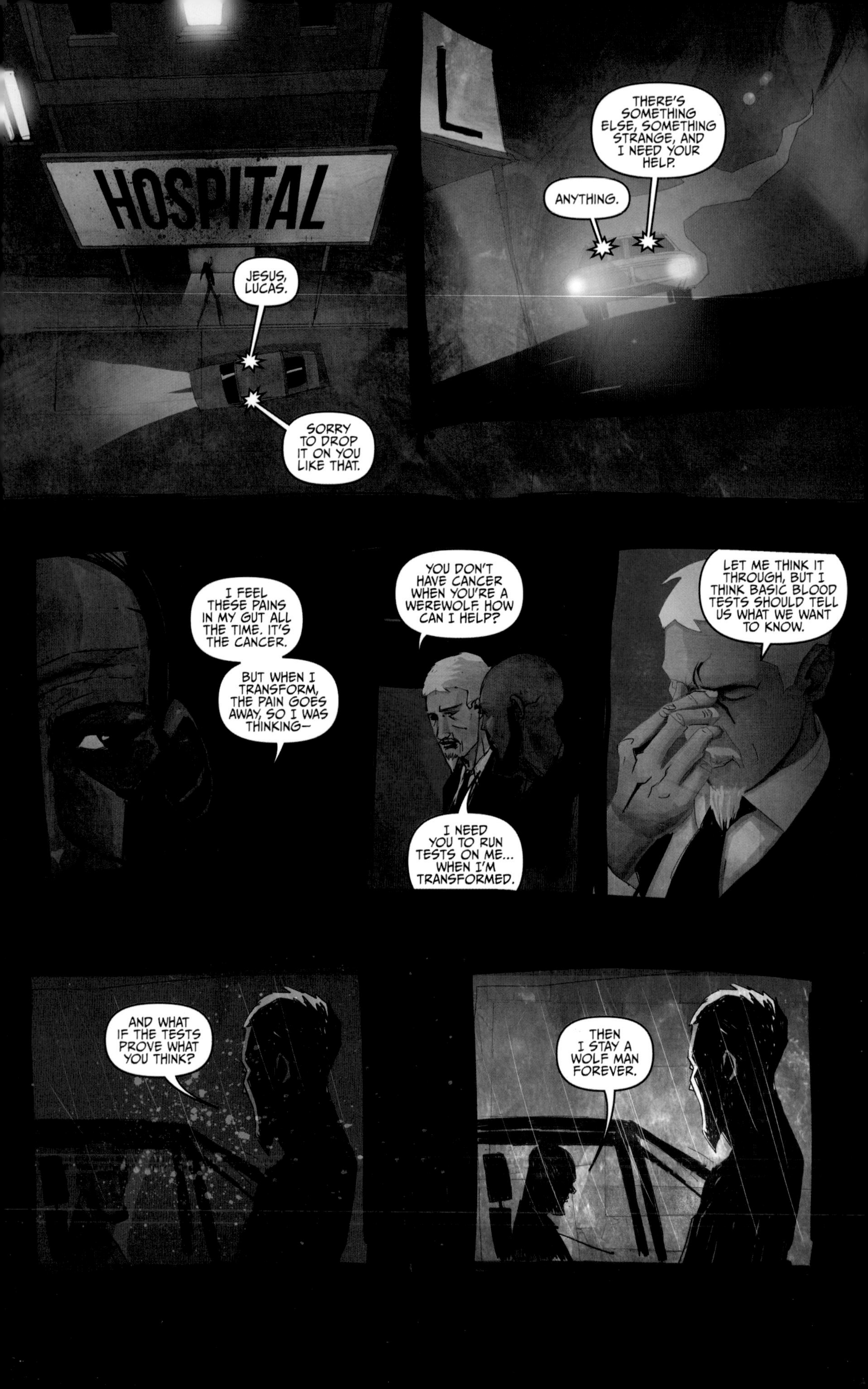
HOSPITAL
JESUS, LUCAS.
SORRY TO DROP IT ON YOU LIKE THAT.
THERE'S SOMETHING ELSE, SOMETHING STRANGE, AND I NEED YOUR HELP.
ANYTHING.
I FEEL THESE PAINS IN MY GUT ALL THE TIME. IT'S THE CANCER.
BUT WHEN I TRANSFORM, THE PAIN GOES AWAY, SO I WAS THINKING–
YOU DON'T HAVE CANCER WHEN YOU'RE A WEREWOLF. HOW CAN I HELP?
I NEED YOU TO RUN TESTS ON ME... WHEN I'M TRANSFORMED.
LET ME THINK IT THROUGH, BUT I THINK BASIC BLOOD TESTS SHOULD TELL US WHAT WE WANT TO KNOW.
AND WHAT IF THE TESTS PROVE WHAT YOU THINK?
THEN I STAY A WOLF MAN FOREVER.

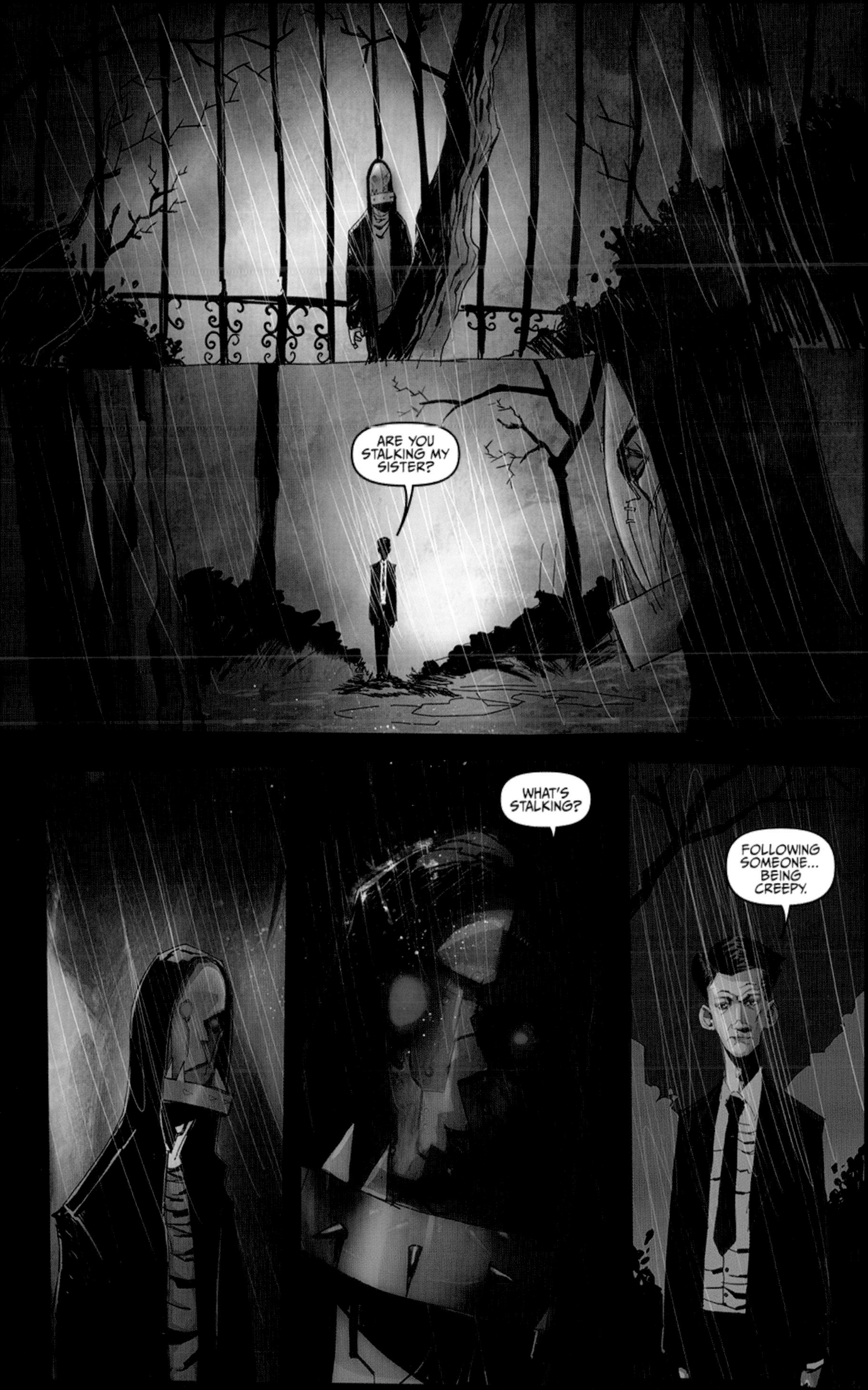
ARE YOU STALKING MY SISTER?
WHAT'S STALKING?
FOLLOWING SOMEONE... BEING CREEPY.

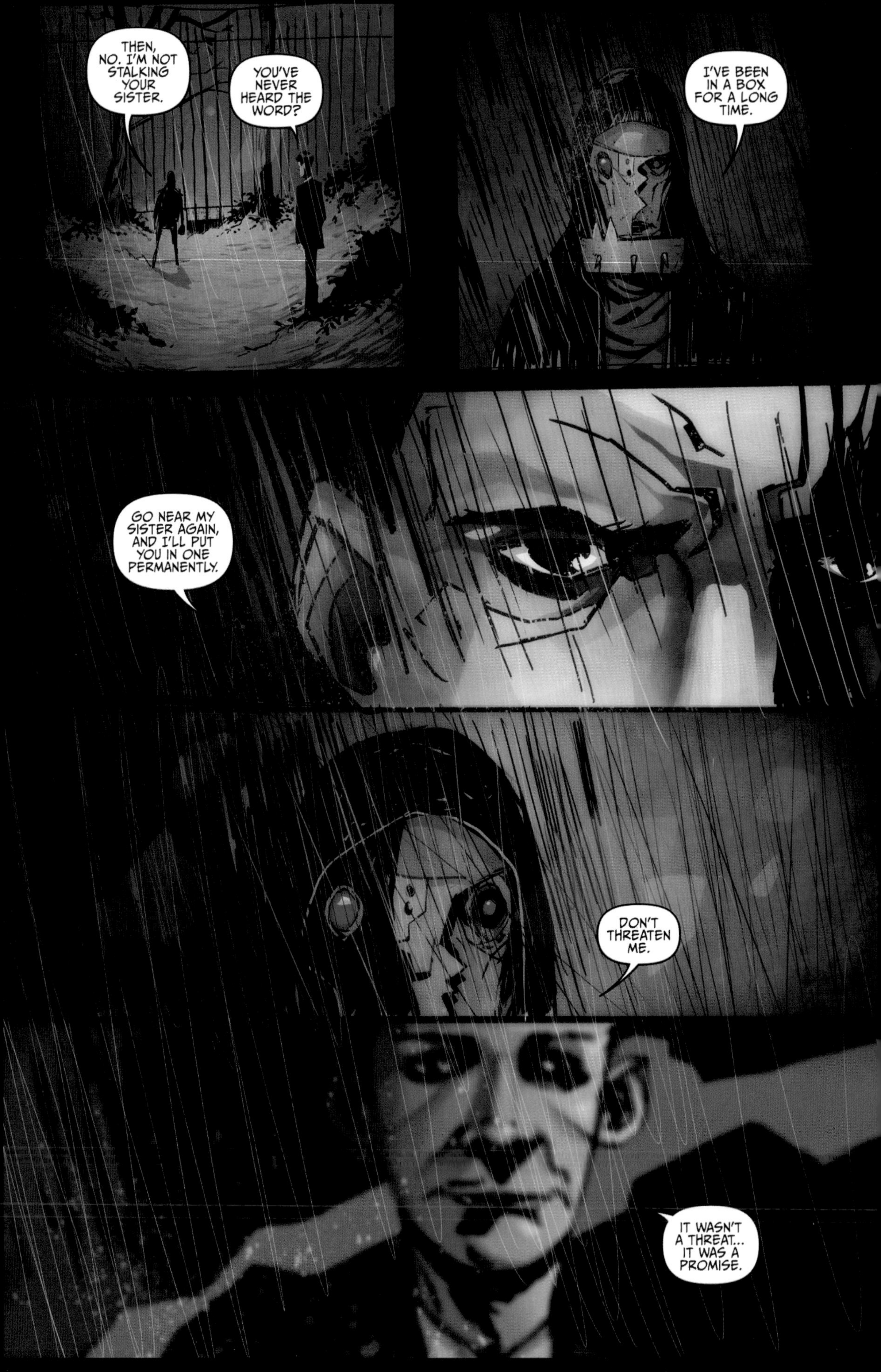
THEN, NO. I'M NOT STALKING YOUR SISTER.
YOU'VE NEVER HEARD THE WORD?
I'VE BEEN IN A BOX FOR A LONG TIME.
GO NEAR MY SISTER AGAIN, AND I'LL PUT YOU IN ONE PERMANENTLY.
DON'T THREATEN ME.
IT WASN'T A THREAT... IT WAS A PROMISE.

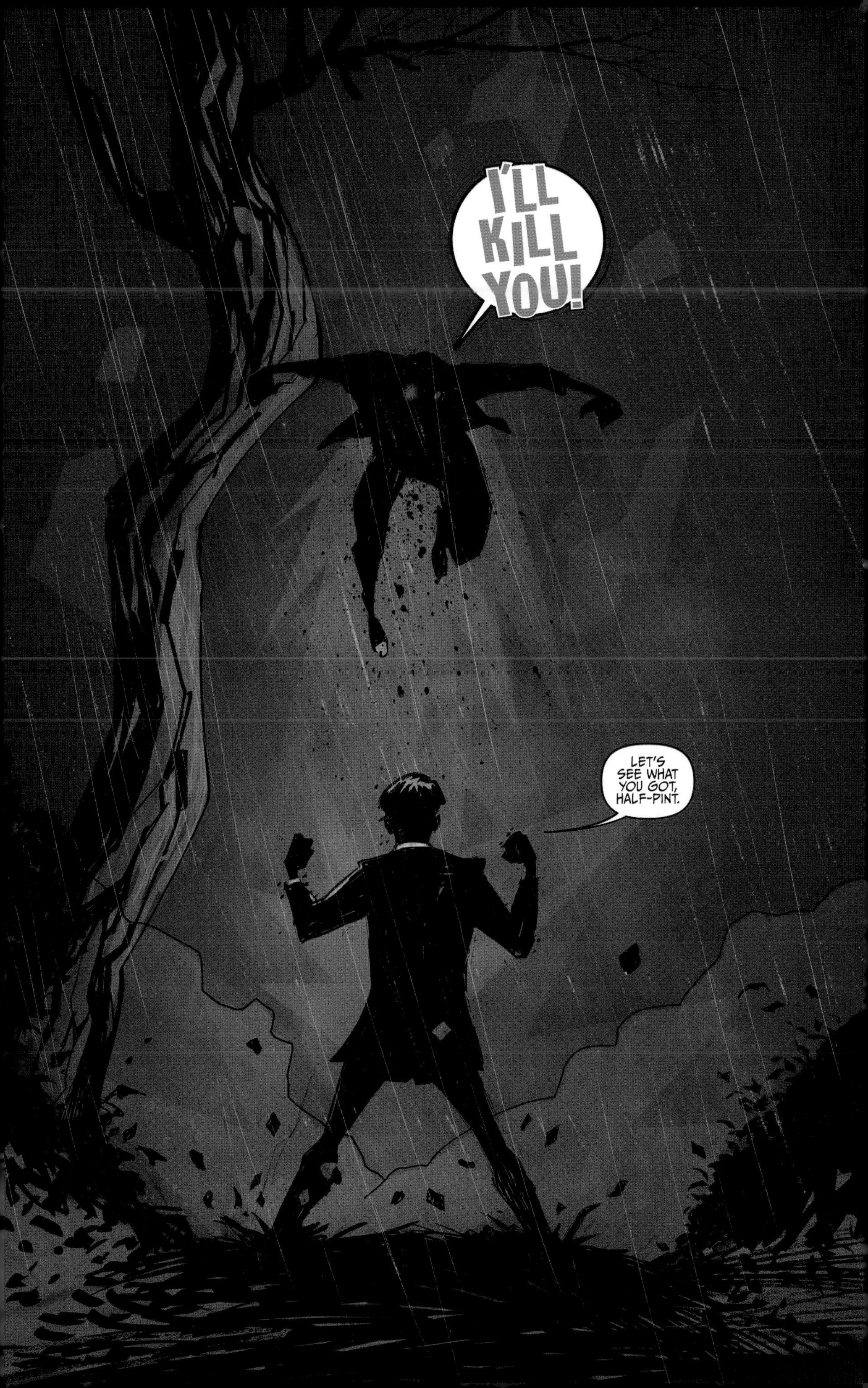
I'LL KILL YOU!
LET'S SEE WHAT YOU GOT, HALF-PINT.

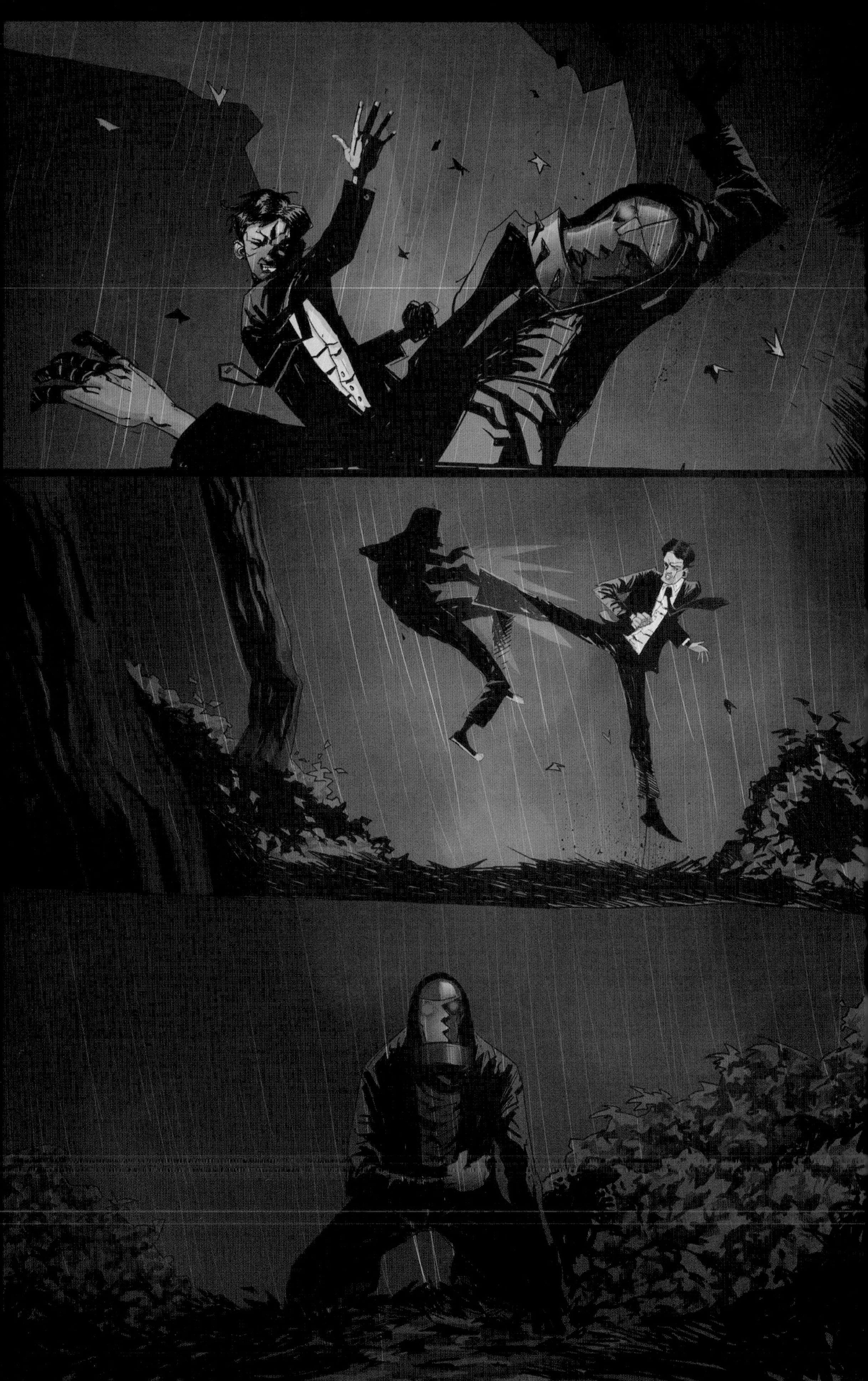

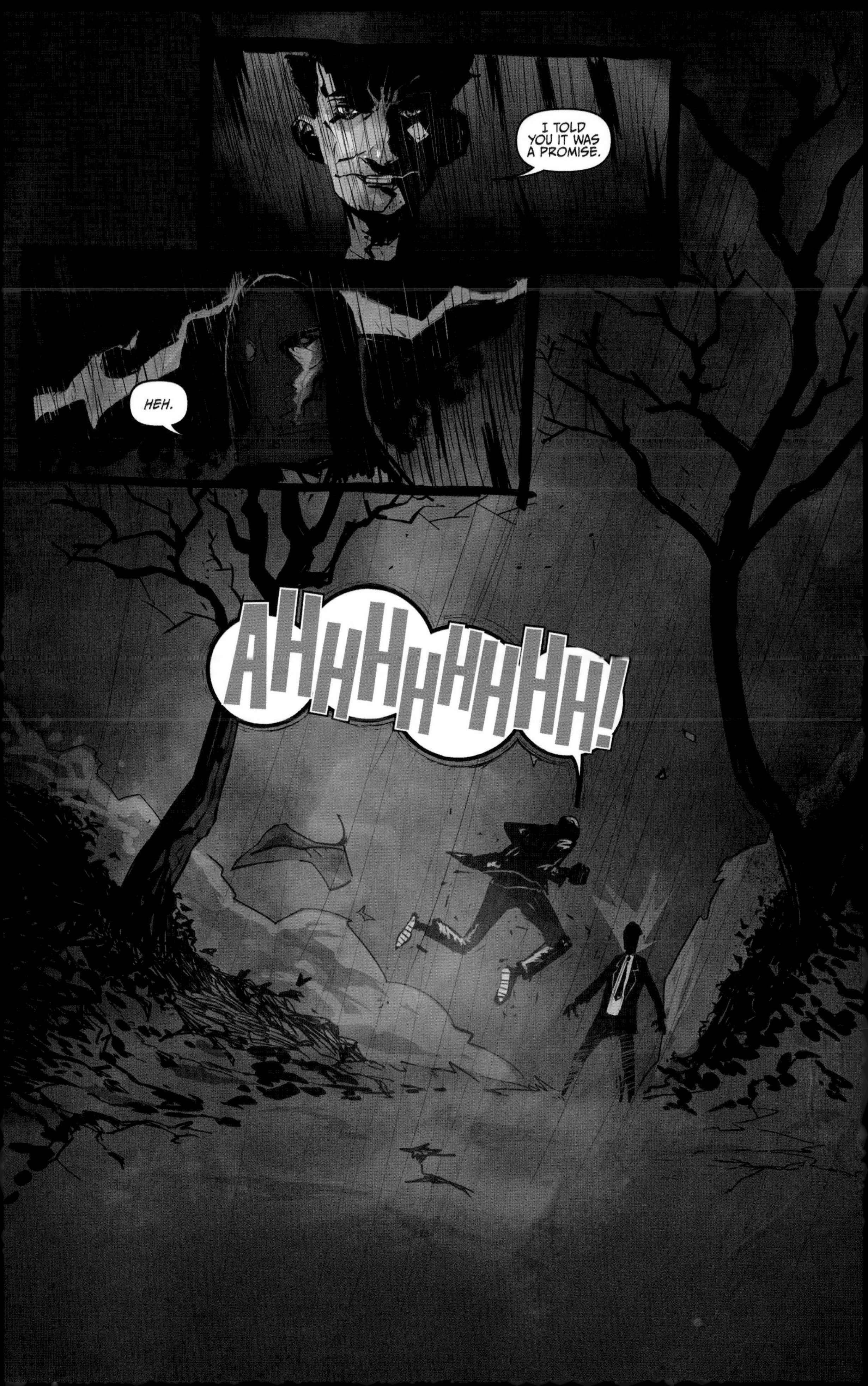
I TOLD YOU IT WAS A PROMISE.
HEH.
AHHHHHHHHH!

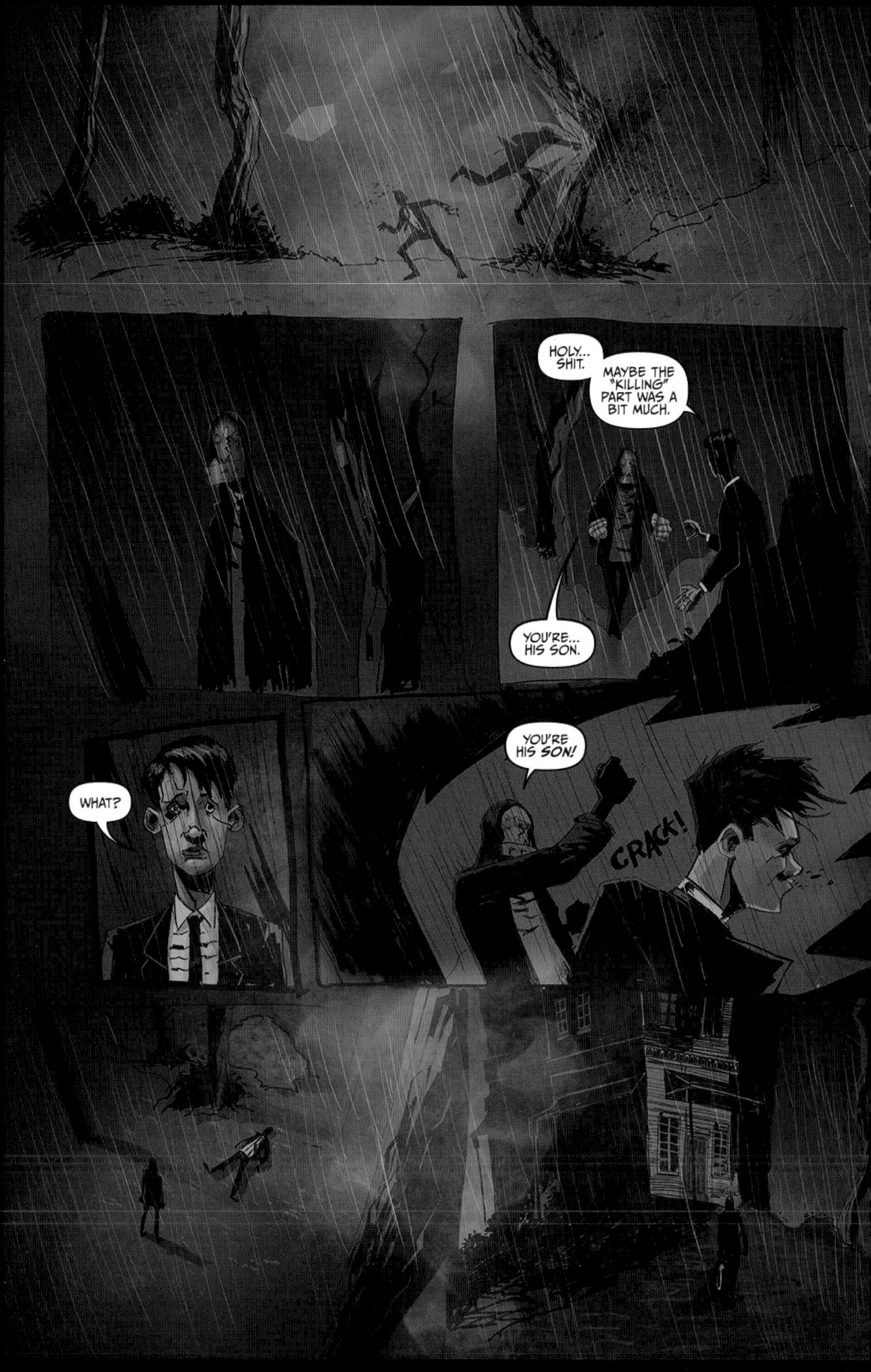

HOLY... SHIT.
MAYBE THE "KILLING" PART WAS A BIT MUCH.
YOU'RE... HIS SON.
WHAT?
YOU'RE HIS SON!
CRACK!

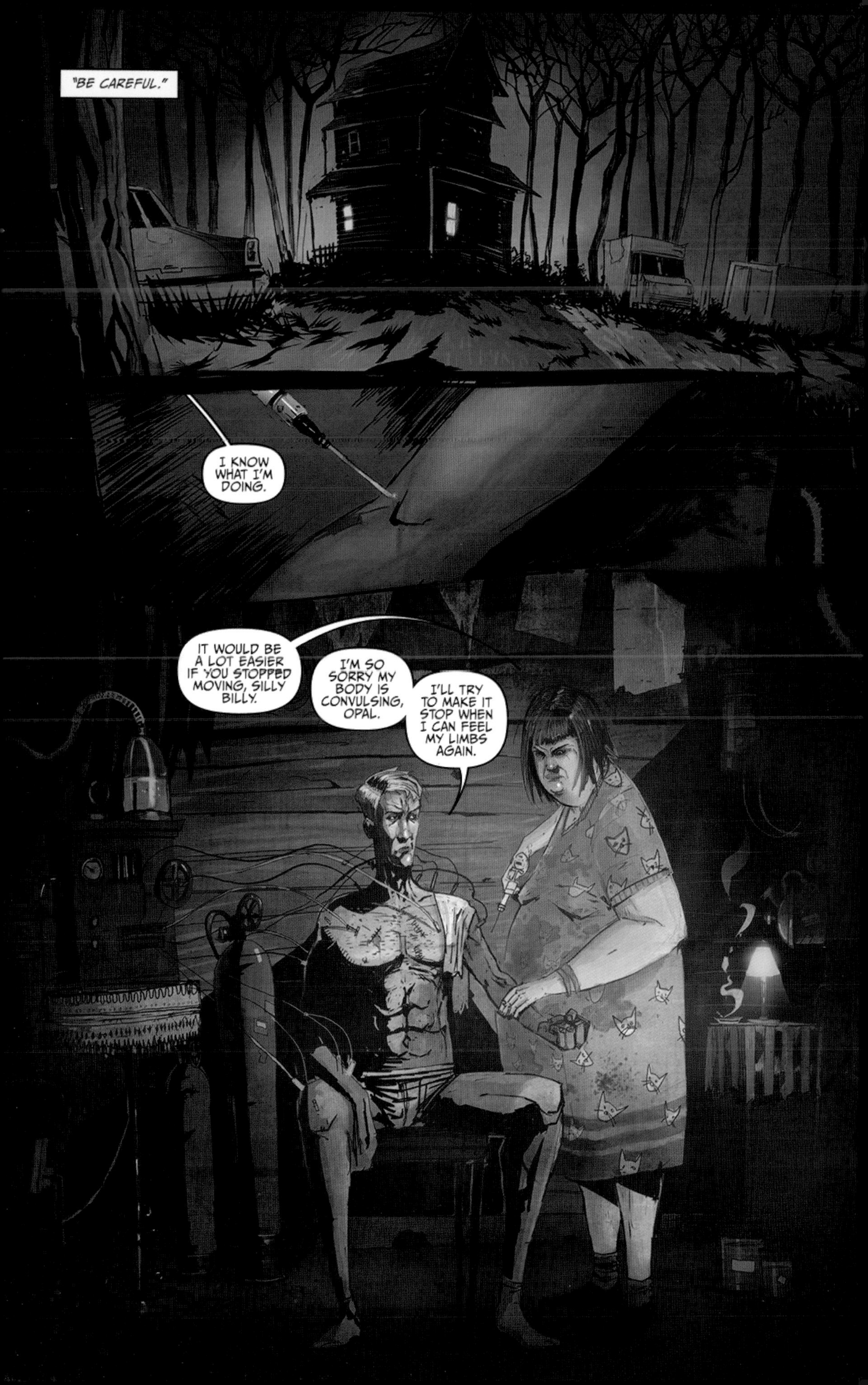
"BE CAREFUL."
I KNOW WHAT I'M DOING.
IT WOULD BE A LOT EASIER IF YOU STOPPED MOVING, SILLY BILLY.
I'M SO SORRY MY BODY IS CONVULSING, OPAL.
I'LL TRY TO MAKE IT STOP WHEN I CAN FEEL MY LIMBS AGAIN.

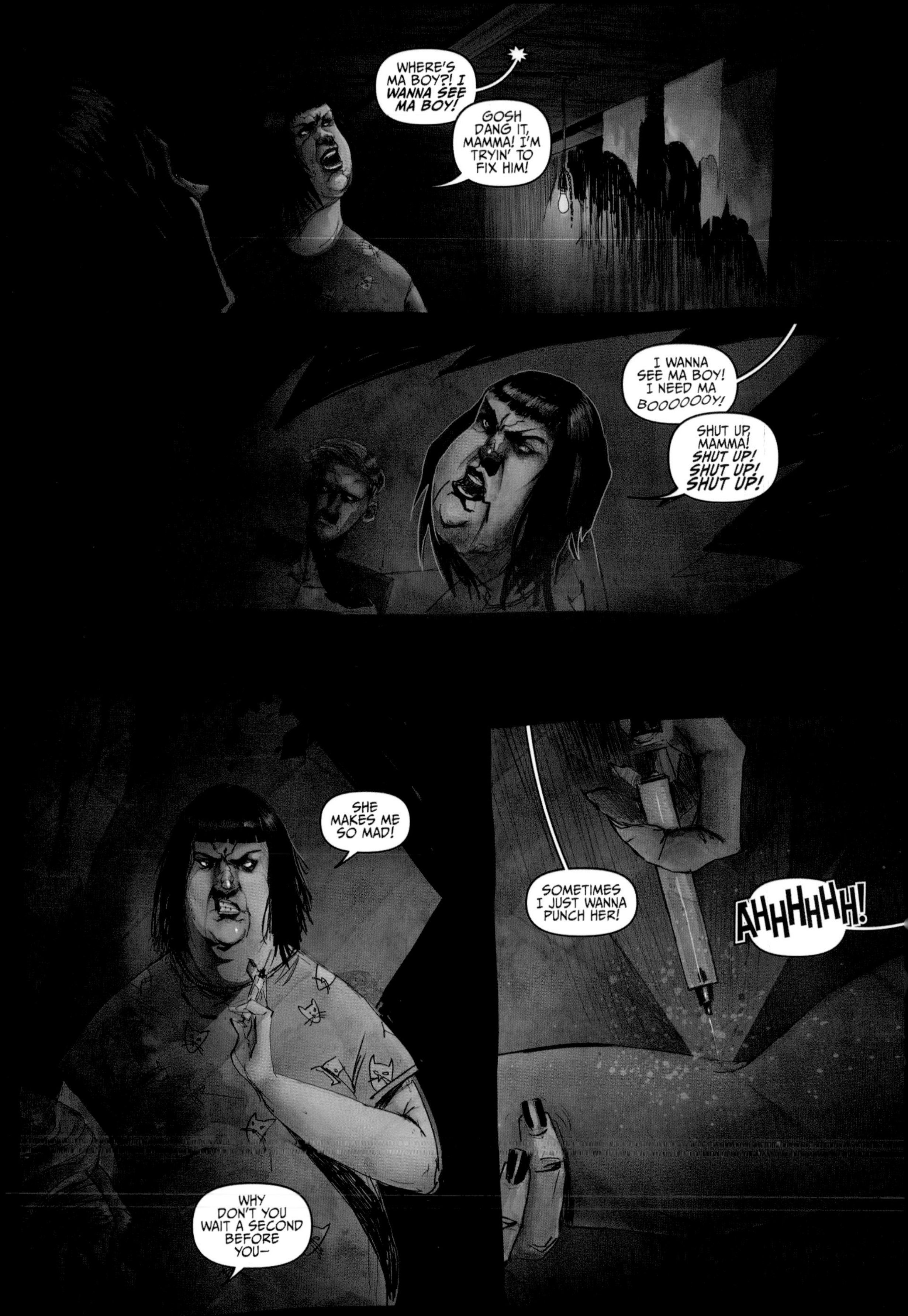
WHERE'S MA BOY?! I WANNA SEE MA BOY!
GOSH DANG IT, MAMMA! I'M TRYIN' TO FIX HIM!
I WANNA SEE MA BOY! I NEED MA BOOOOOOY!
SHUT UP, MAMMA! SHUT UP! SHUT UP! SHUT UP!
SHE MAKES ME SO MAD!
WHY DON'T YOU WAIT A SECOND BEFORE YOU--
SOMETIMES I JUST WANNA PUNCH HER!
AHHHHHH!

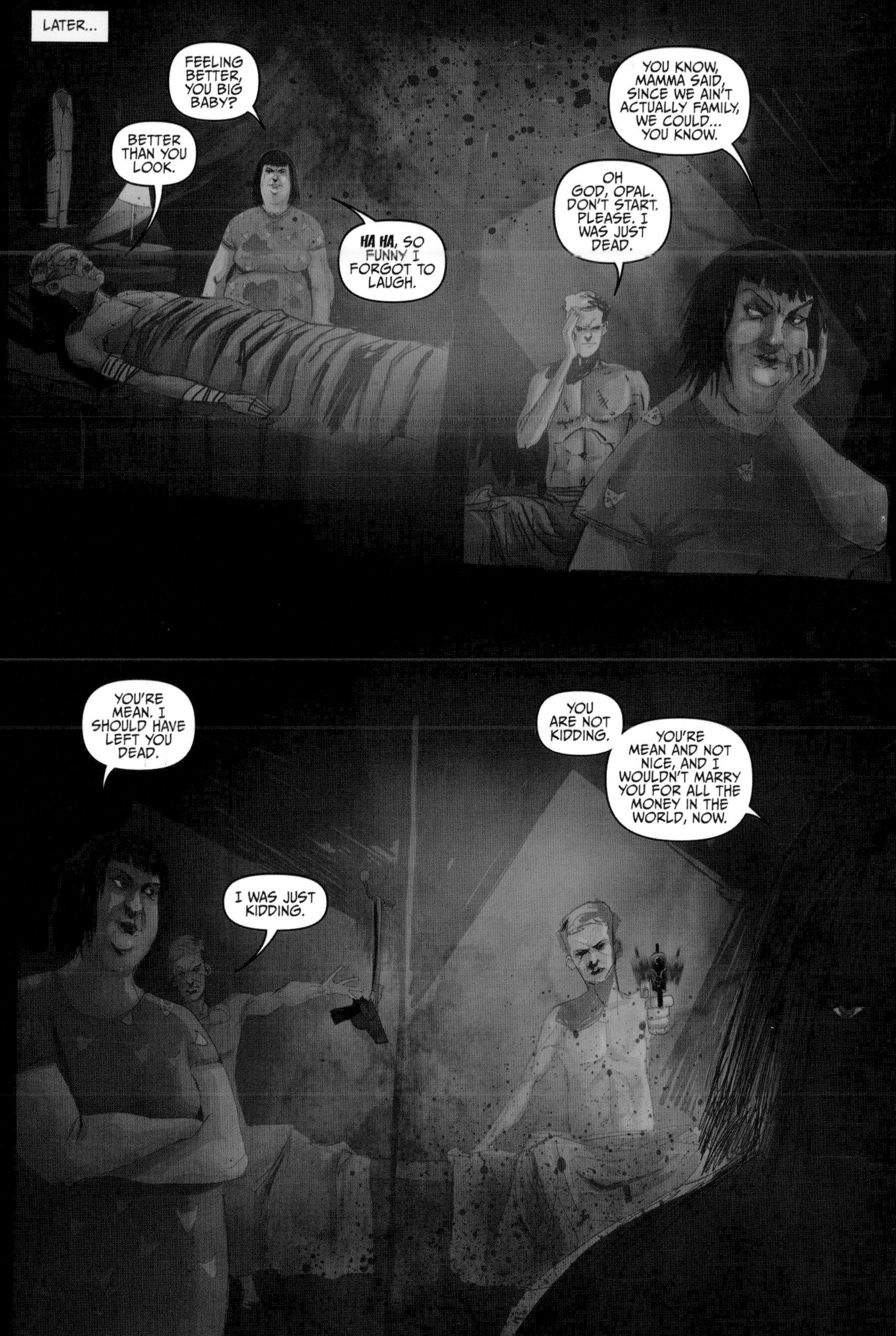
LATER...
FEELING BETTER, YOU BIG BABY?
BETTER THAN YOU LOOK.
HA HA, SO FUNNY I FORGOT TO LAUGH.
YOU KNOW, MAMMA SAID, SINCE WE AIN'T ACTUALLY FAMILY, WE COULD... YOU KNOW.
OH GOD, OPAL. DON'T START. PLEASE. I WAS JUST DEAD.
YOU'RE MEAN. I SHOULD HAVE LEFT YOU DEAD.
I WAS JUST KIDDING.
YOU ARE NOT KIDDING.
YOU'RE MEAN AND NOT NICE, AND I WOULDN'T MARRY YOU FOR ALL THE MONEY IN THE WORLD, NOW.

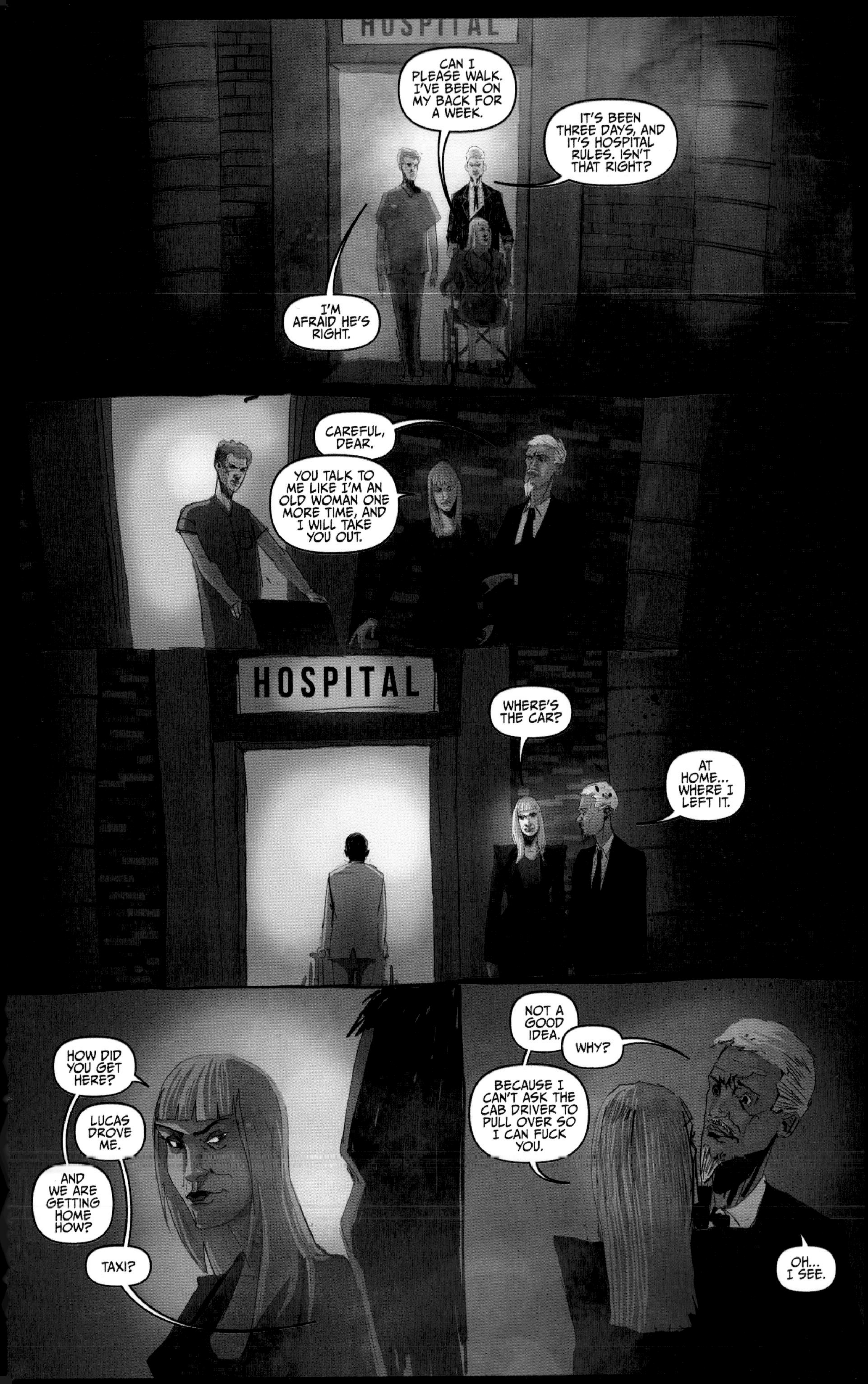
HOSPITAL
CAN I PLEASE WALK. I'VE BEEN ON MY BACK FOR A WEEK.
IT'S BEEN THREE DAYS, AND IT'S HOSPITAL RULES. ISN'T THAT RIGHT?
I'M AFRAID HE'S RIGHT.
CAREFUL, DEAR.
YOU TALK TO ME LIKE I'M AN OLD WOMAN ONE MORE TIME, AND I WILL TAKE YOU OUT.
HOSPITAL
WHERE'S THE CAR?
AT HOME... WHERE I LEFT IT.
HOW DID YOU GET HERE?
LUCAS DROVE ME.
AND WE ARE GETTING HOME HOW?
TAXI?
NOT A GOOD IDEA.
WHY?
BECAUSE I CAN'T ASK THE CAB DRIVER TO PULL OVER SO I CAN FUCK YOU.
OH... I SEE.

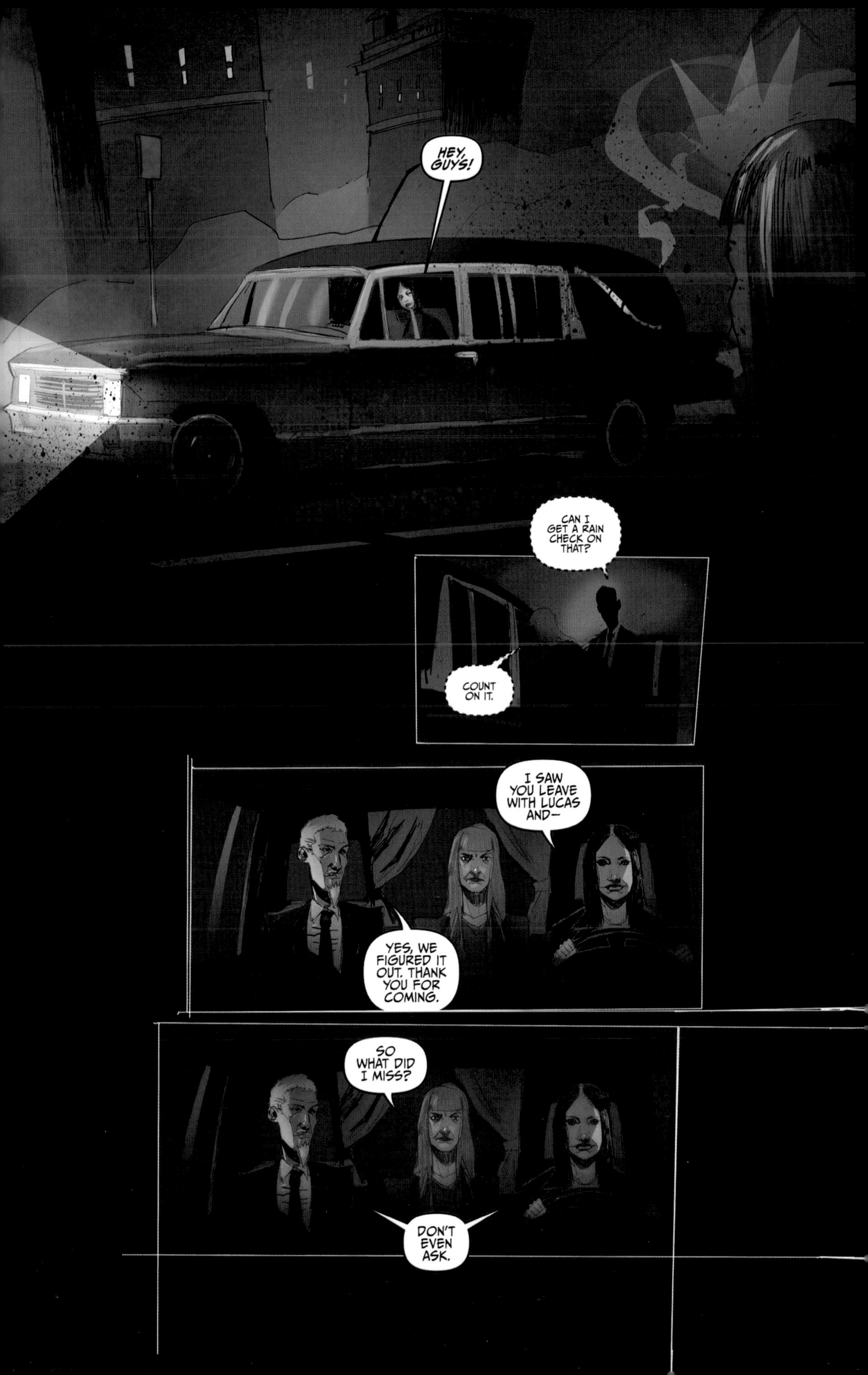
HEY, GUYS!
CAN I GET A RAIN CHECK ON THAT?
COUNT ON IT.
I SAW YOU LEAVE WITH LUCAS AND—
YES, WE FIGURED IT OUT. THANK YOU FOR COMING.
SO WHAT DID I MISS?
DON'T EVEN ASK.

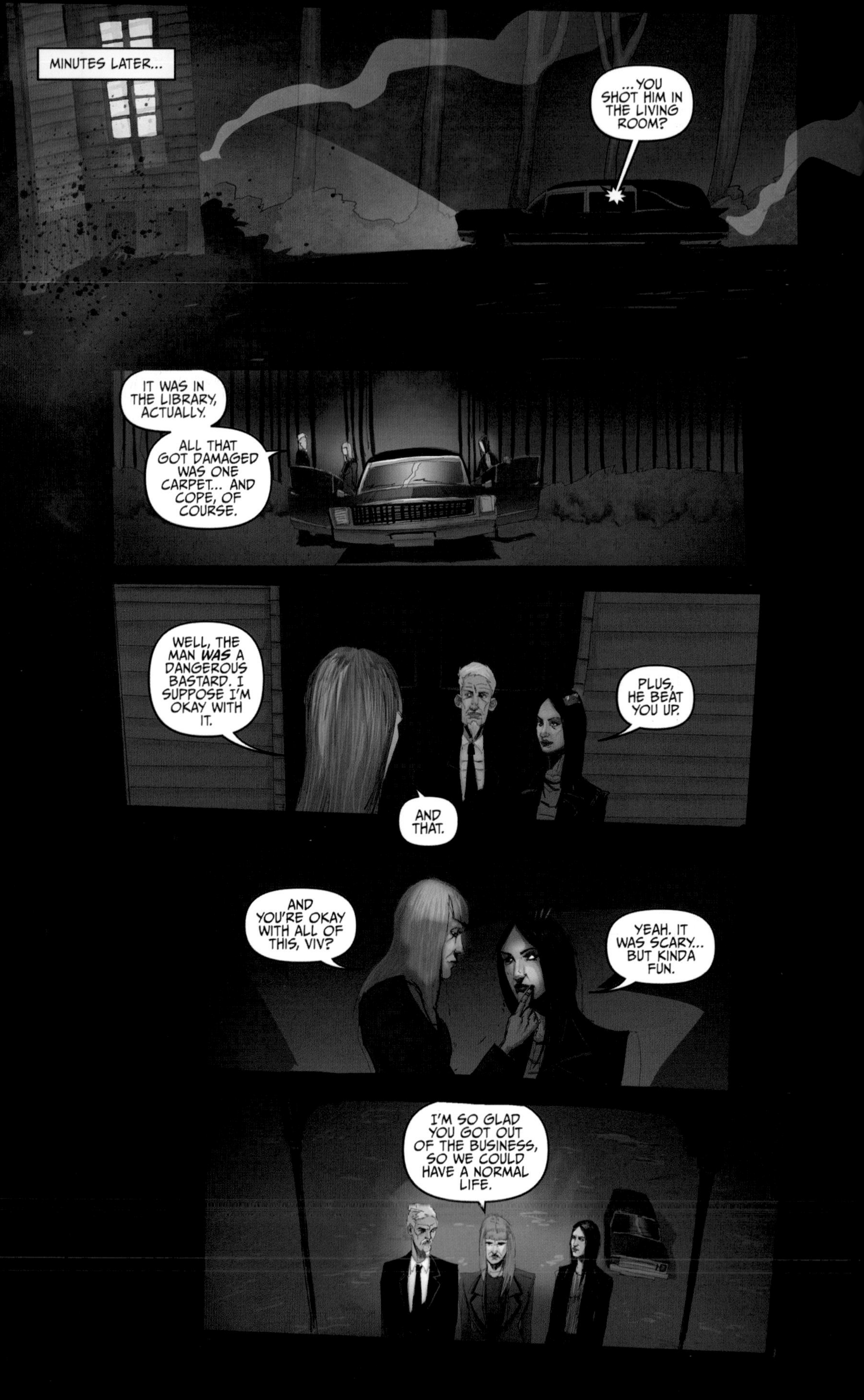
MINUTES LATER...
...YOU SHOT HIM IN THE LIVING ROOM?
IT WAS IN THE LIBRARY, ACTUALLY.
ALL THAT GOT DAMAGED WAS ONE CARPET... AND COPE, OF COURSE.
WELL, THE MAN WAS A DANGEROUS BASTARD. I SUPPOSE I'M OKAY WITH IT.
PLUS, HE BEAT YOU UP.
AND THAT.
AND YOU'RE OKAY WITH ALL OF THIS, VIV?
YEAH. IT WAS SCARY... BUT KINDA FUN.
I'M SO GLAD YOU GOT OUT OF THE BUSINESS, SO WE COULD HAVE A NORMAL LIFE.

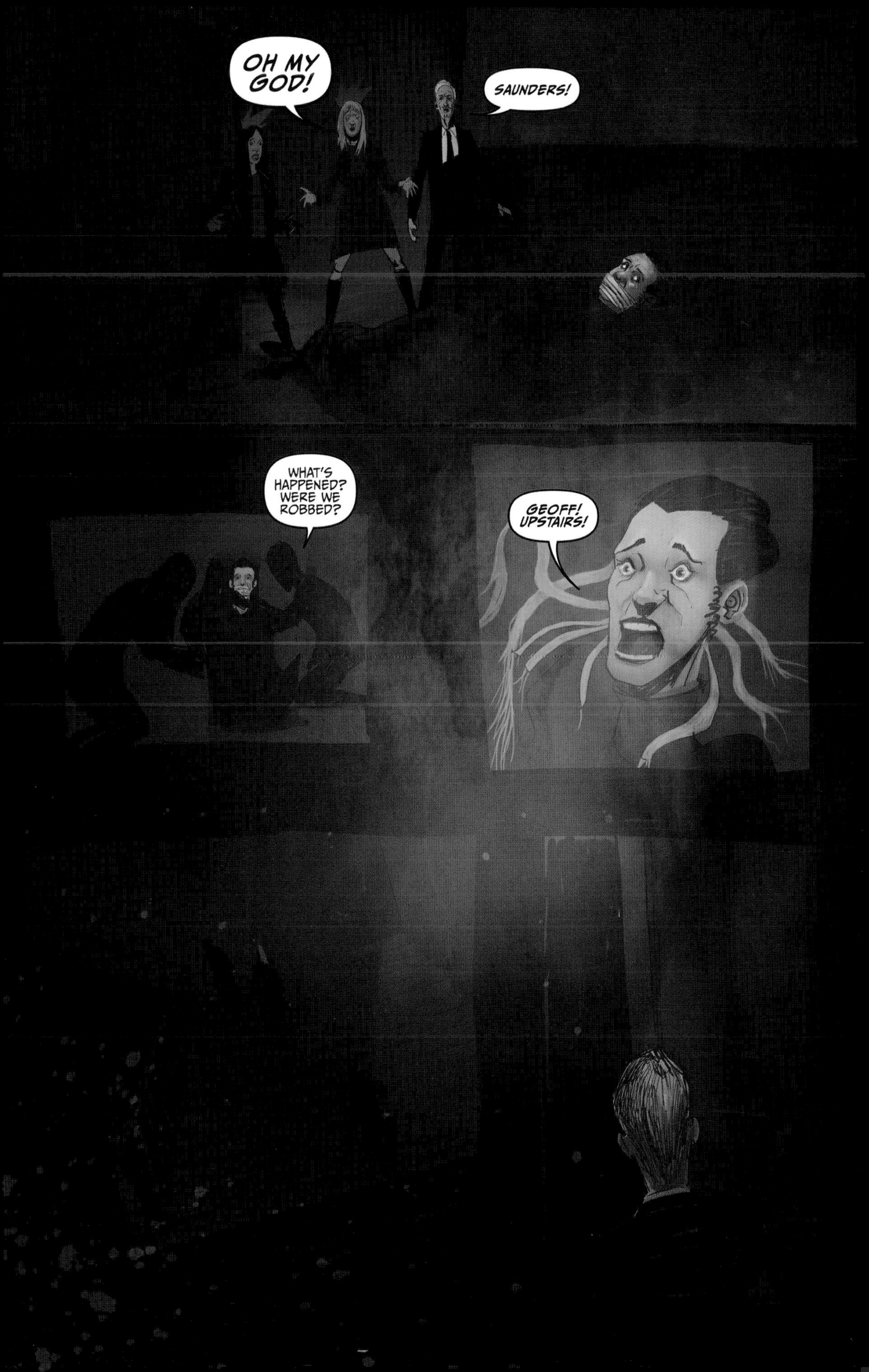
OH MY GOD!
SAUNDERS!
WHAT'S HAPPENED? WERE WE ROBBED?
GEOFF! UPSTAIRS!

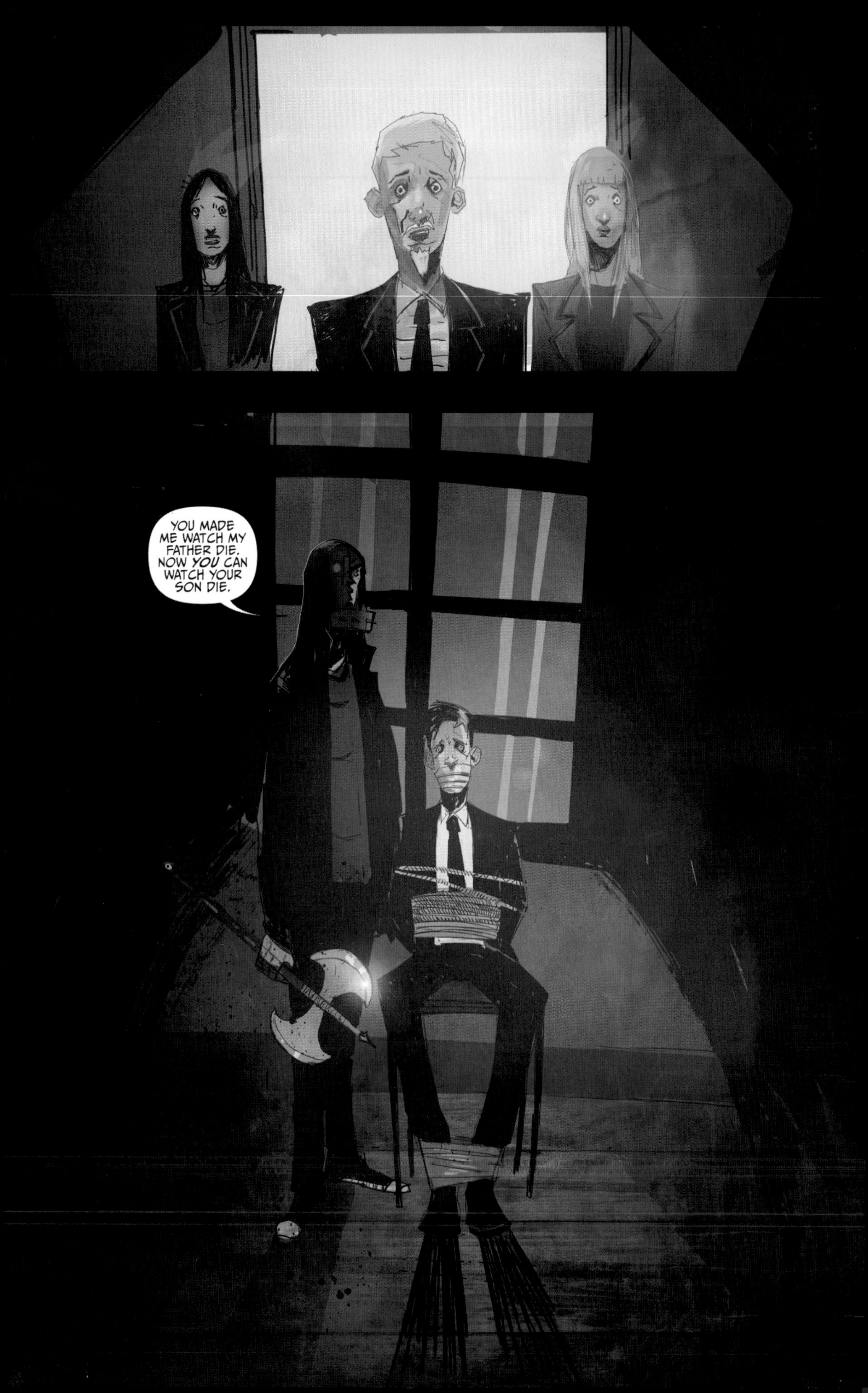
YOU MADE ME WATCH MY FATHER DIE. NOW *YOU* CAN WATCH YOUR SON DIE.

Z

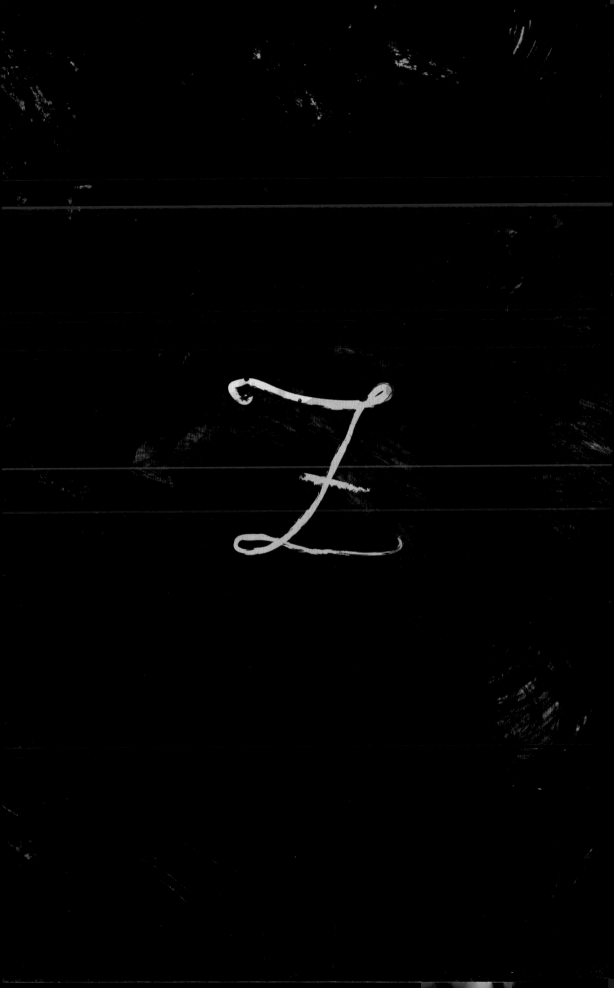

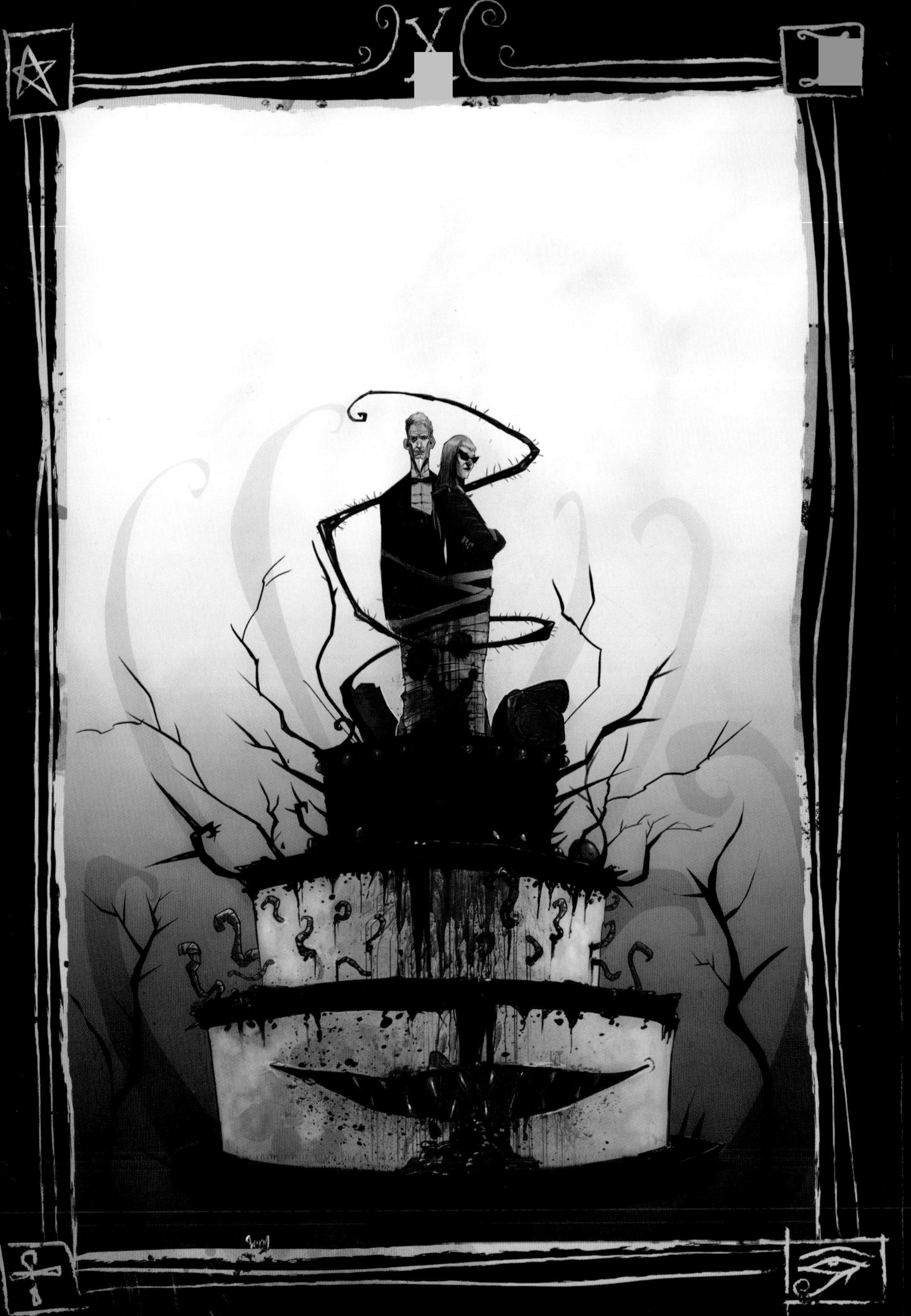
X

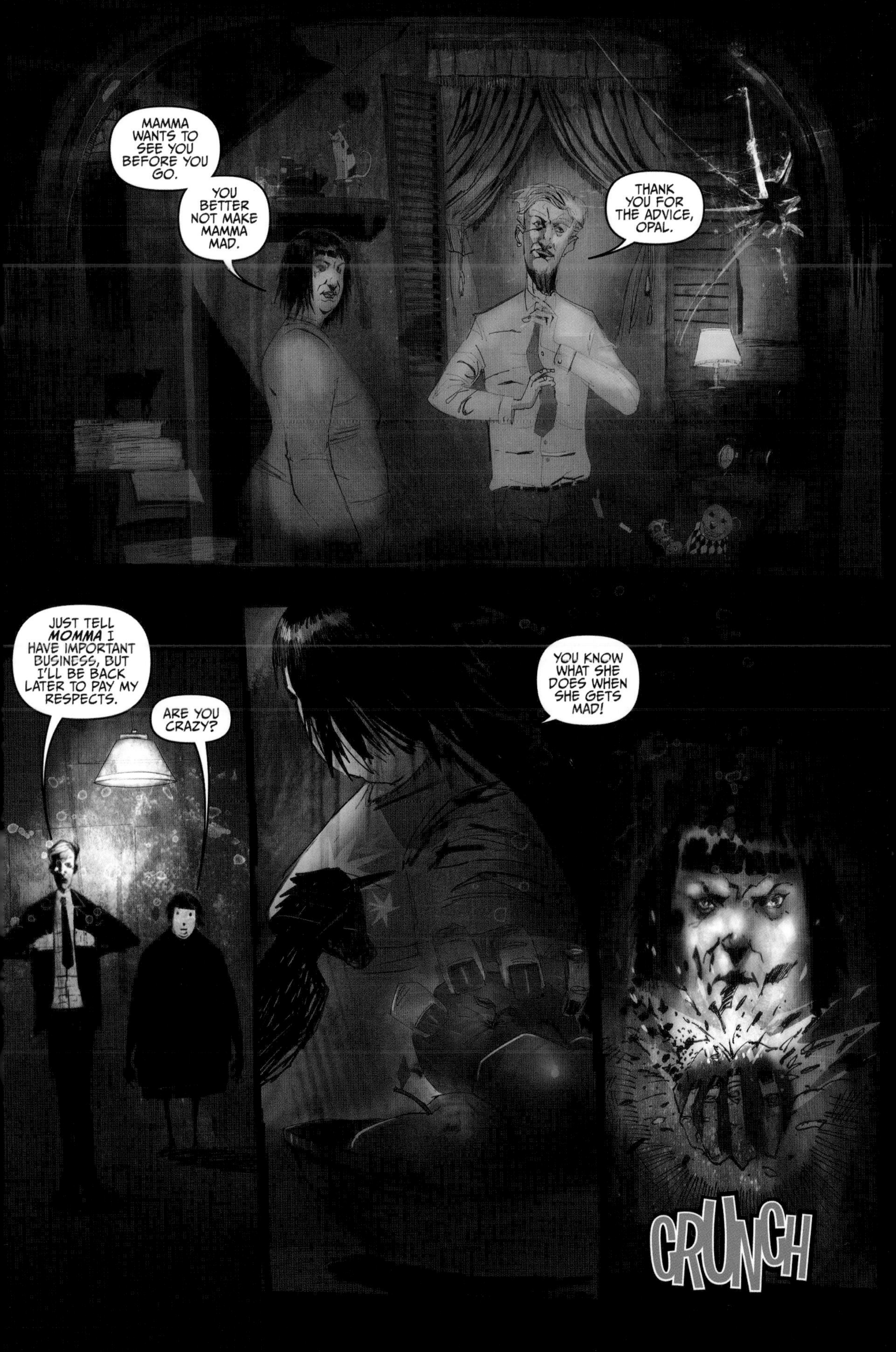
MAMMA WANTS TO SEE YOU BEFORE YOU GO.
YOU BETTER NOT MAKE MAMMA MAD.
THANK YOU FOR THE ADVICE, OPAL.
JUST TELL *MOMMA* I HAVE IMPORTANT BUSINESS, BUT I'LL BE BACK LATER TO PAY MY RESPECTS.
ARE YOU CRAZY?
YOU KNOW WHAT SHE DOES WHEN SHE GETS MAD!
CRUNCH

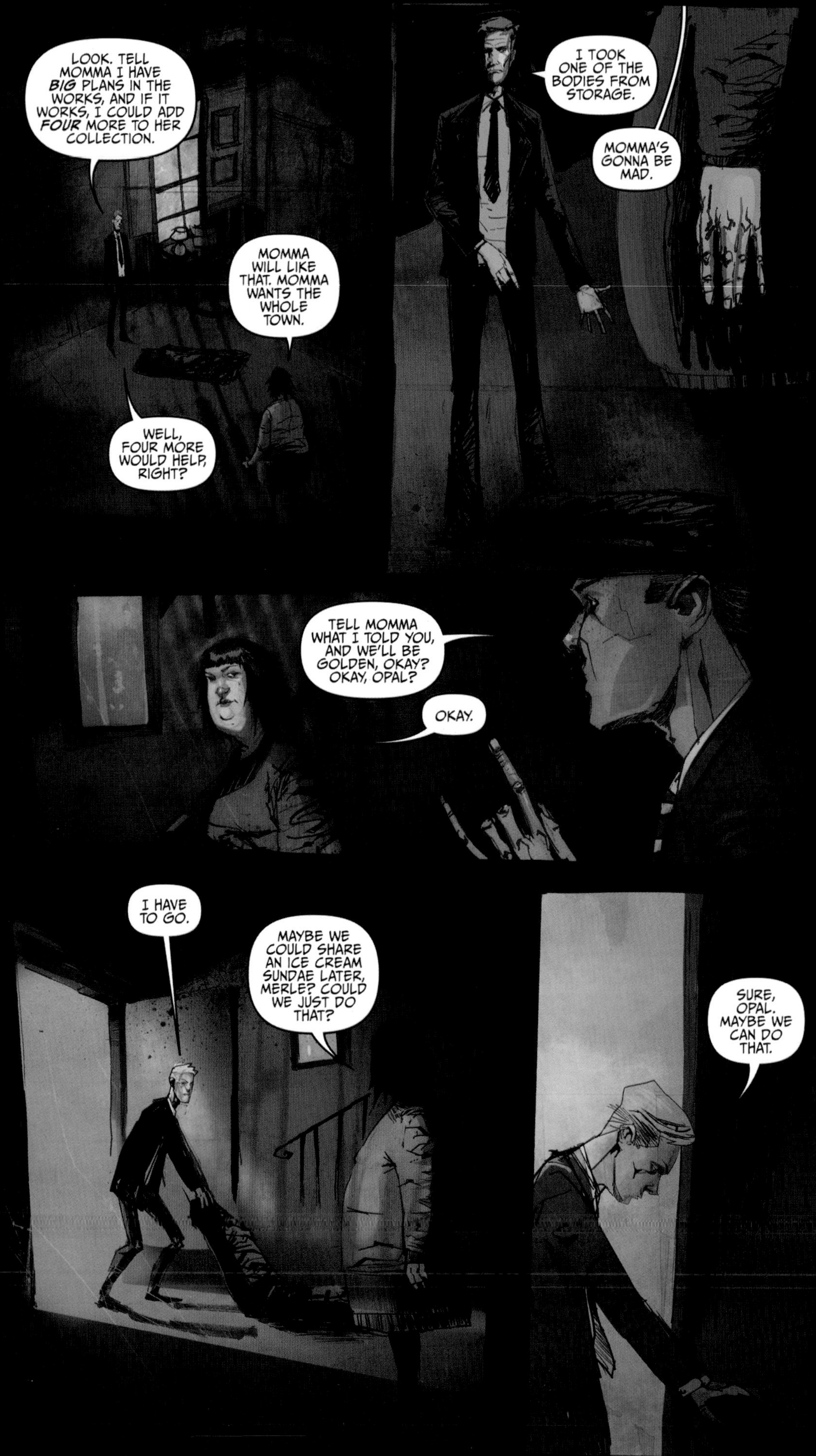

LOOK. TELL MOMMA I HAVE BIG PLANS IN THE WORKS, AND IF IT WORKS, I COULD ADD FOUR MORE TO HER COLLECTION.
MOMMA WILL LIKE THAT. MOMMA WANTS THE WHOLE TOWN.
WELL, FOUR MORE WOULD HELP, RIGHT?
I TOOK ONE OF THE BODIES FROM STORAGE.
MOMMA'S GONNA BE MAD.
TELL MOMMA WHAT I TOLD YOU, AND WE'LL BE GOLDEN, OKAY? OKAY, OPAL?
OKAY.
I HAVE TO GO.
MAYBE WE COULD SHARE AN ICE CREAM SUNDAE LATER, MERLE? COULD WE JUST DO THAT?
SURE, OPAL. MAYBE WE CAN DO THAT.

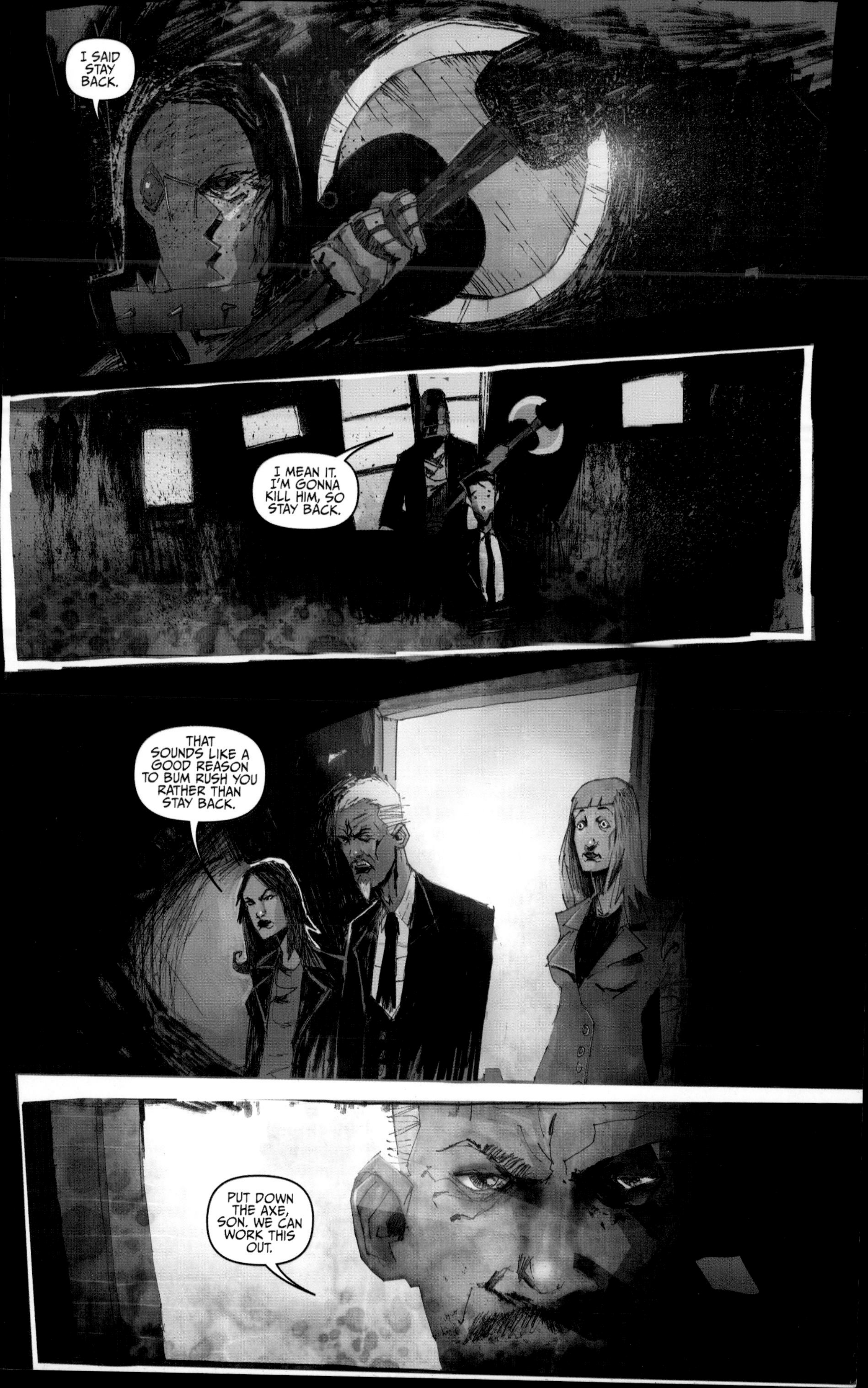
I SAID STAY BACK.
I MEAN IT. I'M GONNA KILL HIM, SO STAY BACK.
THAT SOUNDS LIKE A GOOD REASON TO BUM RUSH YOU RATHER THAN STAY BACK.
PUT DOWN THE AXE, SON. WE CAN WORK THIS OUT.

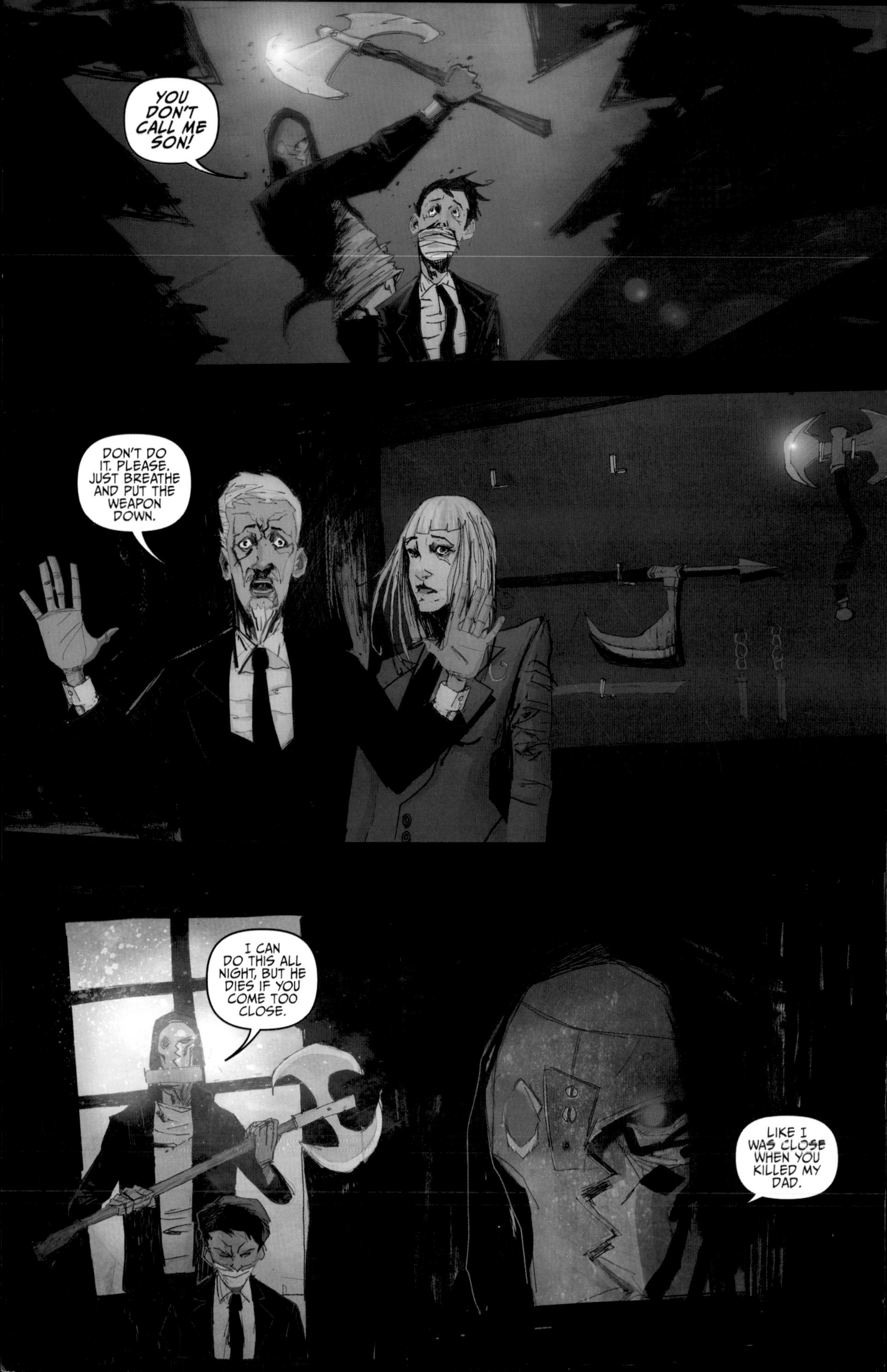
YOU DON'T CALL ME SON!
DON'T DO IT. PLEASE. JUST BREATHE AND PUT THE WEAPON DOWN.
I CAN DO THIS ALL NIGHT, BUT HE DIES IF YOU COME TOO CLOSE.
LIKE I WAS CLOSE WHEN YOU KILLED MY DAD.

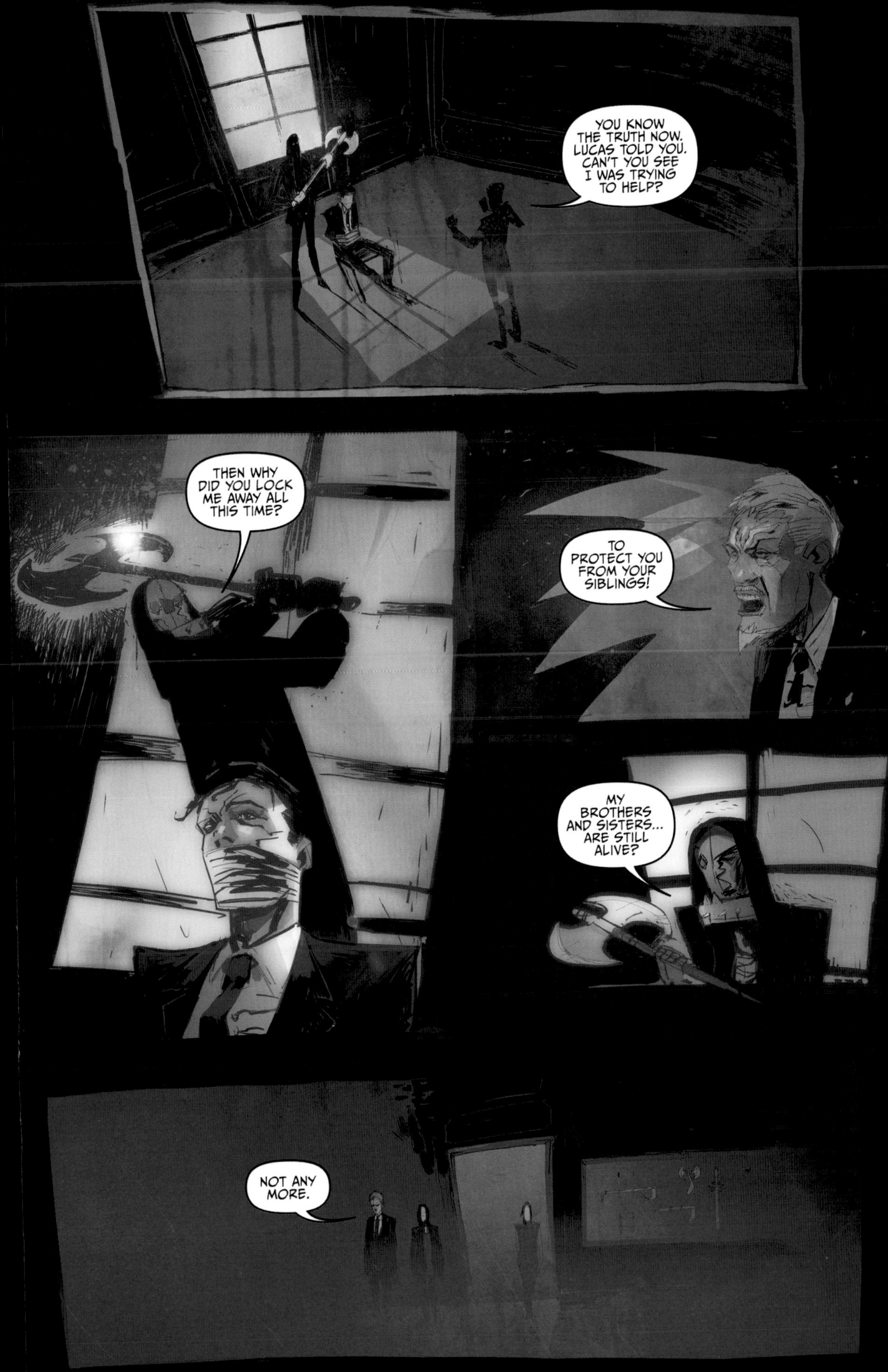
YOU KNOW THE TRUTH NOW. LUCAS TOLD YOU. CAN'T YOU SEE I WAS TRYING TO HELP?
THEN WHY DID YOU LOCK ME AWAY ALL THIS TIME?
TO PROTECT YOU FROM YOUR SIBLINGS!
MY BROTHERS AND SISTERS... ARE STILL ALIVE?
NOT ANY MORE.

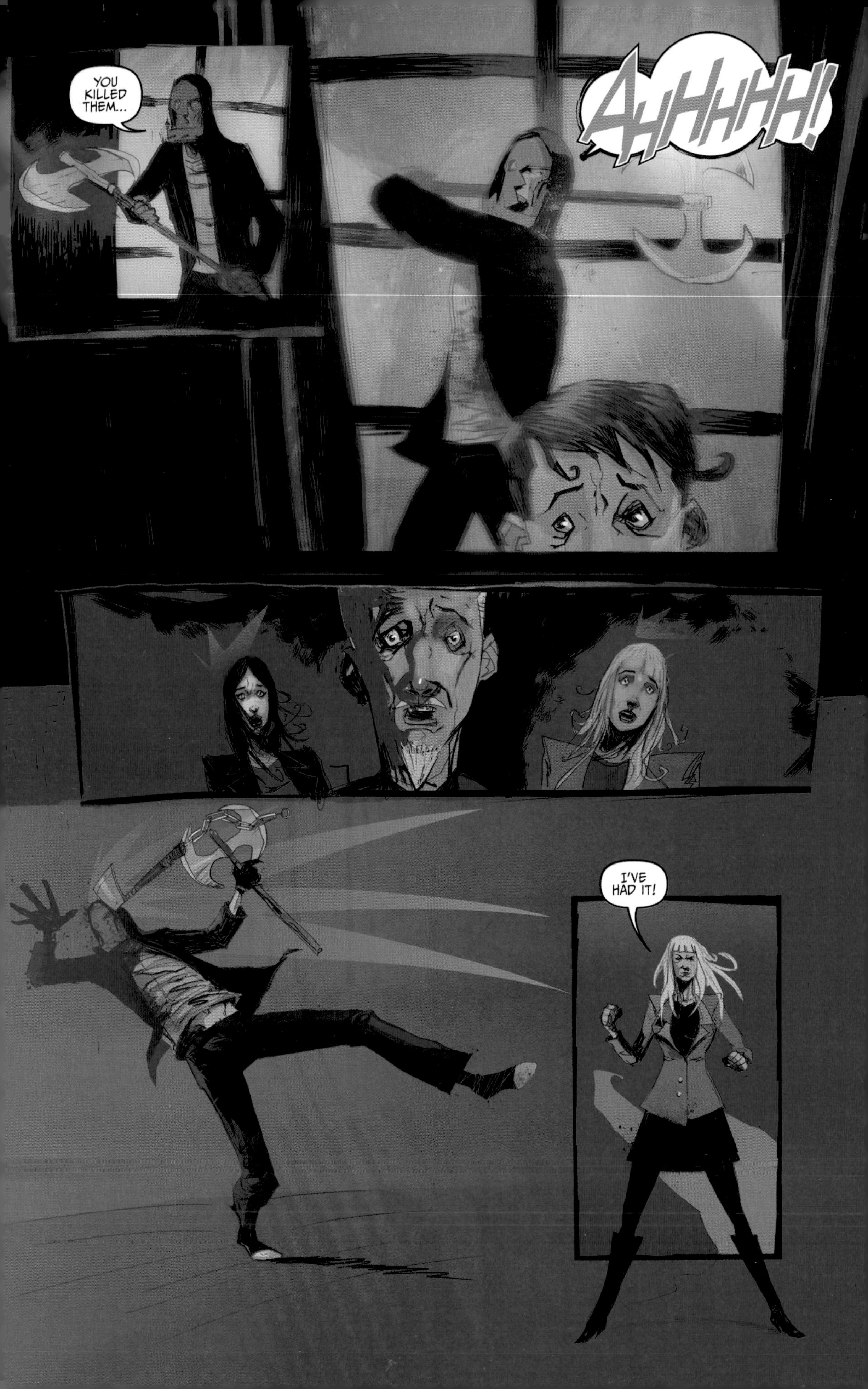
YOU KILLED THEM...
AHHHHH!
I'VE HAD IT!

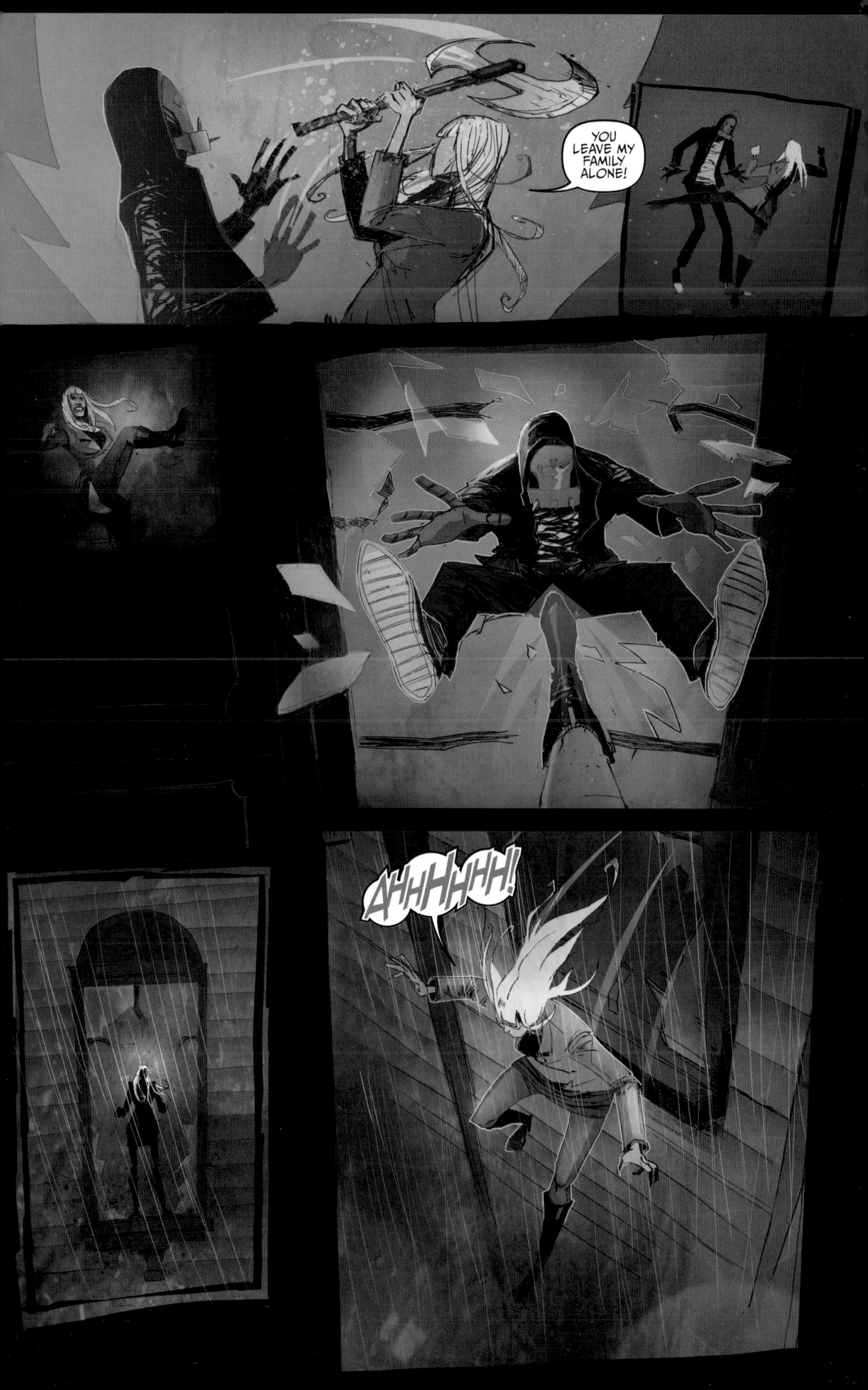
YOU LEAVE MY FAMILY ALONE!
AHHHHHH!

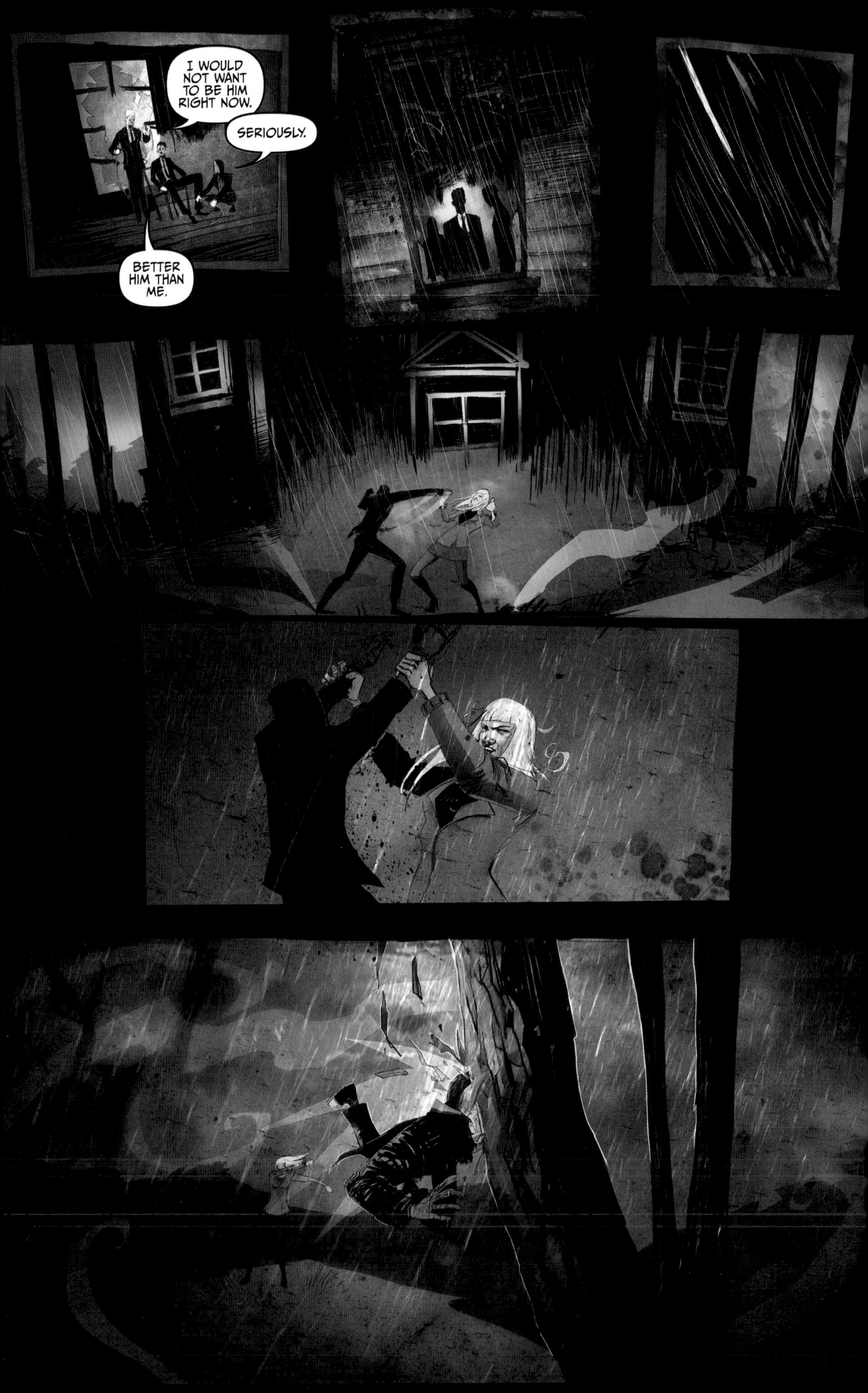
I WOULD NOT WANT TO BE HIM RIGHT NOW.
SERIOUSLY.
BETTER HIM THAN ME.

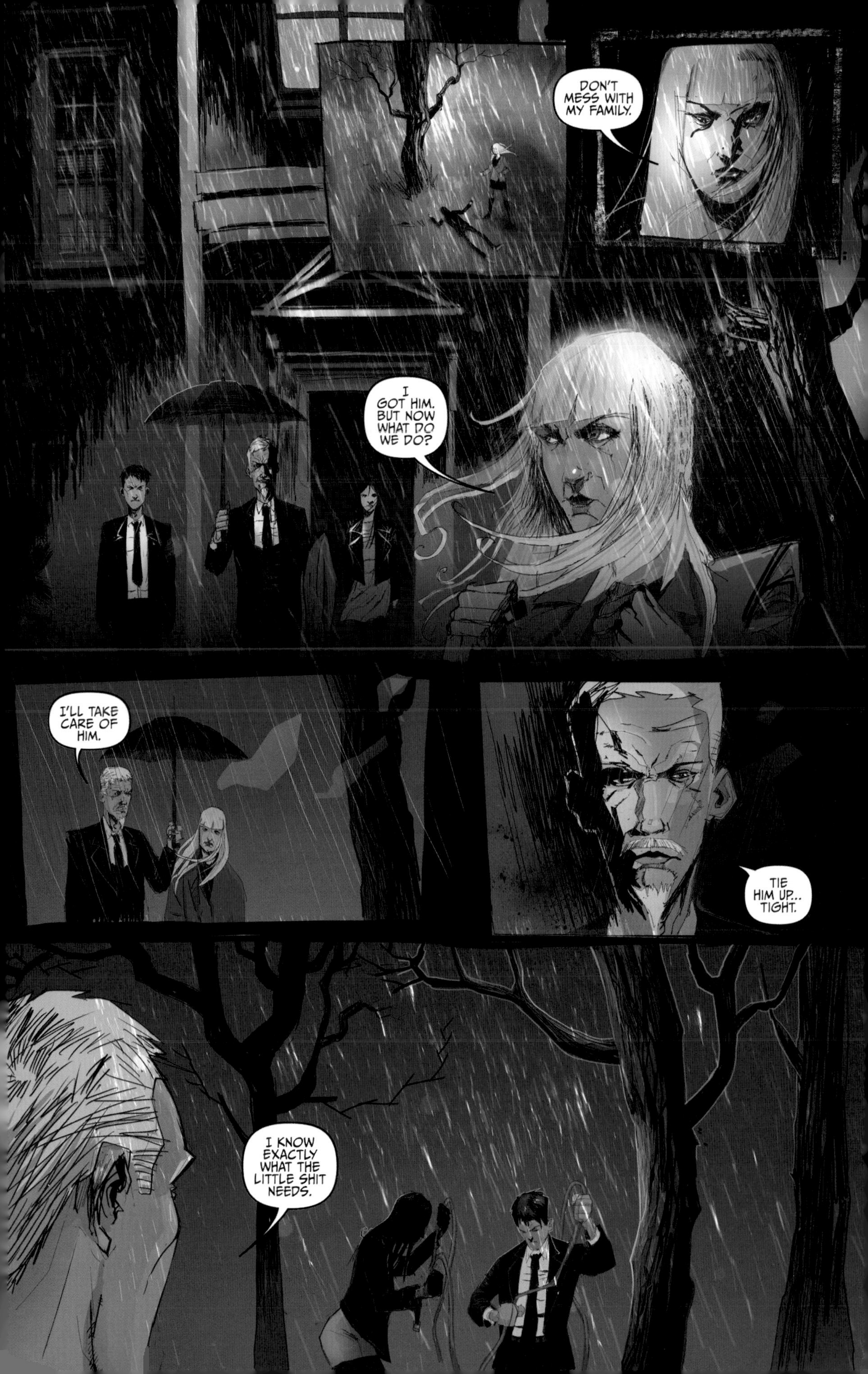
DON'T MESS WITH MY FAMILY.
I GOT HIM. BUT NOW WHAT DO WE DO?
I'LL TAKE CARE OF HIM.
TIE HIM UP... TIGHT.
I KNOW EXACTLY WHAT THE LITTLE SHIT NEEDS.

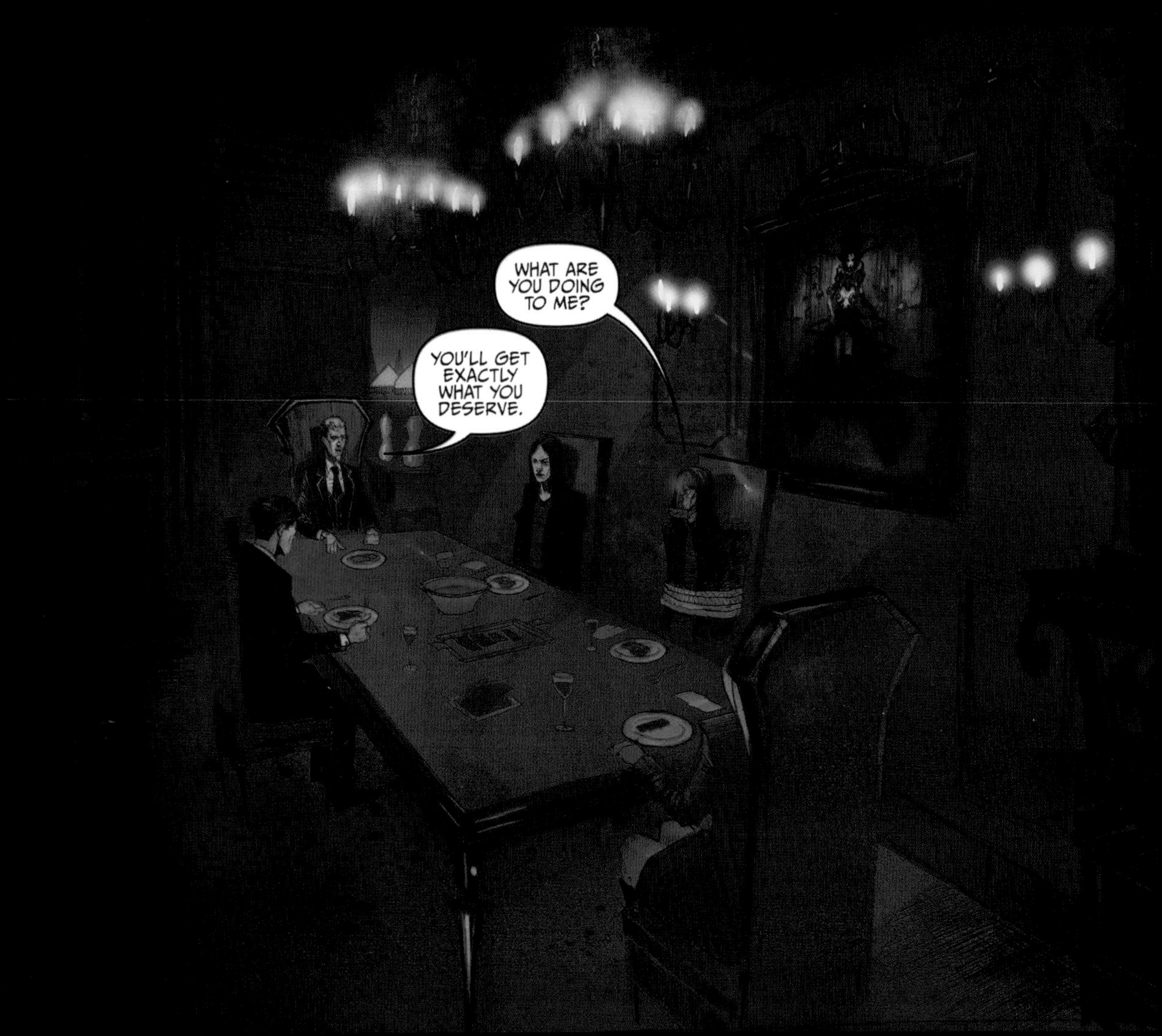
WHAT ARE YOU DOING TO ME?
YOU'LL GET EXACTLY WHAT YOU DESERVE.

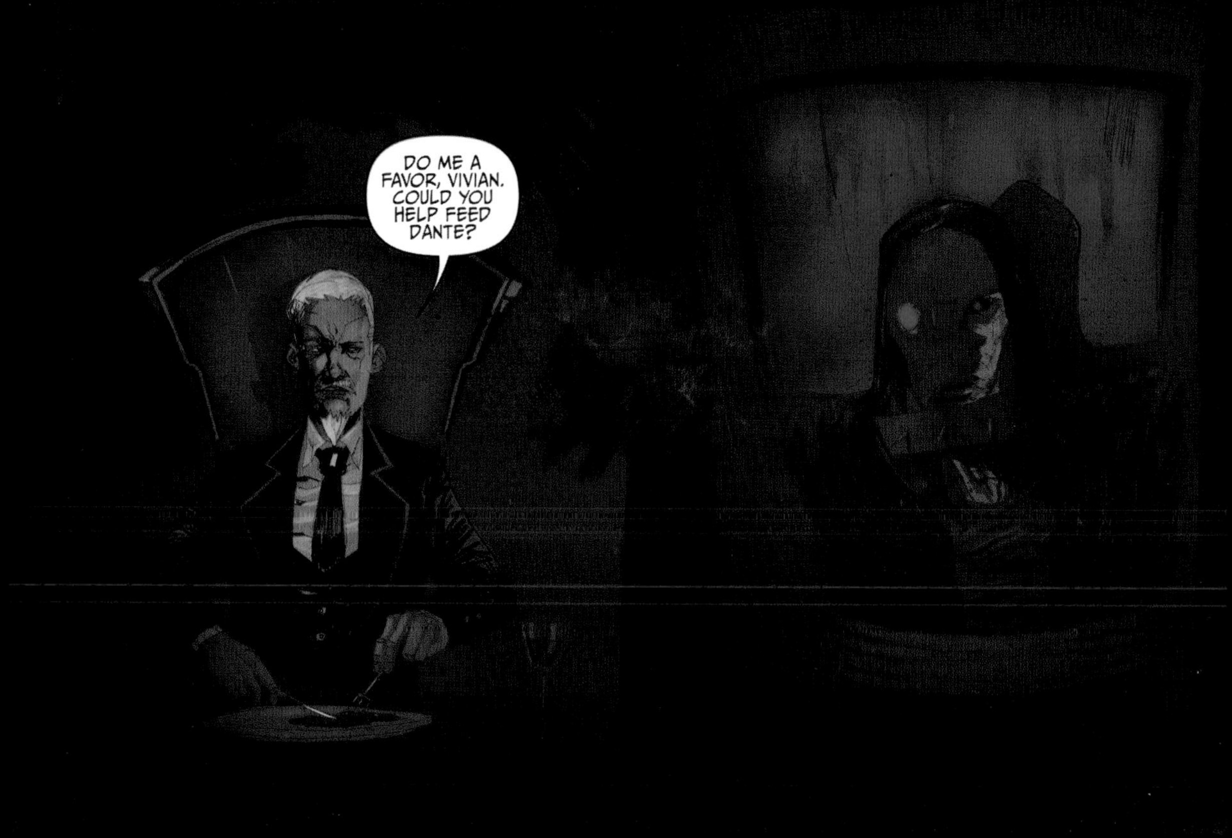
DO ME A FAVOR, VIVIAN. COULD YOU HELP FEED DANTE?

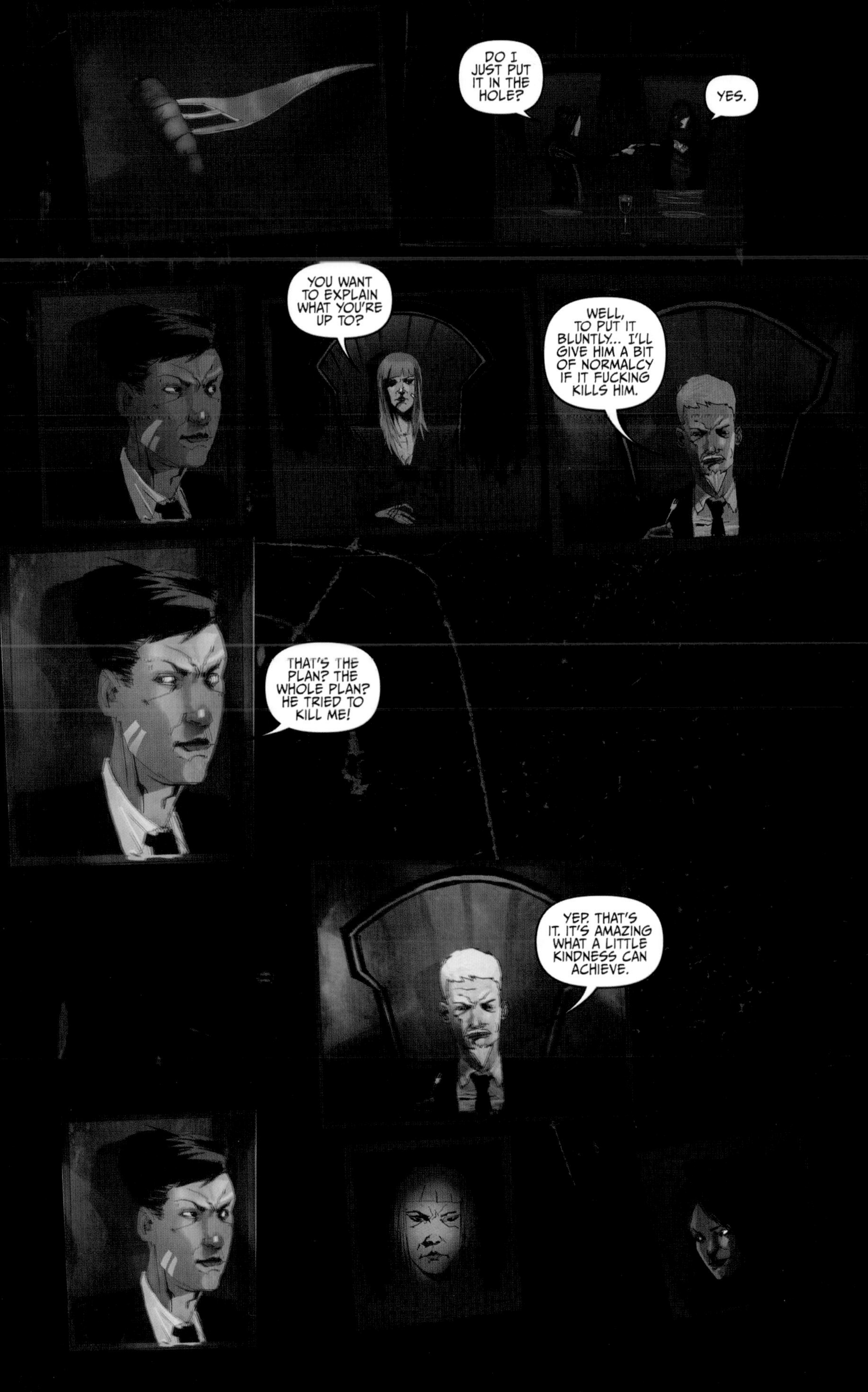
DO I JUST PUT IT IN THE HOLE?
YES.
YOU WANT TO EXPLAIN WHAT YOU'RE UP TO?
WELL, TO PUT IT BLUNTLY... I'LL GIVE HIM A BIT OF NORMALCY IF IT FUCKING KILLS HIM.
THAT'S THE PLAN? THE WHOLE PLAN? HE TRIED TO KILL ME!
YEP. THAT'S IT. IT'S AMAZING WHAT A LITTLE KINDNESS CAN ACHIEVE.

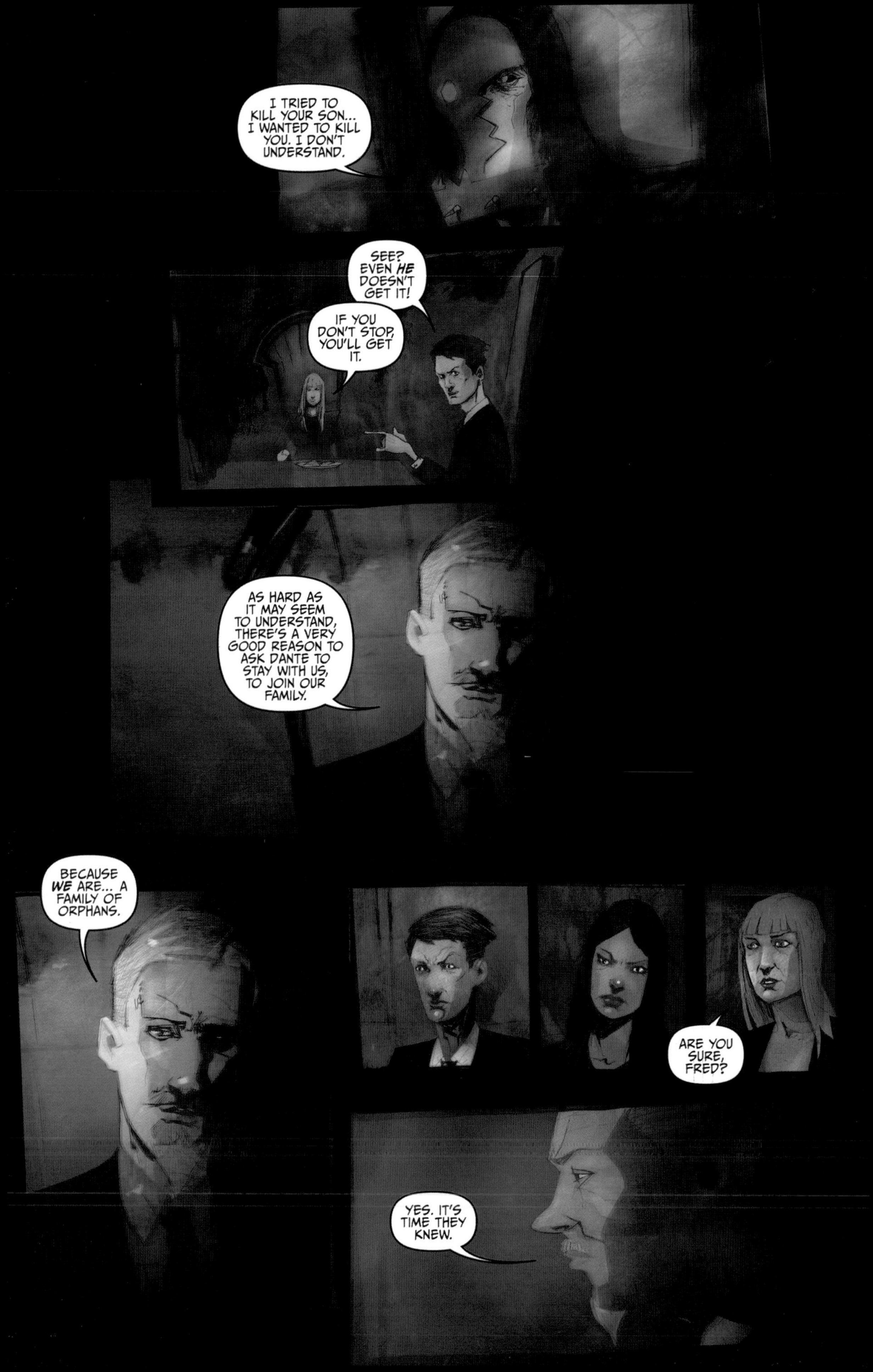
I TRIED TO KILL YOUR SON... I WANTED TO KILL YOU. I DON'T UNDERSTAND.
SEE? EVEN *HE* DOESN'T GET IT!
IF YOU DON'T STOP, YOU'LL GET IT.
AS HARD AS IT MAY SEEM TO UNDERSTAND, THERE'S A VERY GOOD REASON TO ASK DANTE TO STAY WITH US, TO JOIN OUR FAMILY.
BECAUSE *WE* ARE... A FAMILY OF ORPHANS.
ARE YOU SURE, FRED?
YES. IT'S TIME THEY KNEW.

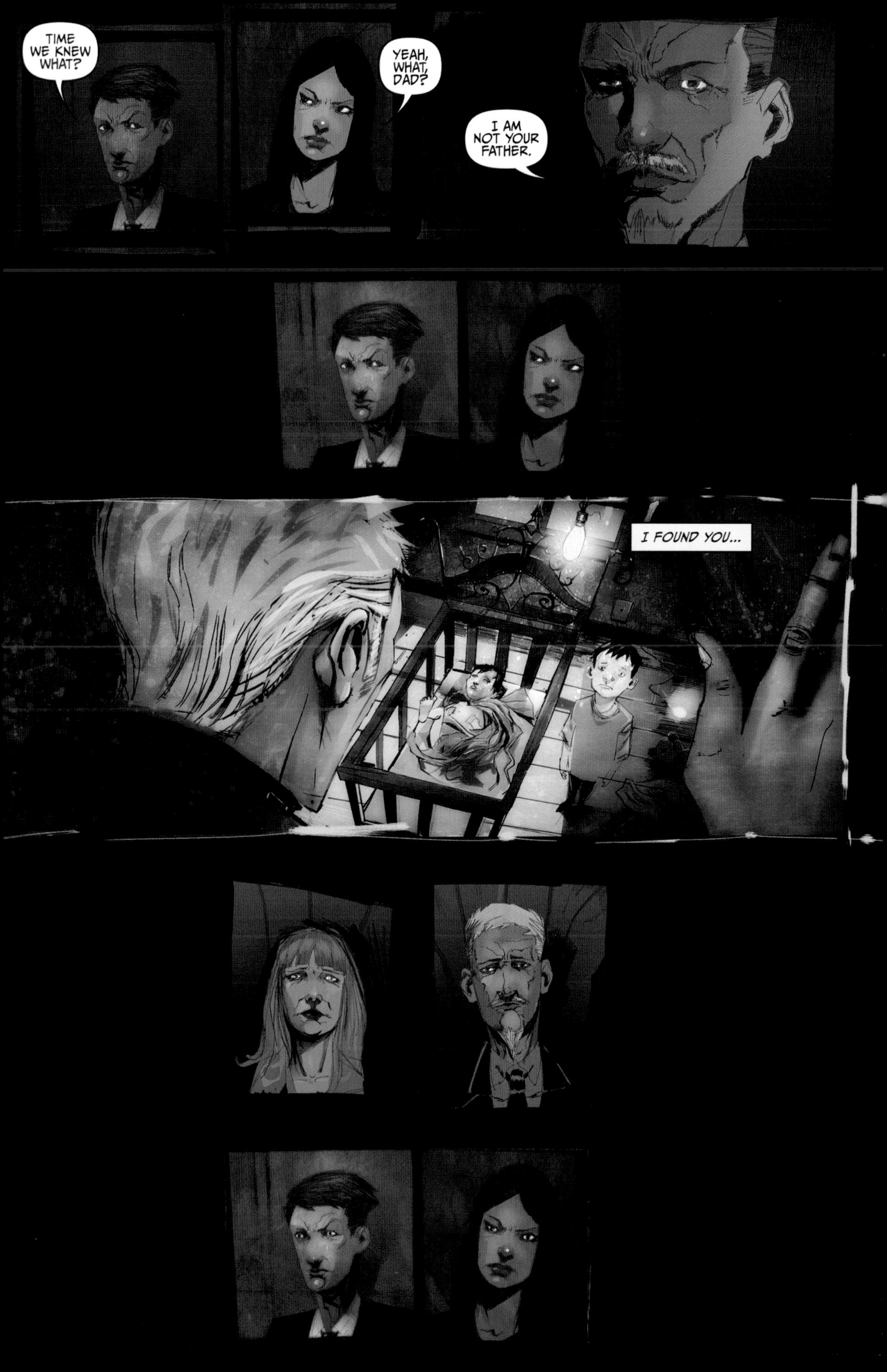
TIME WE KNEW WHAT?
YEAH, WHAT, DAD?
I AM NOT YOUR FATHER.
I FOUND YOU...

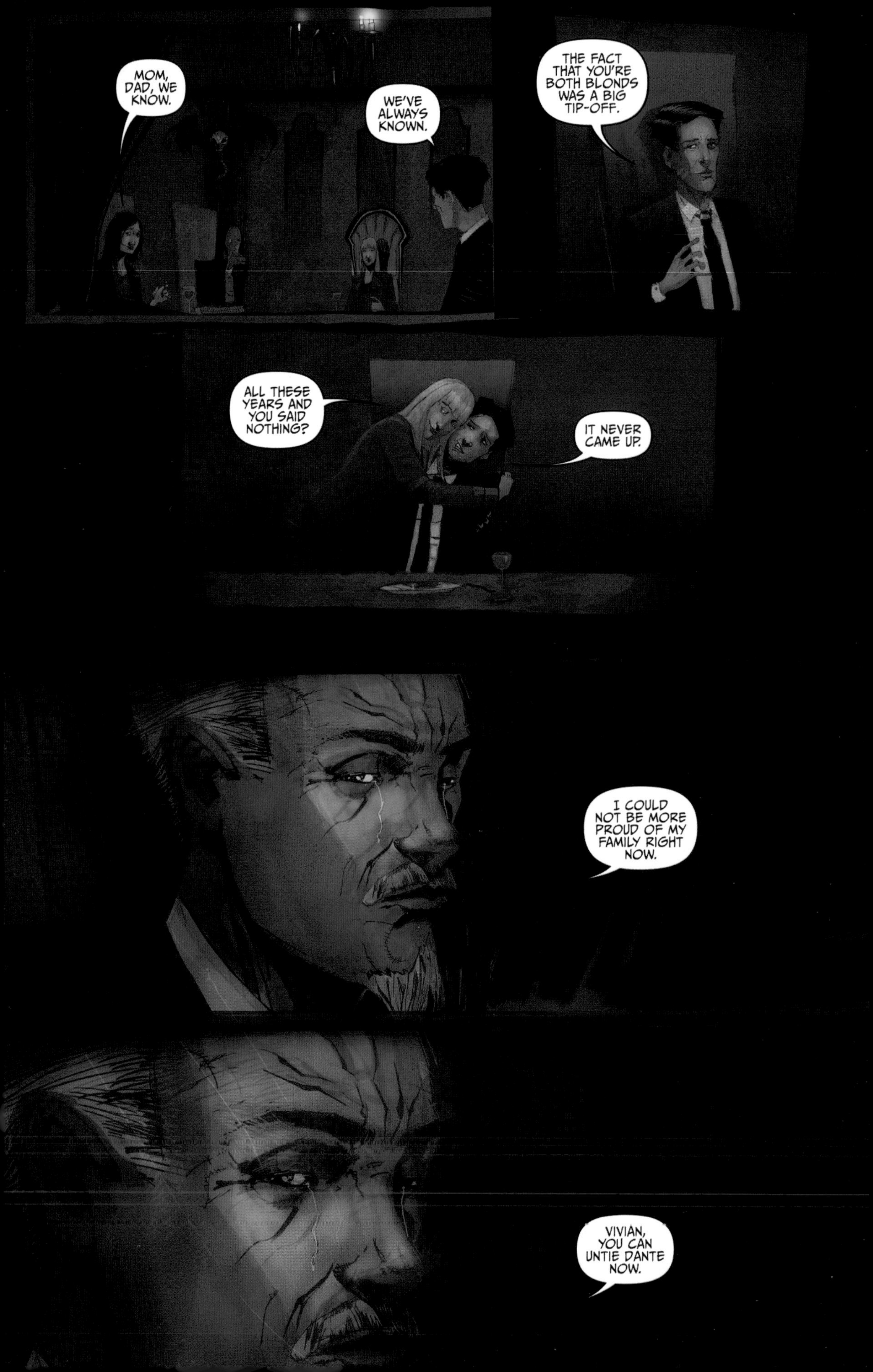
MOM, DAD, WE KNOW.
WE'VE ALWAYS KNOWN.
THE FACT THAT YOU'RE BOTH BLONDS WAS A BIG TIP-OFF.
ALL THESE YEARS AND YOU SAID NOTHING?
IT NEVER CAME UP.
I COULD NOT BE MORE PROUD OF MY FAMILY RIGHT NOW.
VIVIAN, YOU CAN UNTIE DANTE NOW.

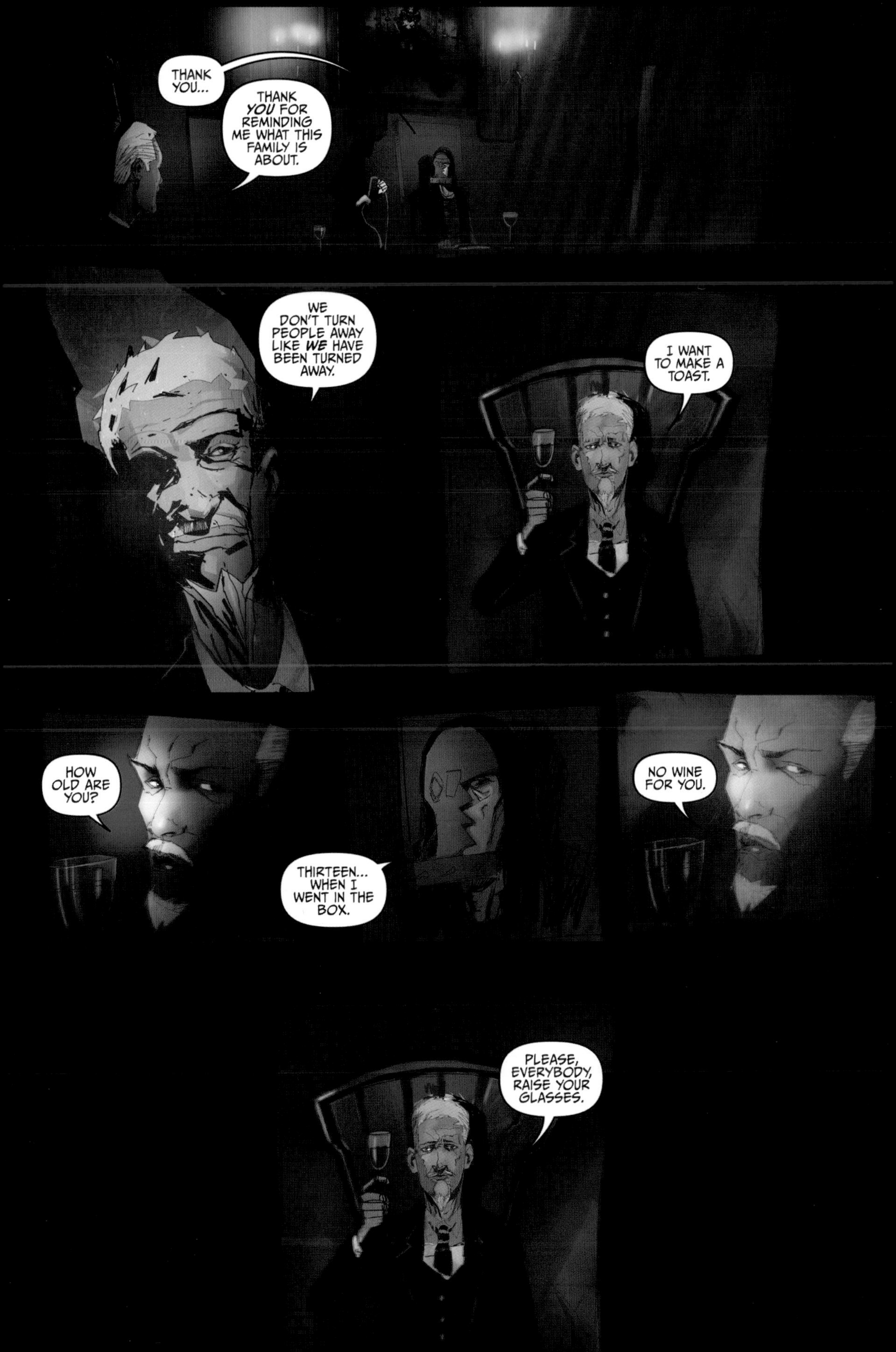
THANK YOU...
THANK YOU FOR REMINDING ME WHAT THIS FAMILY IS ABOUT.
WE DON'T TURN PEOPLE AWAY LIKE WE HAVE BEEN TURNED AWAY.
I WANT TO MAKE A TOAST.
HOW OLD ARE YOU?
THIRTEEN... WHEN I WENT IN THE BOX.
NO WINE FOR YOU.
PLEASE, EVERYBODY, RAISE YOUR GLASSES.

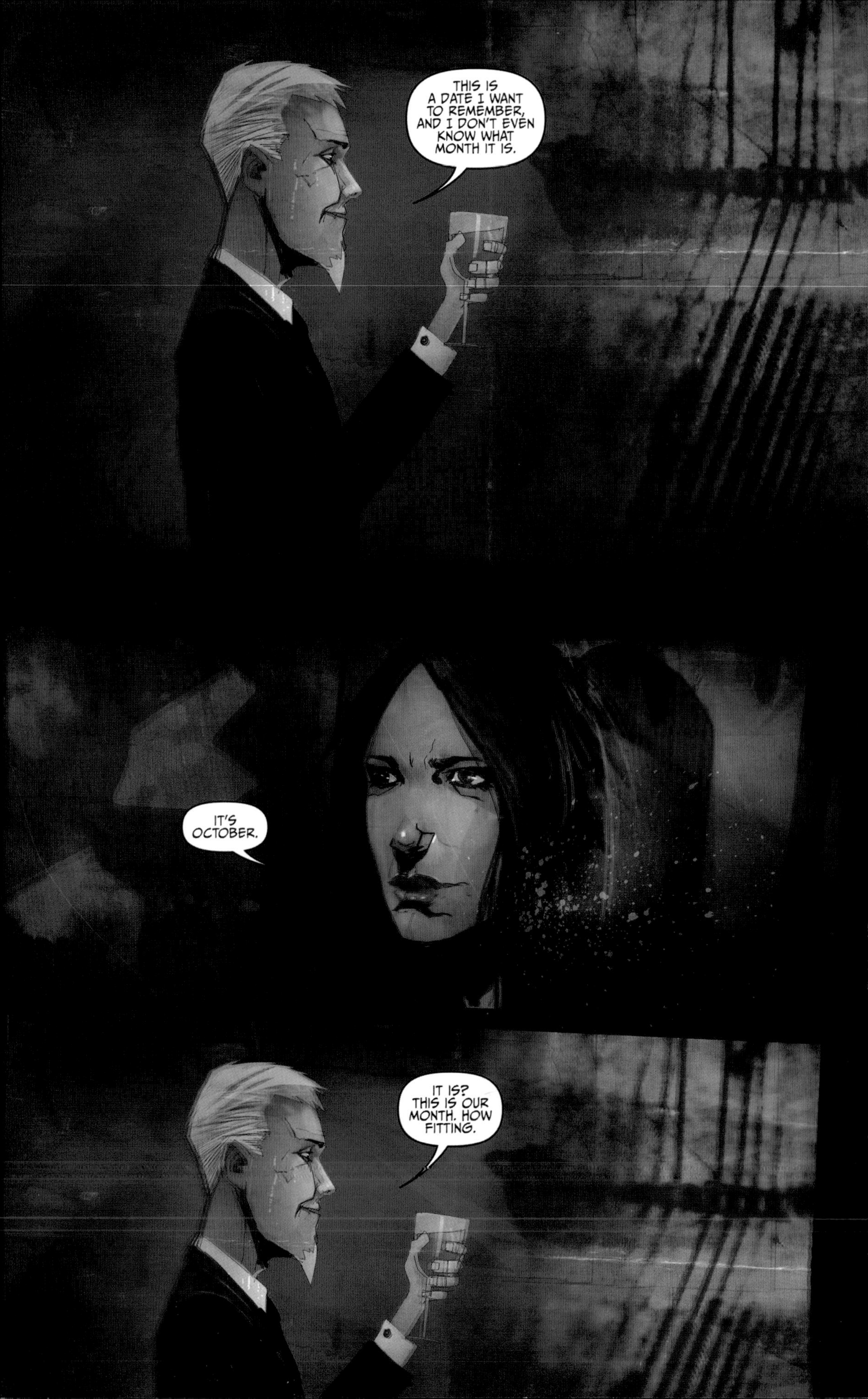
THIS IS A DATE I WANT TO REMEMBER, AND I DON'T EVEN KNOW WHAT MONTH IT IS.
IT'S OCTOBER.
IT IS? THIS IS OUR MONTH. HOW FITTING.

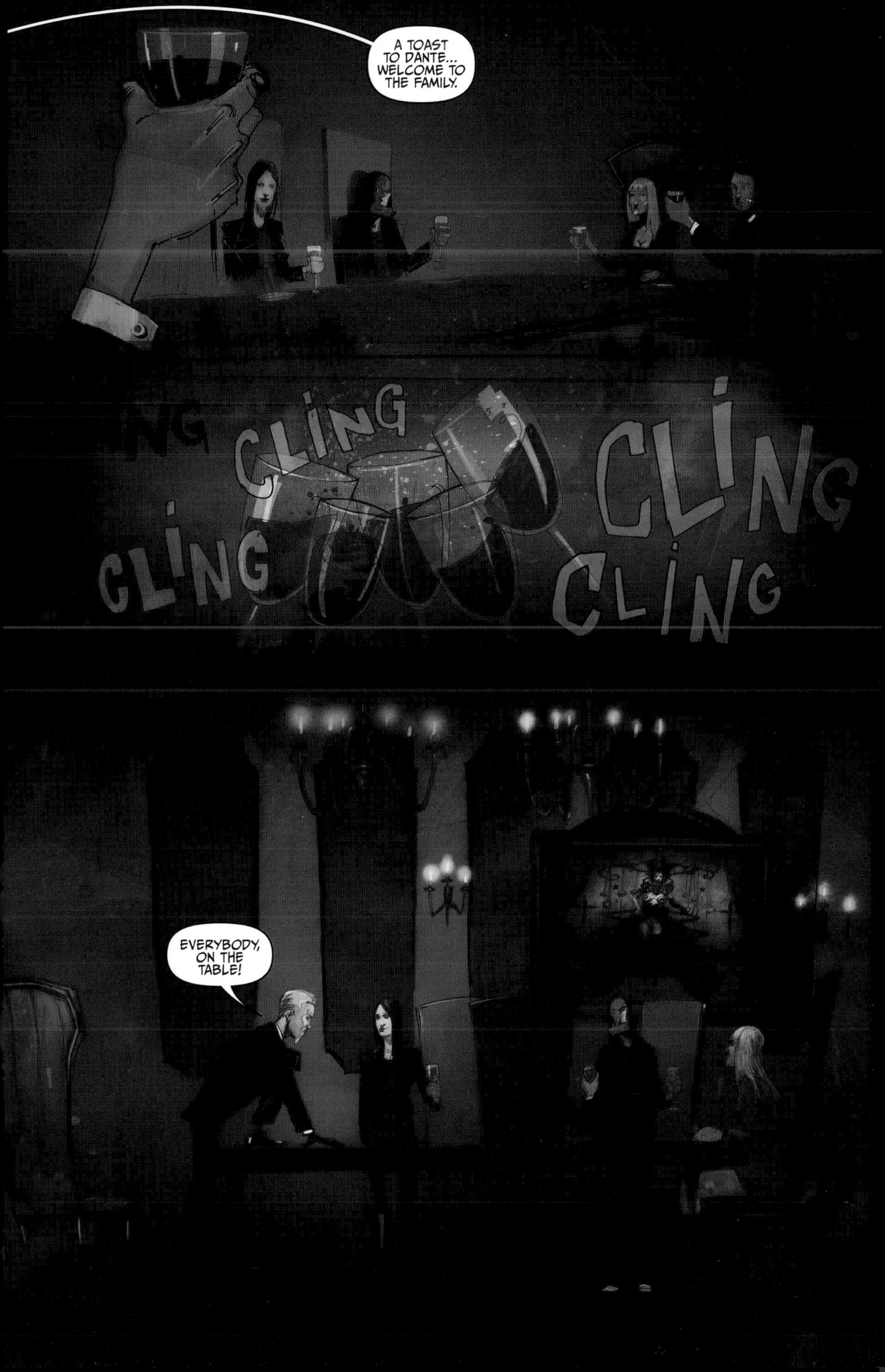
A TOAST TO DANTE... WELCOME TO THE FAMILY.
CLING
CLING
CLING
CLING
EVERYBODY, ON THE TABLE!

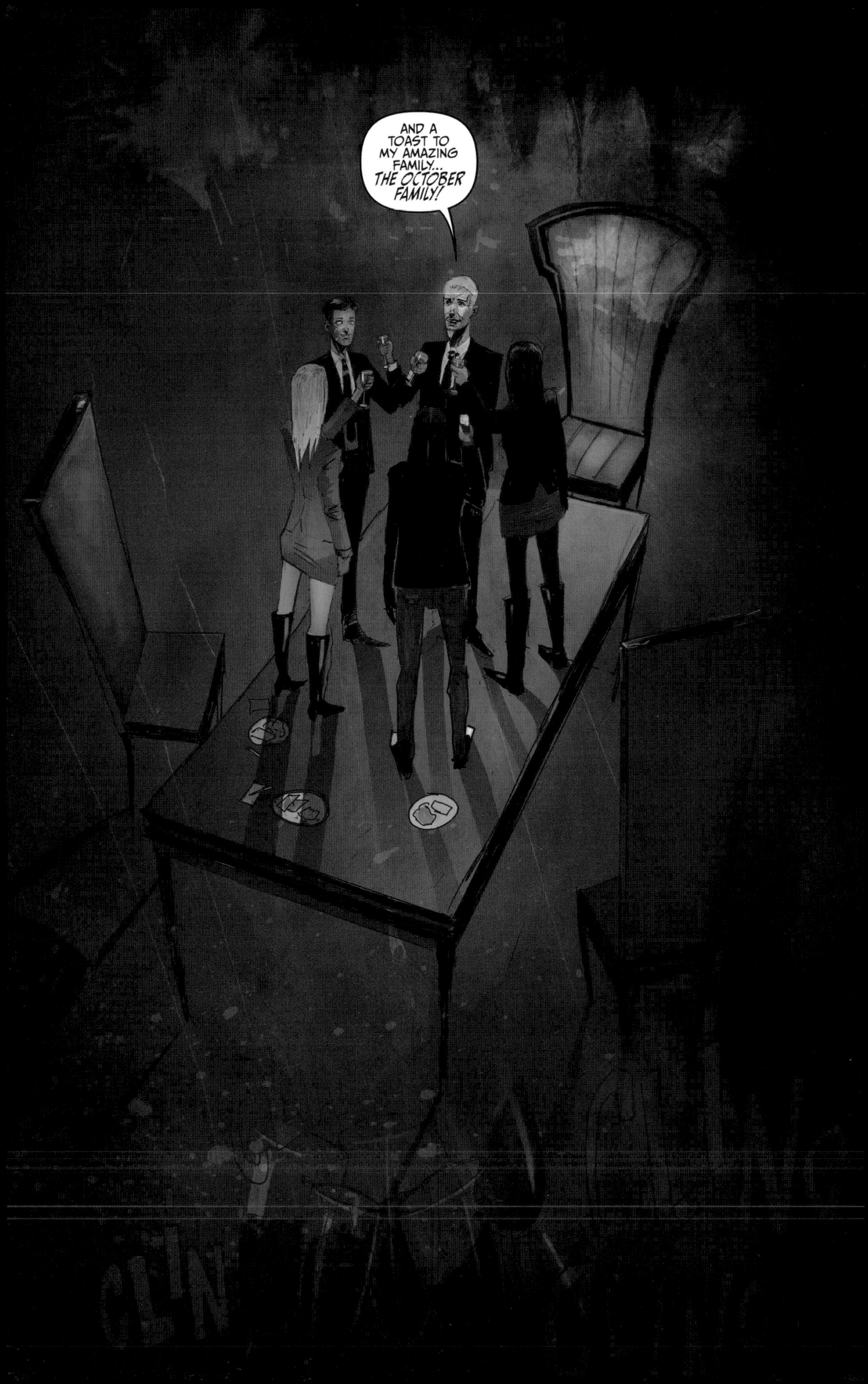
AND A TOAST TO MY AMAZING FAMILY... *THE OCTOBER FAMILY!*

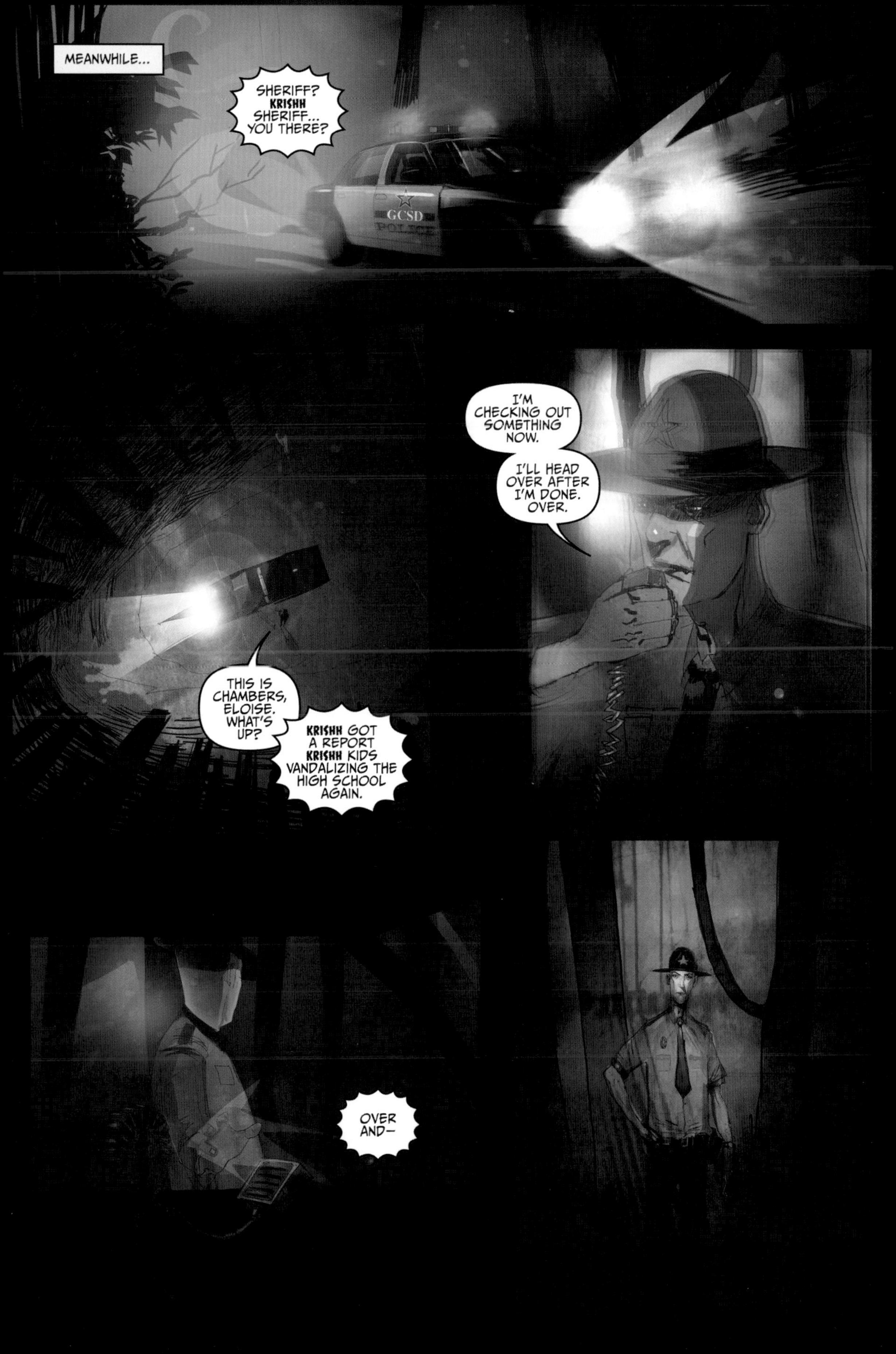
MEANWHILE...
SHERIFF? KRISHH SHERIFF... YOU THERE?
THIS IS CHAMBERS, ELOISE. WHAT'S UP?
KRISHH GOT A REPORT KRISHH KIDS VANDALIZING THE HIGH SCHOOL AGAIN.
I'M CHECKING OUT SOMETHING NOW.
I'LL HEAD OVER AFTER I'M DONE. OVER.
OVER AND—

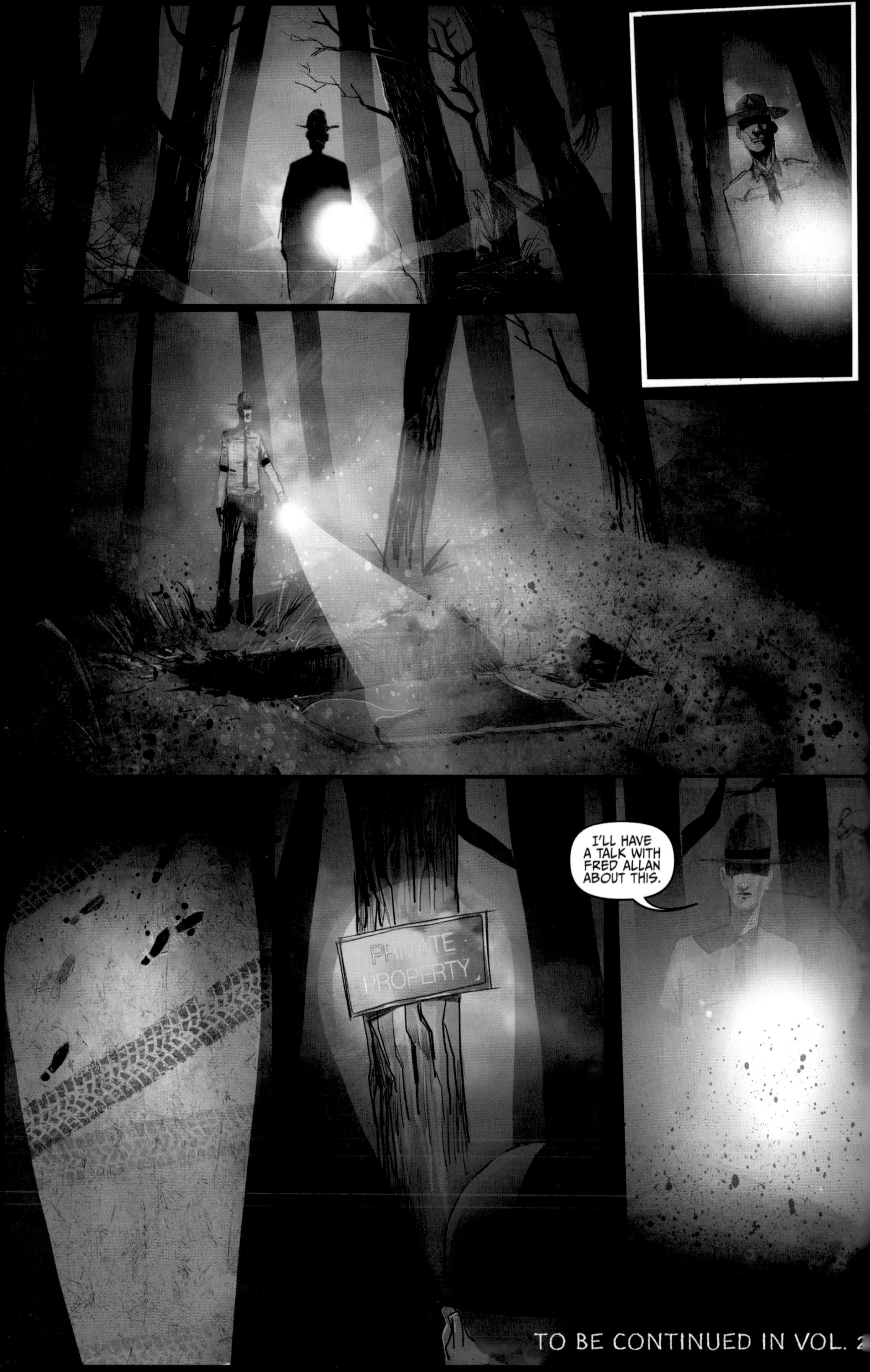
PRIVATE PROPERTY
I'LL HAVE A TALK WITH FRED ALLAN ABOUT THIS.
TO BE CONTINUED IN VOL. 2

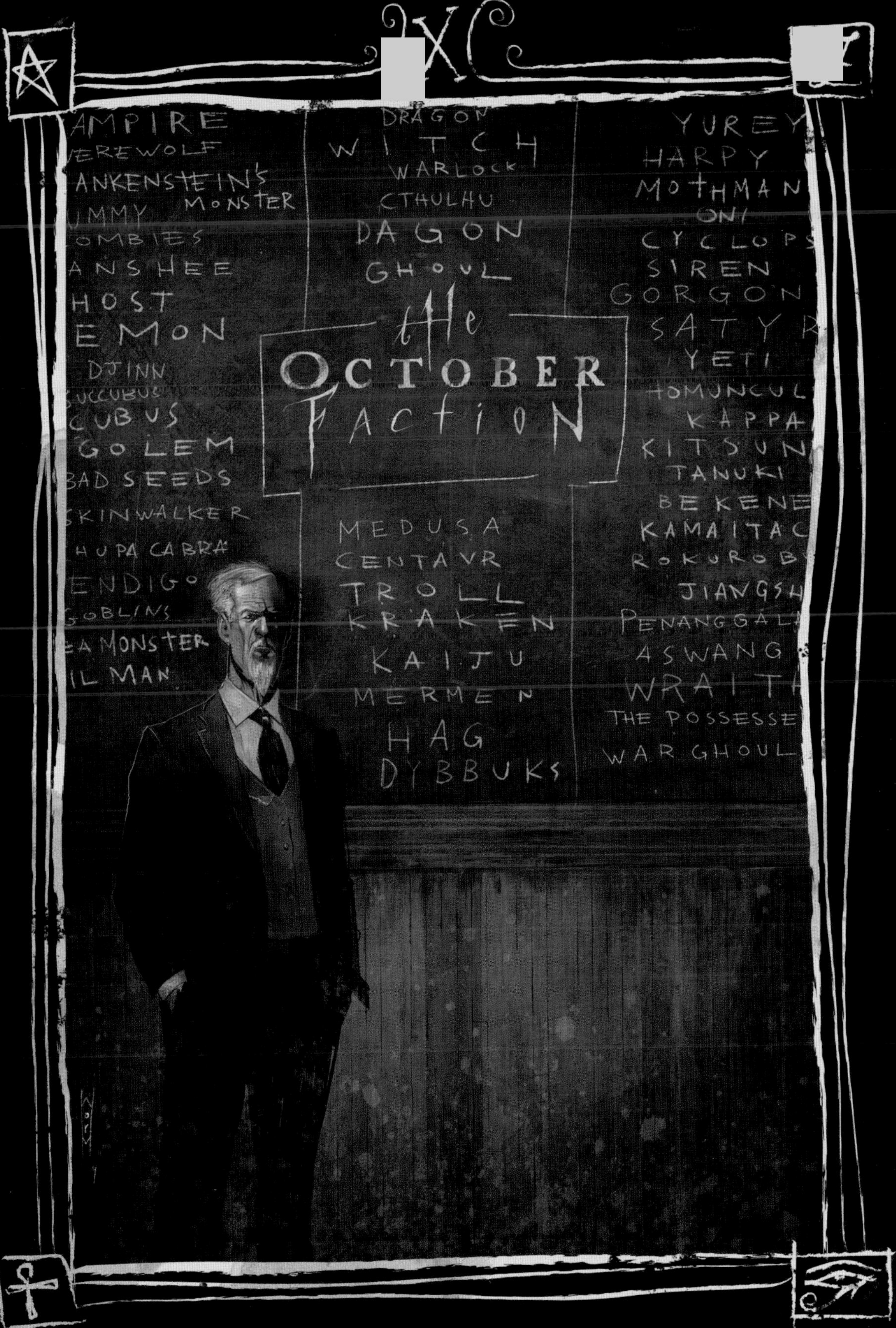
the OCTOBER FACTION
AMPIRE
EREWOLF
ANKENSTEIN'S MONSTER
UMMY
OMBIES
ANSHEE
HOST
EMON
DJINN
UCCUBUS
CUBUS
GOLEM
BAD SEEDS
SKINWALKER
HUPA CABRA
ENDIGO
GOBLINS
EA MONSTER
IL MAN
DRAGON
WITCH
WARLOCK
CTHULHU
DAGON
GHOUL
MEDUSA
CENTAVR
TROLL
KRAKEN
KAIJU
MERMEN
HAG
DYBBUKS
YUREY
HARPY
MOTHMAN
ONI
CYCLOPS
SIREN
GORGON
SATYR
YETI
HOMUNCUL
KAPPA
KITSUN
TANUKI
BEKENE
KAMAITAC
ROKUROB
JIANGSH
PENANGGAL
ASWANG
WRAIT
THE POSSESSE
WAR GHOUL

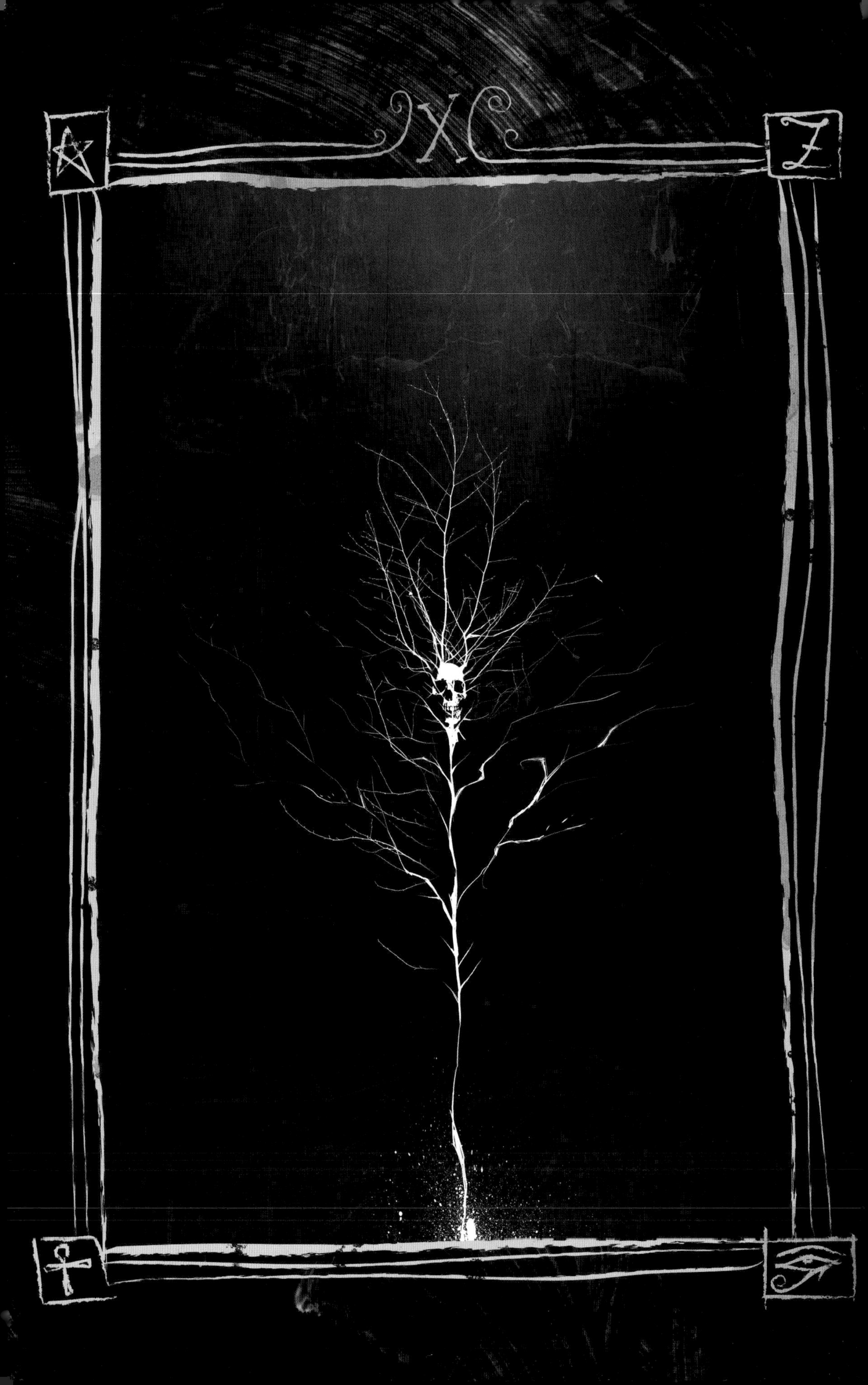
X

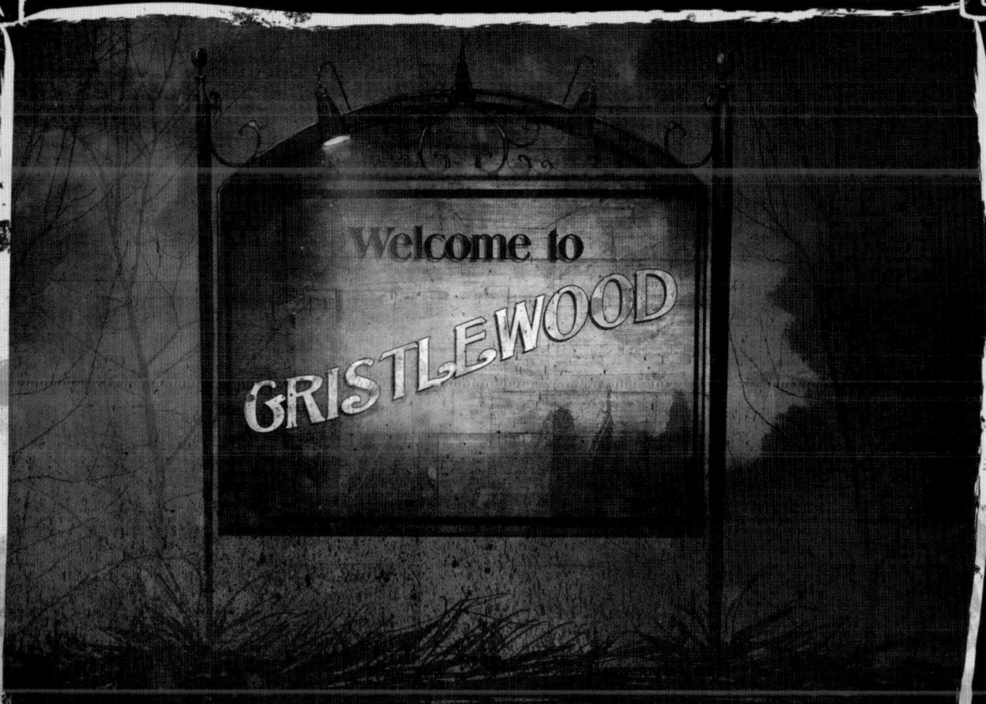
Welcome to
GRISTLEWOOD

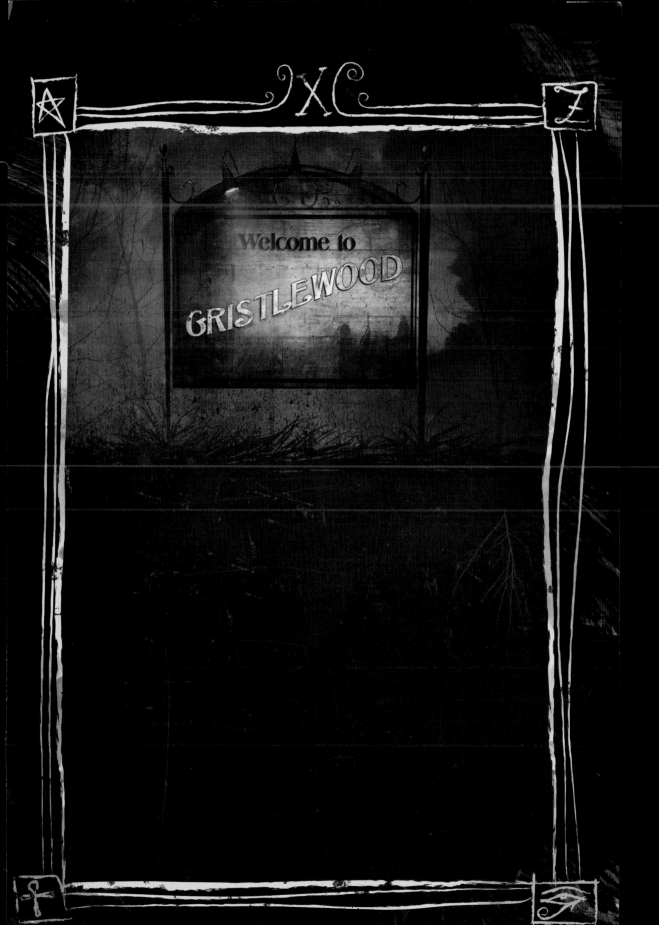

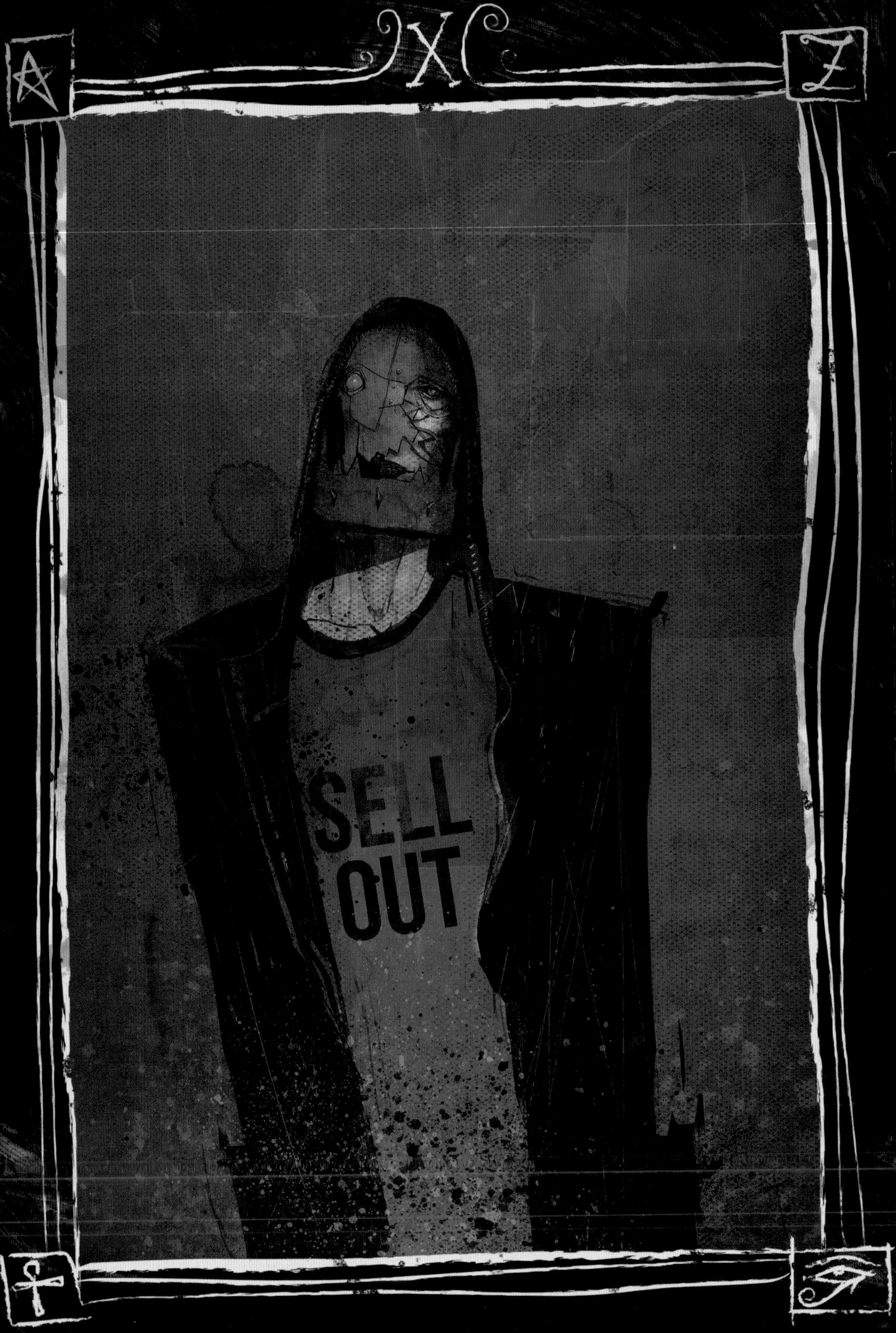
X
SELL
OUT

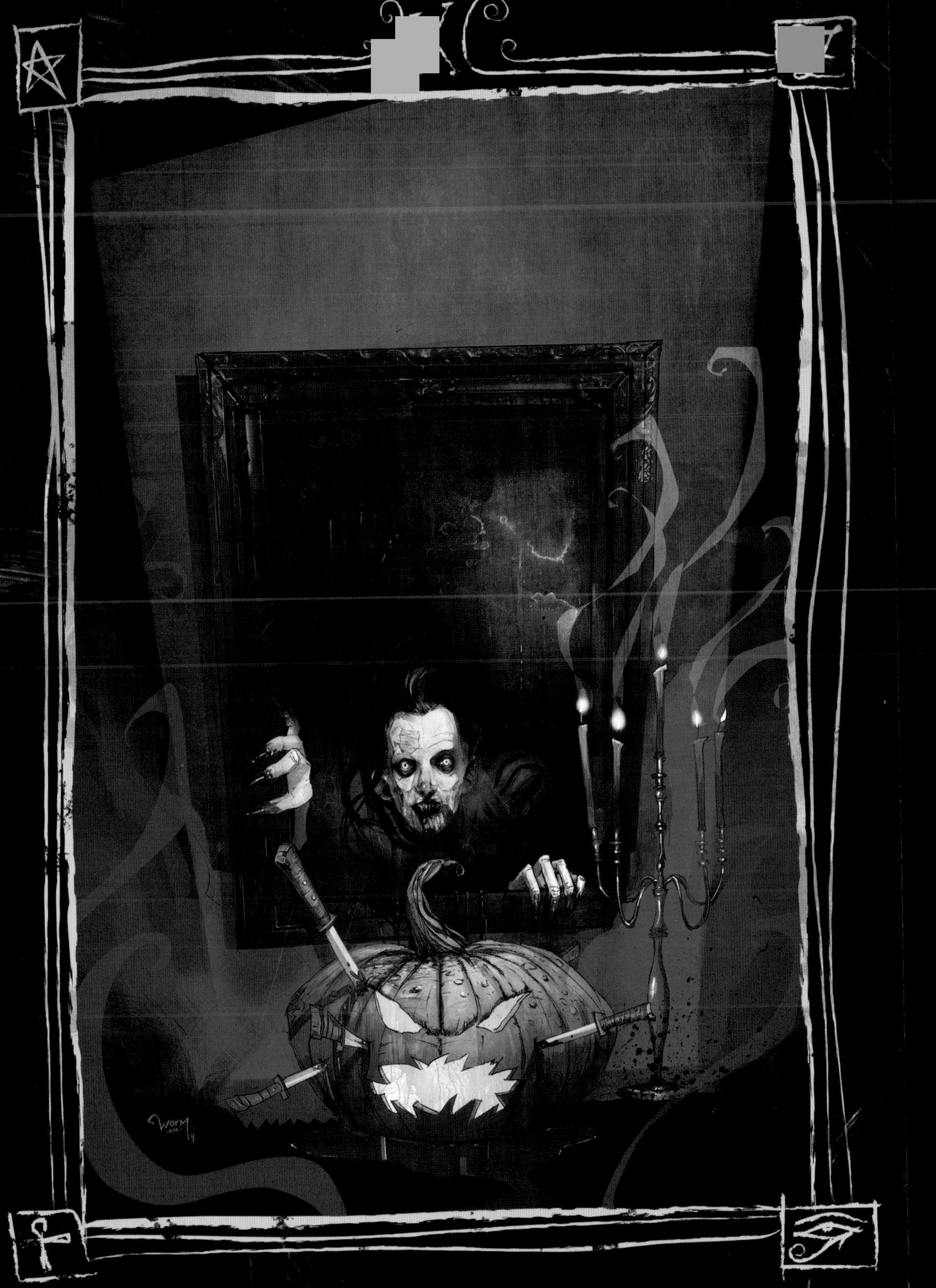
WORM

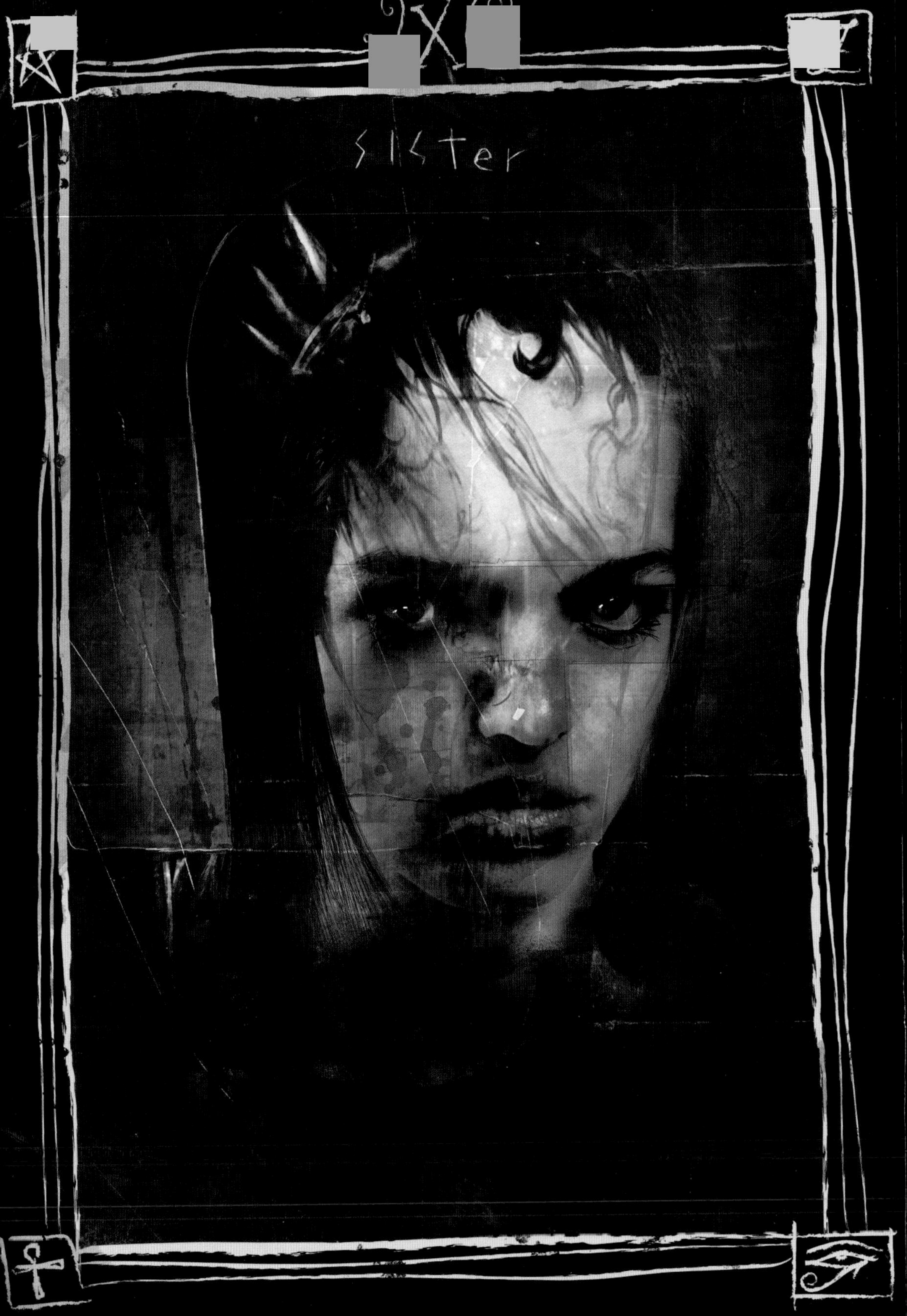
sister

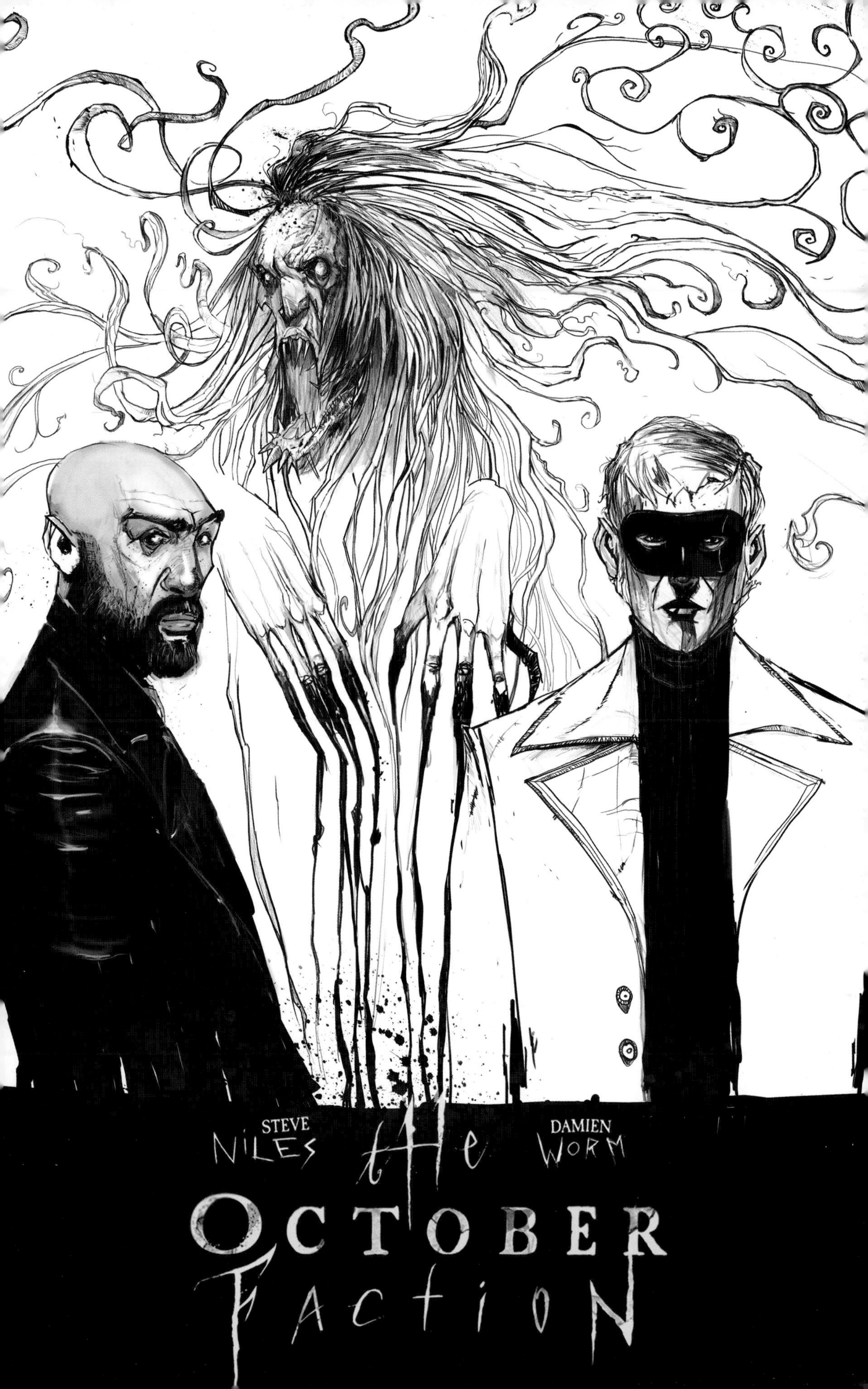
STEVE
NILES
DAMIEN
WORM
tHe
OCTOBER
FACTION

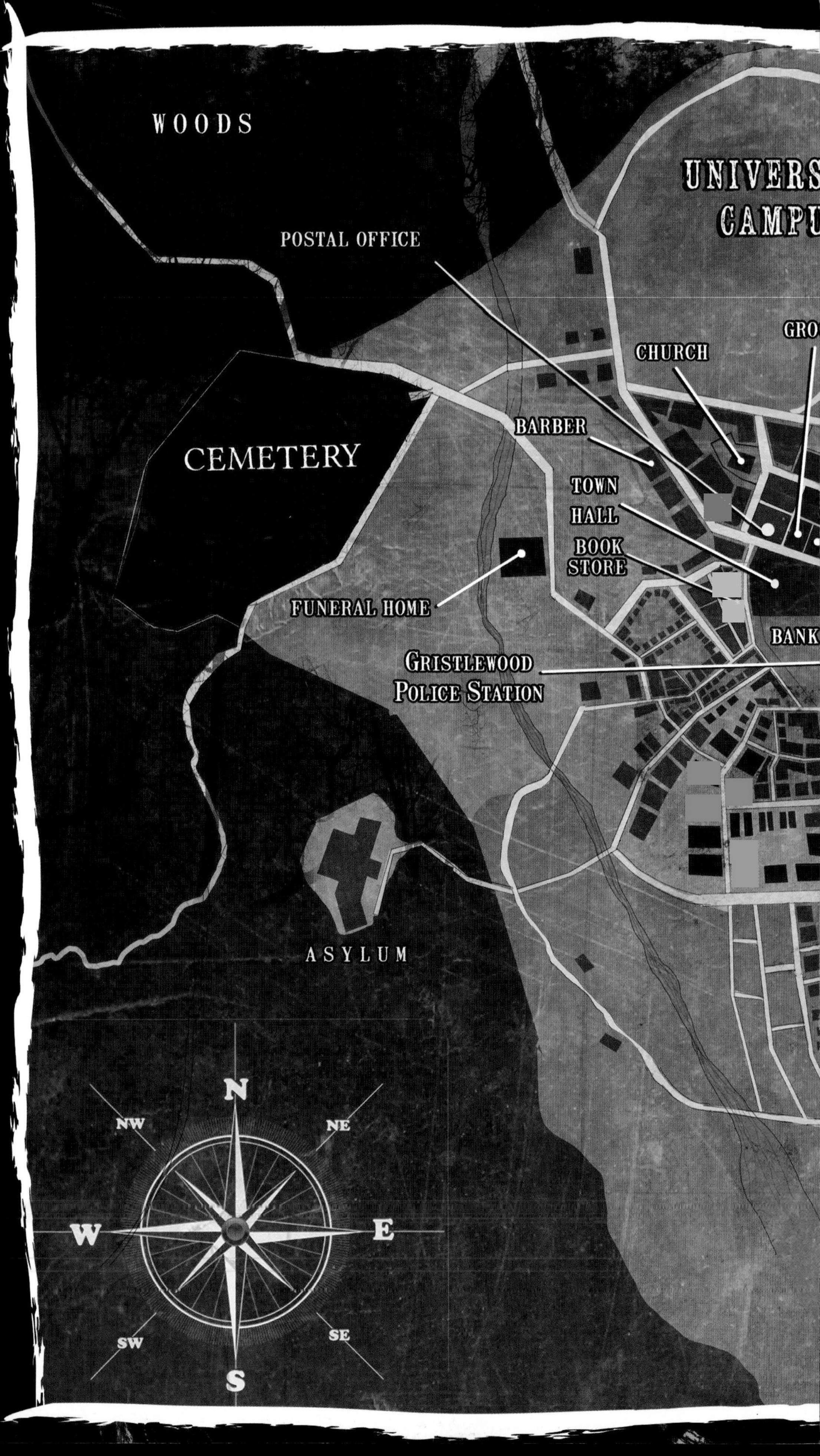
WOODS
UNIVERS
CAMPU
POSTAL OFFICE
GRO
CHURCH
CEMETERY
BARBER
TOWN
HALL
BOOK
STORE
FUNERAL HOME
BANK
GRISTLEWOOD
POLICE STATION
ASYLUM
N
NW
NE
W
E
SW
SE
S

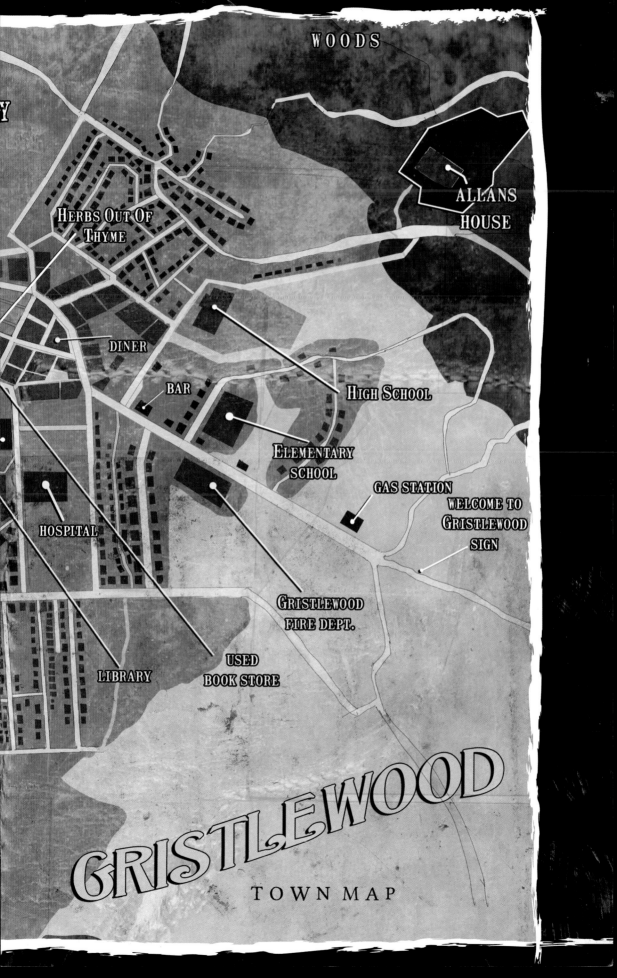

WOODS

ALLANS
HOUSE

HERBS OUT OF
THYME

DINER

BAR

HIGH SCHOOL

ELEMENTARY
SCHOOL

GAS STATION

WELCOME TO
GRISTLEWOOD
SIGN

HOSPITAL

GRISTLEWOOD
FIRE DEPT.

LIBRARY

USED
BOOK STORE

GRISTLEWOOD

TOWN MAP

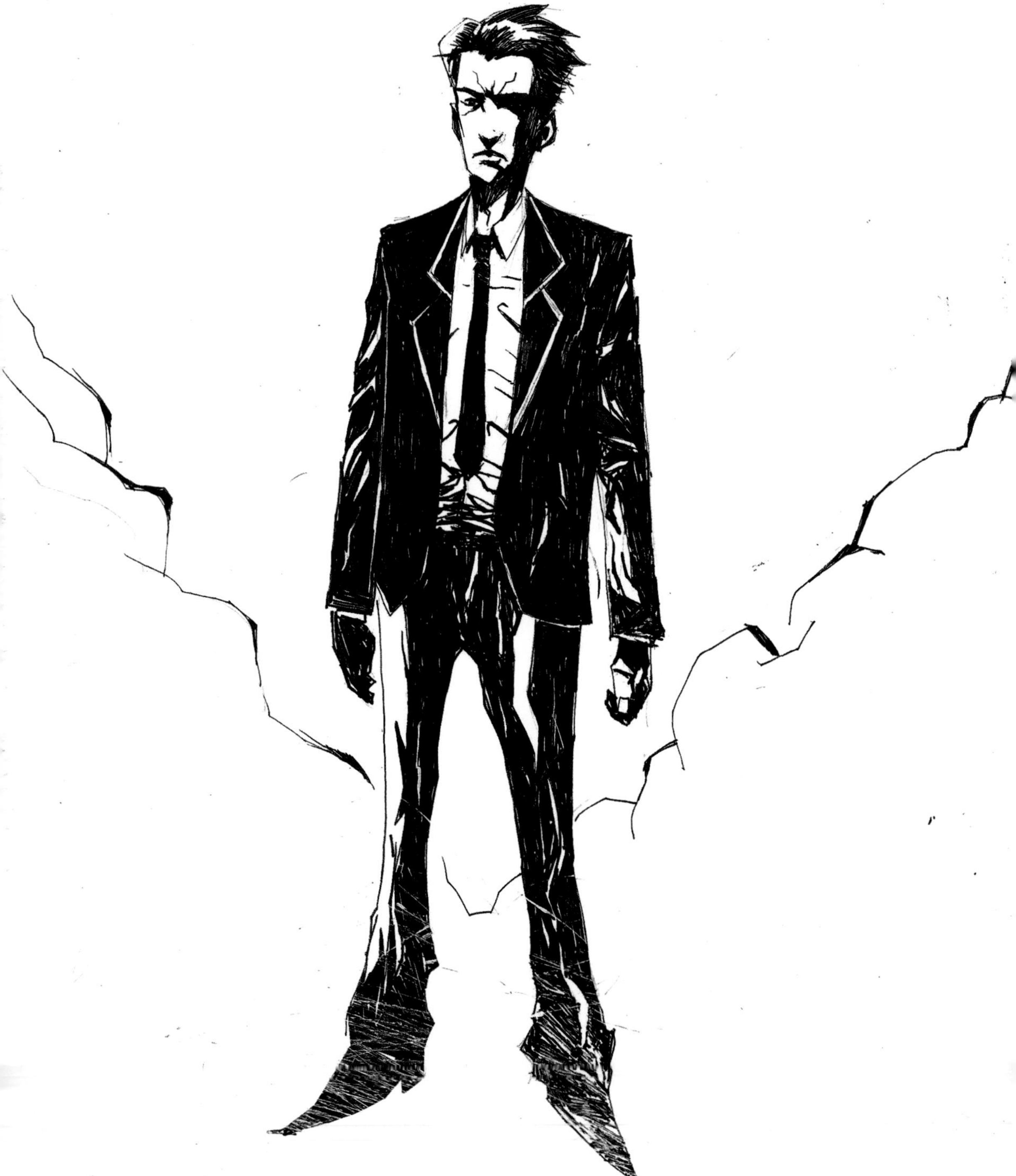

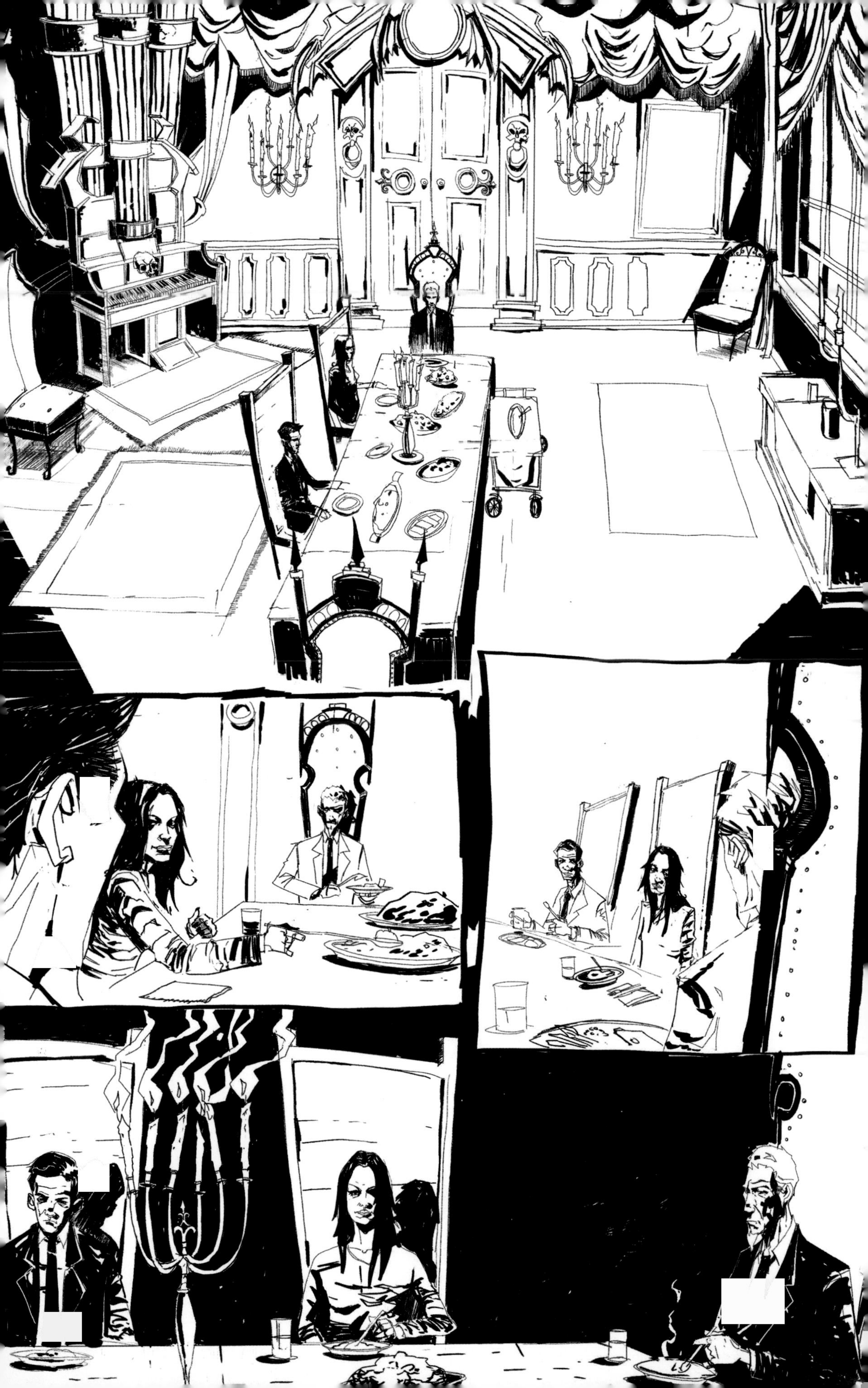

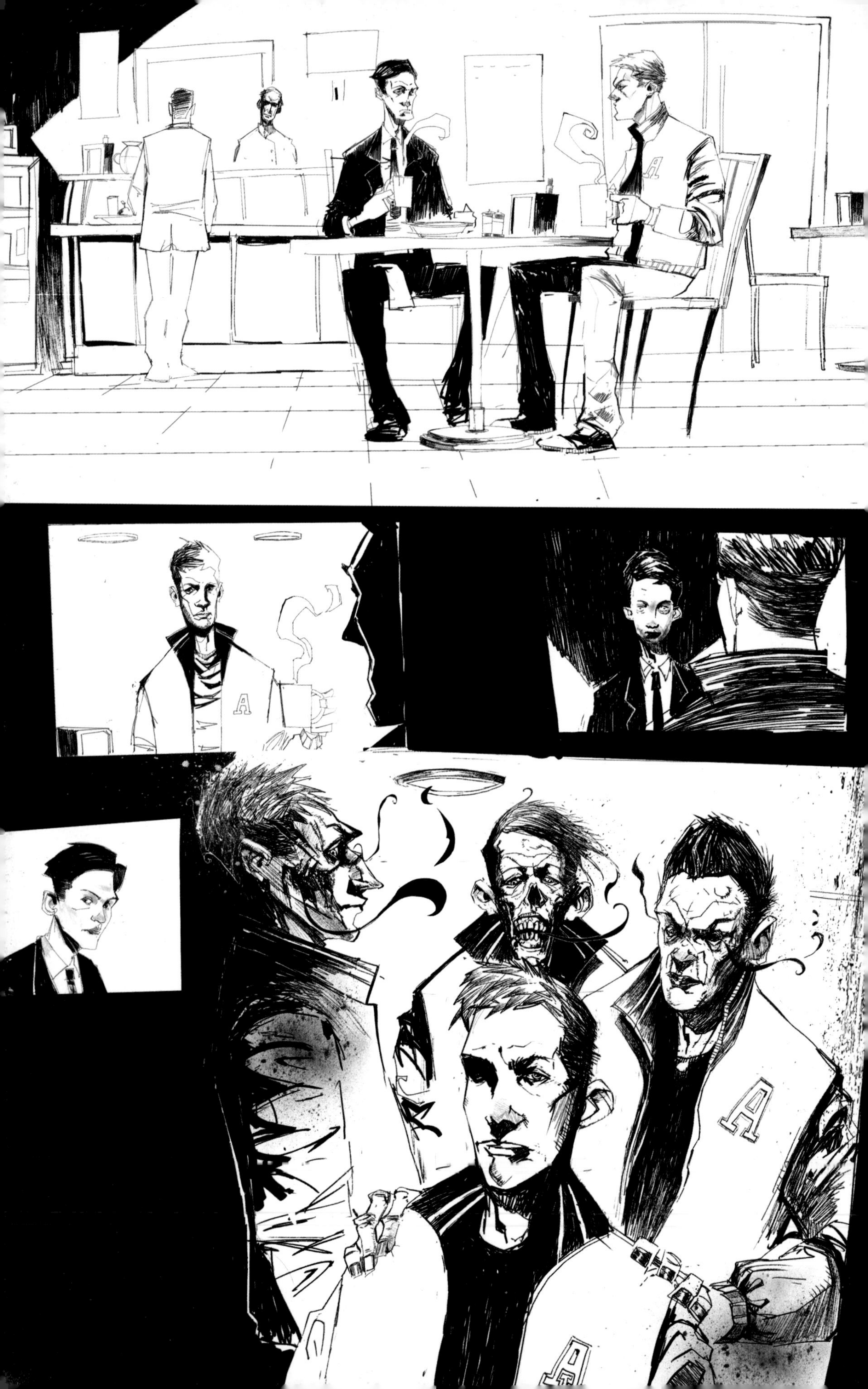

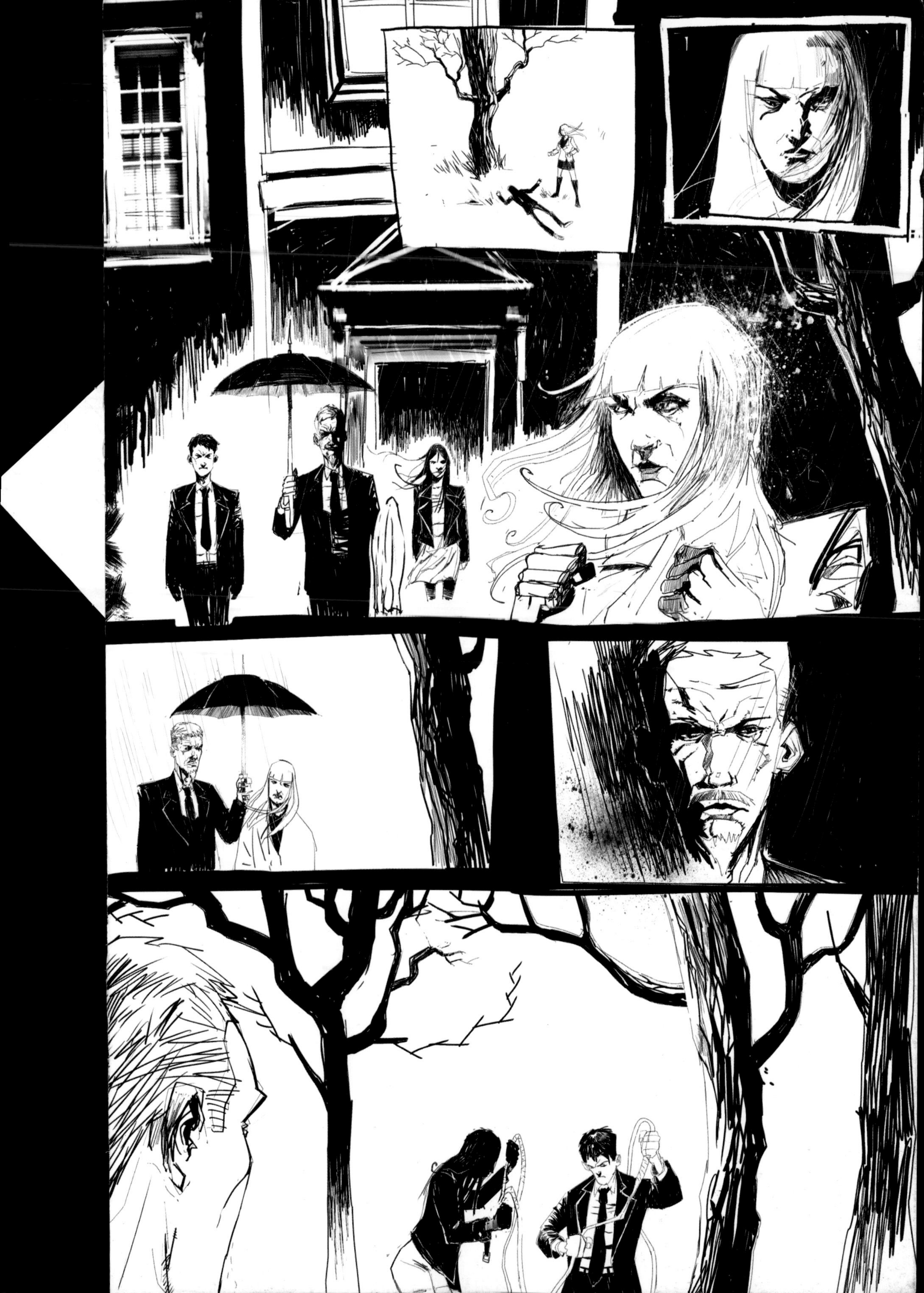